Practical Education Law

Related titles available from Law Society Publishing:

Child Abuse Compensation Claims
Elizabeth-Anne Gumbel, Malcolm Johnson and Richard Scorer

Child Law Handbook
Liz Goldthorpe with Pat Monro

Elderly Client Handbook (3rd edition)
General Editors: Caroline Bielanska and Martin Terrell.
Consultant Editor: Gordon R. Ashton

Family Law Protocol (2nd edition due December 2005)
The Law Society with Resolution, Cafcass, LSC and DCA

Good Practice in Child Care Cases
A Guide for Solicitors Acting in Public Law Children Act Proceedings Including Cases Involving Adoption
The Law Society in association with ALC, CCJLG and SFLA

Health and Social Care Handbook (due February 2006)
Fiona Scolding, Alison Millar and Frances Swaine

All books from Law Society Publishing can be ordered from good bookshops or direct from our distributors, Marston Book Services, by telephone 01235 465656 or email law.society@marston.co.uk. Please confirm the price before ordering.

For further information or a catalogue, please email our editorial and marketing office: publishing@lawsociety.co.uk.

PRACTICAL EDUCATION LAW

Angela Jackman, Deborah Hay and Pat Wilkins

The Law Society

All rights reserved. No part of this publication may be reproduced in any material form, whether by photocopying, scanning, downloading onto computer or otherwise without the written permission of the Law Society and the author except in accordance with the provisions of the Copyright, Designs and Patents Act 1988. Applications should be addressed in the first instance, in writing, to Law Society Publishing.

The views expressed in this publication should be taken as those of the authors only unless it is specifically indicated that the Law Society has given its endorsement.

The authors have asserted the right under the Copyright, Designs and Patents Act 1988 to be identified as the authors of this work.

© Angela Jackman, Deborah Hay and Pat Wilkins 2005

ISBN 10: 1–85328–816–0
ISBN 13: 978–1–85328–816–6

Crown copyright material is reproduced with the permission of the Controller of Her Majesty's Stationery Office

Published in 2005 by Law Society Publishing
113 Chancery Lane, London WC2A 1PL

Typeset by J&L Composition, Filey, North Yorkshire
Printed by TJ International Ltd, Padstow, Cornwall

Contents

Preface x
List of abbreviations xii
Table of cases xiv
Table of statutes xxiv
Table of statutory instruments xxviii

1 Structure of the school system   1

    1.1 Categorisation of schools   1
    1.2 Administration and decision-making   3
    1.3 Inspection and regulation   13

2 Planning and policy decisions and remedies   16

    2.1 School provision: planning and policy decisions   16
    2.2 Challenges to planning and policy decisions: the main remedies   21
    2.3 Judicial review   26
    2.4 Claims for breaches of human rights   38

3 Admissions   41

    3.1 Introduction   41
    3.2 Who is the client?   41
    3.3 The statutory framework   41
    3.4 Admission arrangements   44
    3.5 The adjudicator   50
    3.6 Statutory appeals   51
    3.7 Remedies: judicial review   56

4 School exclusions   60

    4.1 Introduction   60
    4.2 Who is the client?   60

	4.3	The statutory framework	61
	4.4	Types of exclusion	63
	4.5	Removals	65
	4.6	The decision to exclude	65
	4.7	Role of the governing body	72
	4.8	Preparing for the governing body meeting	73
	4.9	The governing body meeting	76
	4.10	Role of the independent appeal panel	79
	4.11	Preparatory procedural issues	80
	4.12	Preparing for the appeal to the independent appeal panel	81
	4.13	The independent appeal panel hearing	82
	4.14	Further remedies	85
	4.15	Legal help/public funding	87

5 Pupils out of school — 88

5.1	Introduction	88
5.2	The statutory framework for educational provision	88
5.3	Guidance	90
5.4	School's duty to excluded pupils	92
5.5	Different modes of provision	92
5.6	Reintegration	93
5.7	Pupils with statements of special educational needs	95
5.8	Damages for pupils out of school	96

6 Negligence — 97

6.1	Introduction	97
6.2	Educational negligence	97
6.3	Who is the client?	99
6.4	The statutory framework	99
6.5	Initial information needed from the client	100
6.6	What does the client need to know?	100
6.7	Duty of care	101
6.8	Damage	102
6.9	Contributory negligence	105
6.10	Procedural issues	105
6.11	Mediation/alternative dispute resolution	106
6.12	Independent schools	107
6.13	Other causes of action	107
6.14	Public funding	108
6.15	Conclusions	108

7	**Special educational needs: identification and assessment**		**109**
	7.1	Introduction	109
	7.2	The statutory framework	109
	7.3	Definitions	110
	7.4	Responsible bodies	111
	7.5	Machinery for identifying and meeting special educational needs	112
	7.6	Procedure for requesting a statutory assessment	119
	7.7	Decision to assess	121
	7.8	The proposed (amended) statement	122
	7.9	Inclusive schooling	127
	7.10	The final statement	128
	7.11	Transport	129
	7.12	Maintenance of statements	129
	7.13	Transfer between different phases	131
	7.14	Annual reviews from Year 9	131
	7.15	Ceasing to maintain a statement	132
	7.16	Transfer of statements	132
8	**Special educational needs: appeals**		**133**
	8.1	The statutory framework	133
	8.2	Whose right of appeal?	134
	8.3	Against which decisions can a parent appeal?	134
	8.4	Timescales and procedure for appeal	134
	8.5	Registration of the appeal	137
	8.6	Post-registration requirements for Part IV appeals	138
	8.7	Hearing date	138
	8.8	Case statement	139
	8.9	After the case statement period	140
	8.10	Late evidence	140
	8.11	Witnesses	141
	8.12	Directions	142
	8.13	Representation	142
	8.14	Views of the child	143
	8.15	The hearing	143
	8.16	Adjournments	144
	8.17	The determination	145
	8.18	Costs	145
	8.19	Enforcement of tribunal determinations	146

CONTENTS

	8.20	Review of the determination	146
	8.21	Statutory appeal	147
	8.22	Concessions of appeal by the local education authority	147
	8.23	Legal help/public funding	147

9 Disability discrimination 148

	9.1	Introduction	148
	9.2	Who is the client?	148
	9.3	The statutory framework	149
	9.4	Definition of disability	150
	9.5	What education settings does Part IV cover?	153
	9.6	What activities are covered by Part IV?	155
	9.7	The discrimination test	156
	9.8	Pre-school provision	161
	9.9	School accessibility strategies	161
	9.10	The local education authority's residual duties	162
	9.11	Appeals to the Special Educational Needs and Disability Tribunal	163
	9.12	Exclusion and admission appeal panels	169
	9.13	Role of the Disability Rights Commission	169
	9.14	Public funding	170

10 School transport 171

	10.1	Introduction	171
	10.2	The statutory framework	171
	10.3	Types of assistance/arrangements	172
	10.4	Who is the client?	173
	10.5	Potential issues	173
	10.6	Remedies	176
	10.7	Public funding	176

Appendices

A	Particulars of claim	177
B	Special educational needs: reasons for appeal	182
C	Special educational needs: parental statement to SENDIST	185
D	Exclusion: grounds of appeal to the independent appeal panel	187
E	Exclusion: judicial review – claim form	189
F	Exclusion: judicial review – application for urgent consideration	195
G	Exclusion: judicial review – counsel's grounds	197

H	Special educational needs: appeals checklist	204
I	Draft claim under the Disability Discrimination Act 1995 to SENDIST	205
J	Pre-action protocol letter	209
K	Case digest: exclusions	212
L	Case digest: special educational needs	220

Index 239

Preface

There is little doubt that education law has become the focus of intense legal activity within the final decade of the twentieth century and the first five years of the new millennium.

The growth in education law has coincided with the development of a comprehensive package of rights for pupils and their parents and the incorporation of the European Convention on Human Rights into our legal framework, which now also includes protection from discriminatory treatment under the Disability Discrimination Act 1995. Simultaneously the development of the common law liability in negligence has provided an increasing safeguard and remedy for pupils and adults whose education was incompetently handled.

We should be proud of the protection that our legislative system affords to pupils, especially that particularly vulnerable group of pupils with special educational needs, through the operation of public law and in particular the statutory appeal processes which exist in relation to the admission and exclusion of pupils from schools and the provision of remediation for their special educational needs.

The enforcement of rights in education, often in relation to exclusions from school, is regular fodder for the media and politicians. Nevertheless we would hope that everyone would endorse the words of former Education Secretary David Blunkett, who has said:

> [Education] is vital to the creation of a fully inclusive society, a society in which all members see themselves as valued for the contribution they make. We owe all children – whatever their particular needs and circumstances – the opportunity to develop to their full potential, to contribute economically, and to play a full [part] as active citizens.
>
> (*Meeting Special Educational Needs: A Programme of Action*, DfEE, Annex B).

In order to ensure that children are provided with that opportunity it may be necessary for children or their parents to seek legal advice and support and for their rights to be enforced. However, the legal position in relation to almost any issue which a child or parent may wish to have considered, is now so complex that the lay person or unrepresented parent of a school-aged child may really struggle to gain any access to the system, which represents such a fundamental and important part of the child's life. Therefore, the need for easily available, local and constructive advice continues to increase as successive administrations change and expand the education legislative framework.

In our work with individuals, usually receiving support through public funding, it is possible to achieve significant and sometimes life-changing outcomes for children and their families, both by successfully utilising the existing statutory or public law remedies, in relation to admissions to schools, exclusions from schools and special educational needs, but more often by simply being aware of how to approach the relevant statutory agency on the specific point at issue and providing the support mechanism to achieve a change in position.

We therefore have tried to fill a perceived need for accessible and clear information on the most usual range of enquiries that we or our colleagues are asked to deal with not only through specialist education law teams or firms, but in everyday practice.

We unashamedly consider issues from the perspective of our usual client group, rather than from the viewpoint of the education authorities or schools. Wherever possible, we would encourage the use of mediation or dispute resolution and have highlighted the possible approaches to and advantages of a practical and non-litigious focus on what will really benefit pupils and/or their families.

We have attempted to provide checklists, flow charts and information in bullet points or tables, to ease rapid reference for the busy practitioner. However, we are conscious that more in-depth consideration of the law will often be necessary and have tried to provide helpful pointers on where practitioners might look for more information.

We have included the most relevant statutory material and precedents in the majority of areas we consider within the book.

At the time of writing the majority of our clients are able to obtain some form of public funding when seeking to enforce public law rights through judicial review. However, despite the prominence of statutory tribunals and appeal panels within the education law context, no public funding is available for representation at what may be lengthy and complex hearings. Some clients are, however, able to obtain public funding in order to obtain expert evidence and we have tried to make clear what financial help can be sought and when, as well as pointing out its restrictions.

The law is stated as at July 2005.

We hope this will prove a useful starting point in this fascinating and rewarding area of law and assist you in finding the initial answer your client may seek with the speed their concerns may merit.

Angela Jackman, Deborah Hay and Pat Wilkins

Abbreviations

AAP	admission appeals panel
the Consolidation Regulations	Education (Special Educational Needs) (England) (Consolidation) Regulations 2001, SI 2001/3455
DDA 1995	Disability Discrimination Act 1995
DfES	Department for Education and Science
DRC	Disability Rights Commission
EA	Education Act
ECHR	European Convention for the Protection of Human Rights and Fundamental Freedoms
IAP	independent appeal panel
IEP	individual education plan
IPS	independent parental supervisor
IPSEA	Independent Panel for Special Educational Advice
LEA	local education authority
LGA 1974	Local Government Act 1974
LMS	local management of schools
LSA	learning support assistant
LSC	Legal Services Commission
Ofsted	Office for Standards in Education
PPO	parent partnership officer
PPS	parent partnership scheme
PRU	pupil referral unit
SEN	special educational needs
SENCO	special educational needs coordinator
SENDA 2001	Special Educational Needs and Disability Act 2001
SENDIST	Special Educational Needs and Disability Tribunal

the SEN Information Regulations	Education (Special Educational Needs) (England) (Information) Regulations 1999, SI 1999/2506
SIA 1996	School Inspections Act 1996
SSFA 1998	School Standards and Framework Act 1998
the Tribunal Regulations	Special Educational Needs Tribunal Regulations 2001, SI 2001/600

Table of cases

A (A Child), Re [2000] ELR 639, QBD 221, 235
A v. Head Teacher and Governors of Lord Grey School [2004] EWCA Civ 382; [2004] QB 1231, CA; *reversing in part* [2003] EWHC 1533; [2003] 4 All ER 1317; [2003] ELR 517, QBD 38, 96, 202, 215, 218
A v. Kirklees MBC [2001] EWCA Civ 582; [2001] ELR 657, CA 226
A v. Special Educational Needs and Disability Tribunal and Barnet LBC [2003] EWHC Admin 3368; [2004] ELR 293, QBD 220, 221, 238
A v. Staffordshire CC (1996) *The Times*, 18 October 214
Abadeh v. British Telecommunications plc [2001] ICR 156; [2001] IRLR 23, EAT 153
Adams v. Bracknell Forest BC [2004] UKHL 29; [2005] 1 AC 76 [2004] 3 WLR 89, HL 103
Alton-Evans v. Leicester Local Education Authority [1998] ELR 237, QBD 225
Anufrijeva v. Southwark LBC [2003] EWCA Civ 1406; [2004] QB 1124; [2004] 2 WLR 603, CA 31, 96
Associated Provincial Picture Houses Ltd v. Wednesbury Corp [1948] 1 KB 223, CA 202
B v. Harrow LBC (No. 1) [2000] 1 WLR 223; [2000] ELR 109, HL; *reversing* [1998] 3 FCR 231; [1998] ELR 351, CA 42, 222, 229, 231
B v. Harrow LBC (No. 2) [2000] ELR 1, QBD 232
B v. Harrow LBC and Special Educational Needs Tribunal *See* B v. Harrow LBC (No. 1)
B v. Isle of Wight Council [1997] ELR 279, QBD 220
B v. Secretary of State for the Home Department [2000] 2 CMLR 1086; [2000] UKHRR 498, CA 202
Belgian Linguistic (No. 2) (A/6) (1979–80) 1 EHRR 252, ECHR 39
Bolam v. Friern Barnet Hospital Management Committee [1957] 1 WLR 582, QBD 99, 102, 236
Bradford-Smart v. West Sussex CC [2002] EWCA Civ 7; [2002] 1 FCR 425; [2002] ELR 139, CA 108
Bromley LBC v. Special Educational Needs Tribunal (No. 2) [1999] 3 All ER 587; [1999] ELR 260, CA 221, 228, 232
C v. Buckinghamshire CC [1999] BLGR 321; [1999] ELR 179, CA 223, 232
C v. Lambeth LBC [2003] EWHC 1195 221
C v. Lambeth LBC and Special Educational Needs Tribunal [1999] ELR 350, QBD 230

TABLE OF CASES

C v. Lancashire CC [1997] 3 FCR 587; [1997] ELR 377, QBD 222
C (Shirley) v. Brent LBC [2003] EWCA Civ 1773; [2003] EWHC Admin 1590 . . .223
CB v. Merton LBC and Special Educational Needs and Disability Tribunal [2002]
    EWHC 877; [2002] ELR 441, QBD 223
Carty v. Croydon LBC [2005] EWCA Civ 19; [2005] 1 WLR 2312, CA 98
Catchpole v. Buckinghamshire CC See C v. Buckinghamshire CC
Christmas v. Hampshire CC [1998] ELR 1, QBD 104
College of Ripon and York St John v. Hobbs [2002] IRLR 185, EAT 150
Crean v. Somerset CC [2002] ELR 152, QBD 145, 226
Cruickshank v. Vaw Motorcast Ltd [2002] ICR 729, EAT 153
DM and KC v. Essex CC and Special Educational Needs Tribunal [2003] EWHC
    Admin 135; [2003] ELR 419, QBD 236
DN v. Greenwich LBC [2004] EWCA Civ 1659; [2005] 1 FCR 112; [2005] ELR
    133, CA 101, 104–5
DR v. Sheffield City Council [2002] EWHC Admin 528 222
E v. Hampshire CC [2000] ELR 652, CA 223
E v. Newham LBC [2003] EWCA Civ 9; [2003] ELR 286, CA 222, 231
E v. Oxfordshire CC [2001] EWHC Admin 816; [2001] ELR 256, QBD 230, 233
E v. Rotherham MBC [2001] EWHC Admin 432; [2002] ELR 266, QBD 221
E (A Child) v. Flintshire CC and Special Educational Needs and Disability
    Tribunal [2002] EWHC Admin 388; [2002] ELR 378, QBD 220, 221
Ekpe v. Metropolitan Police Commissioner [2001] IRLR 605, EAT 153
Ellison v. Hampshire CC (unreported, 24 February 2000) 233
F v. Humberside CC [1997] 1 All ER 183; [1997] ELR 12, QBD 227
Faulkner v. Enfield LBC [2003] ELR 426, QBD 108
Fisher v. Hughes [1998] ELR 475, QBD 229
G v. Barnet LBC and Special Educational Needs and Disability Tribunal [1998]
    ELR 480, QBD 220
G v. South Gloucestershire CC and Special Educational Needs Tribunal [2000]
    ELR 136, QBD 235
G v. Wakefield MBC (1998) 96 LGR 69 220
Ghosh v. General Medical Council [2001] UKPC 29; [2001] 1 WLR 1915, PC . .202
Goodwin v. Patent Office [1999] ICR 302, EAT 151
Governing Body of PPC v. DS [2005] EWHC 1036; [2005] All ER (D) 64,
    QBD 156, 159
H v. Kent CC [2000] ELR 660, QBD 226, 235
H v. Leicestershire CC [2000] ELR 471, QBD 221
Havering LBC v. Special Educational Needs Tribunal [1996] EWHC 73 231
Hereford and Worcester CC v. Lane [1998] ELR 319, CA 232
JD v. Devon CC [2001] EWHC Admin 958, QBD 226
James v. Post Office [2001] EWCA Civ 558, CA 165
Joyce v. Dorset CC [1997] ELR 26, QBD 229, 230
Kirton v. Tetrosyl Ltd [2003] EWCA Civ 619; [2003] ILR 353, CA 152
Knight v. Dorset CC [1997] COD 256, QBD 231
L, (a Minor), Re, by his father and Litigation Friend [2003] UKHL 9; [2003]
    2 AC 633; [2003] ELR 309, HL 84, 85
L v. Clarke and Somerset CC [1998] ELR 129, QBD 183, 221, 226, 234
L v. Hereford and Worcester CC and Hughes [2000] ELR 375, QBD 229

xv

TABLE OF CASES

Latchman v. Reed Business Information Ltd [2002] ILR 1453, EAT 152
Leonard v. Southern Derbyshire Chamber of Commerce [2001] IRLR 19,
    EAT 151
Linford Cash and Carry Ltd v. Thompson [1989] IRLR 235, EAT 216
Locabail (UK) Ltd v. Bayfield Properties [2000] QB 451, CA 233
M (A Minor), Re [1996] ELR 135, CA 225
M v. Brighton and Hove City Council [2003] EWHC Admin 1722; [2003] ELR
    752, QBD 221
McAuley Catholic High School v. C [2003] EWHC Admin 3045; [2004] 2 All ER
    436, QBD 157, 159, 164
McKeown v. Appeal Committee and Governors of Cardinal Heenan High School
    and Leeds City Council [1998] ELR 578, QBD 59
McNicol v. Balfour Beatty Rail Maintenance Ltd [2002] EWCA Civ 1074; [2002]
    ICR 1498, CA 150
Mayor and Burgesses of Camden LBC v. Hodin and White [1996] ELR 430,
    QBD 228
Nichol v. Gateshead MBC (1988) 87 LGR 435, CA 29
O v. Harrow LBC [2001] EWCA Civ 2046; [2002] 1 WLR 928, CA 224
O'Rourke v. Camden LBC [1998] AC 188, HL 31
O'Rourke v. United Kingdom (unreported, 26 June 2001) 31
Oxfordshire CC v. GB [2001] EWCA 1358; [2002] ELR 8, CA 223, 230, 235
Oxfordshire CC v. M and Special Educational Needs Tribunal [2002] EWHC
    Admin 2908; [2003] ELR 718, QBD 236
P v. National Association of Schoolmasters Union of Women Teachers
    (NASUWT) [2003] UKHL 8; [2003] 2 AC 663; [2003] ELR 357, HL 84
Palmer v. RSA; Palmer v. AQA (unreported, 26 March 2004), Central London
    County Court 154
Phelps v. Hillingdon LBC [2001] 2 AC 619, HL 98, 101, 103, 104, 108, 236
Porter v. Magill [2001] UKHL 67; [2002] 2 AC 357, HL 233
Practice Statement (Administrative Court: Administration of Justice) [2002]
    1 WLR 810 ....33, 35
R. (on the application of A) v. Cambridgeshire CC and Lorn [2002] EWHC
    Admin 2391; [2003] ELR 464, QBD 222
R. (on the application of A) v. Head Teacher of North Westminster Community
    School [2002] EWHC Admin 2351; [2003] ELR 378, QBD 86, 217, 219
R. (on the application of A (A Child)) v. Kingsmead School Governors; R.
    (on the application of AM) v. Kingsmead School Governors; R. (on
    the application of DR) v. St George's Catholic School Head Teacher;
    R. (on the application of D) v. St George's Catholic School Head
    Teacher [2002] EWCA Civ 1822, [2003] ELR 104; (2002) The Times, 19
    December, CA 74, 76, 86, 215, 216, 219
R. (on the application of A) v. Lambeth LBC [2001] EWHC Admin 379; [2002]
    ELR 231, QBD 226, 235
R. (on the application of AM) v. Governing Body of K School and Independent
    Appeal Panel of E LBC. See R. (on the application of A (A Child)) v.
    Kingsmead School Governors
R. (on the application of B) v. Head Teacher of Alperton Community School
    [2001] EWHC Admin 229; [2001] ELR 359, QBD 39, 57, 212

xvi

TABLE OF CASES

R. (on the application of B) v. Head Teacher and Governors of Denbigh High School. *See* R. (on the application of Begum) v. Head Teacher and Governors of Denbigh High School
R. (on the application of B) v. Vale of Glamorgan CBC and Confrey [2001] ELR 529, QBD 226, 235
R. (on the application of Begum) v. Head Teacher and Governors of Denbigh High School [2005] EWCA Civ 199; [2005] 2 All ER 396, CA; *reversing* [2004] EWHC Admin 1389; [2004] ELR 374, QBD 40, 214
R. (on the application of Bernard) v. Enfield LBC [2002] EWHC Admin 2282; [2003] HRLR 4, QBD 31
R. (on the application of Boulton) v. Leeds School Organisation Committee [2002] EWCA Civ 884, CA 29
R. (on the application of Burkett) v. Hammersmith and Fulham LBC [2002] UKHL 23; [2002] 1 WLR 1593, HL 27
R. (on the application of C) v. Governing Body of Cardinal Newman High School [2001] EWHC Admin 299; [2001] ELR 359 .... 55, 57
R. (on the application of C) v. Governors of B School [2001] ELR 285, CA 85
R. (on the application of C) v. Sefton MBC Independent Appeals Panel and Governors of Hillside High School [2001] ELR 393, QBD 214
R. (on the application of Cowl) v. Plymouth CC [2001] EWCA Civ 1935; [2002] 1 WLR 803, CA 176, 235
R. (on the application of DR) v. Head Teacher and Governing Body and Independent Appeal Panel of W City Council. *See* R. (on the application of A (A Child)) v. Kingsmead School Governors
R. (on the application of Daly) v. Home Secretary [2001] UKHL 26; [2001] 2 AC 532, HL 202
R. (on the application of Douglas) v. North Tyneside MBC [2003] EWCA 1847; [2004] 1 WLR 2363 39
R. (on the application of Elliot) v. Electoral Commission [2003] EWHC 395, QBD 28
R. (on the application of G) v. Westminster CC [2004] EWCA Civ 45; [2004] 1 WLR 1113; [2004] ELR 135, CA 89
R. (on the application of H) v. R School and Special Educational Needs Tribunal [2004] EWHC Admin 981; [2005] ELR 67 .... 151, 167
R. (on the application of IPSEA Ltd) v. Secretary of State for Education and Skills [2003] EWCA Civ 7; [2003] ELR 393, CA; [2002] EWHC Admin 504 .... 124, 221, 231
R. (on the application of J) v. A School [2003] All ER (D) 158 217
R. (on the application of Jones) v. Ceredigion CC [2004] EWHC Admin 1376; [2004] ELR 506, QBD 173
R. (on the application of K) v. Governors of W School and West Sussex CC [2001] ELR 311 217
R. (on the application of K) v. Newham LBC [2002] EWHC Admin 405; [2002] ELR 390, QBD 46, 57, 175
R. (on the application of KB) v. Mental Health Review Tribunal [2003] EWHC Admin 193; [2004] QB 936; [2003] 3 WLR 185, QBD 31

xvii

TABLE OF CASES

R. (on the application of KW) v. Special Educational Needs and Disability
  Tribunal and Rochdale MBC [2003] EWHC Admin 1770; [2003] ELR
  566, QBD 222
R. (on the application of L) v. Governors of J School [2003] UKHL 9; [2003]
  2 AC 633; [2003] 1 All ER 1012, HL 212–213
R. (on the application of L) v. Independent Appeal Panel of St Edward's College
  [2001] EWHC Admin 108; [2001] ELR 452, QBD 58
R. (on the application of L) v. Waltham Forest LBC [2003] EWHC Admin 2907;
  [2004] ELR 161, QBD 237
R. (on the application of Louden) v. Bury School Organisation Committee [2002]
  EWHC 2749, QBD 29
R. (on the application of M) v. Brighton and Hove City Council and Special
  Educational Needs and Disability Tribunal [2003] EWHC Admin 1722;
  [2003] ELR 752, QBD 237
R. (on the application of MH) v. Hackney LBC [2001] EWHC Admin 314,
  QBD 225
R. (on the application of MH) v. Special Educational Needs and Disability
  Tribunal and Hounslow LBC [2004] EWCA Civ 770; [2004] ELR
  424, CA 128
R. (on the application of Mayor and Burgesses of Hounslow LBC) v. School
  Admission Appeal Panel for Hounslow LBC [2002] EWCA Civ 900;
  [2002] 1 WLR 3147; [2002] ELR 402, CA 40, 56, 58
R. (on the application of Morris) v. Newham LBC [2002] EWHC Admin 1262,
  QBD 31
R. (on the application of Nash) v. Chelsea College of Art [2001] EWHC Admin
  538; (2001) *The Times*, 25 July, QBD 235
R. (on the application of O) v. St James Roman Catholic Primary School
  Appeal Panel [2001] ELR 469, QBD 40
R. (on the application of Opoku) v. Principle of Southwark College [2002]
  EWHC Admin 2092; [2003] 1 WLR 234, QBD 233
R. (on the application of P (A Child)) v. Oxfordshire CC Exclusion Appeals
  Panel [2002] EWCA Civ 693; [2002] ELR 556, CA 213
R. (on the application of Roberts) v. Chair and Governing Body of Cwmfelinfach
  Primary School [2001] EWHC Admin 242, QBD 214
R. (on the application of S) v. Governing Body of YP School [2003] EWCA Civ
  1306; [2004] ELR 37; [2003] All ER (D) 202, CA 217
R. (on the application of S) v. Head Teacher of C High School [2001] EWHC
  Admin 513; [2002] ELR 73, QBD 216
R. (on the application of S) v. Norfolk CC [2004] EWHC Admin 404; [2004]
  ELR 259, QBD 237
R. (on the application of South Gloucestershire LEA) v. South Gloucestershire
  Schools Appeals Panel [2001] EWHC Admin 732; [2002] ELR 309,
  QBD 57–8
R. (on the application of T) v. Head Teacher of Elliott School [2002] EWCA
  Civ 1349; [2003] ELR 160, CA 216, 217
R. (on the application of T) v. Head Teacher of Wembley High School [2001]
  EWHC Admin 299; [2001] ELR 359, QBD 50
R. (on the application of V) v. Cumbria CC [2003] EWHC Admin 232, QBD ...220

xviii

R. (on the application of W) *v.* Bedfordshire CC [2001] EWHC Admin 47; [2001]
   ELR 645, QBD 226
R. (on the application of W (Jane)) *v.* Blaenau Gwent BC [2003] EWHC Admin
   2880; [2004] ELR 152, QBD 237
R. (on the application of Williamson) v. Secretary of State for Education [2005]
   UKHL 15; [2005] 2 WLR 590, HL; *affirming* [2002] EWCA Civ 1926;
   [2003] QB 1300; [2003] ELR 176, CA 40
R. (on the application of Young) *v.* Oxford City Council [2002] EWCA Civ 990;
   [2003] JPL 232, CA 28
R. *v.* Barnet LBC, *ex p.* B [1998] ELR 281, CA 234
R. *v.* Barnet LBC, *ex p.* Barnett (unreported, 27 November 1995) 224
R. *v.* Barnsley MBC, *ex p.* Hook [1976] 1 WLR 1052, CA 202
R. *v.* Beatrix Potter School, *ex p.* K [1997] ELR 468, QBD 59
R. *v.* Birmingham City Council, *ex p.* L [2000] ELR 543, QBD 59
R. *v.* Birmingham City Council Education Appeal Committee, ex p. B [1999]
   ELR 305 ....54, 59
R. *v.* Board of Governors of Stoke Newington School [1994] ELR 131 ....214, 215
R. *v.* Bradford MBC, *ex p.* Sikander Ali [1994] ELR 299 ....46, 58
R. *v.* Brent and Harrow AHA, *ex p.* Harrow LBC [1997] ELR 187 232
R. *v.* Brent LBC, *ex p.* Baruwa (1997) 29 HLR 915, CA 230
R. *v.* Brighouse School Appeal Committee, ex p. G and B [1997] ELR 39,
   QBD 48
R. *v.* Bryn Elian High School Board of Governors, ex p. W [1999] ELR 380,
   QBD 213
R. *v.* Camden LBC, *ex p.* S (1990) 89 LGR 513, QBD 58
R. *v.* Camden LBC and Governors of Hampstead School, *ex p.* H [1996] ELR
   360, CA 214, 217, 218
R. *v.* Cardinal Newman's School, *ex p.* S [1998] ELR 304 212
R. *v.* Chair of the Governors and Head Teacher of A and S School, *ex p.* T
   [2000] ELR 274, QBD 208, 223
R. *v.* Cleveland CC, *ex p.* Commission for Racial Equality [1994] ELR 44;
   (1993) 1 FCR 597, CA 42
R. *v.* Cobham Hall School, *ex p.* S [1998] ELR 389, QBD 107
R. *v.* Commissioner for Local Administration, *ex p.* H [1999] ELR 314, CA 23
R. *v.* Commissioner for Local Administration, *ex p.* S [1999] ELR 103, QBD 23
R. *v.* Cumbria CC, *ex p.* P [1995] ELR 337, QBD 222
R. *v.* Devon CC, *ex p.* George [1989] AC 573, HL 171, 173, 174
R. *v.* Dorset CC and Further Education Funding Council, *ex p.* Goddard
   [1995] ELR 109, QBD 232
R. *v.* Downes, *ex p.* Wandsworth LBC [2000] ELR 425, QBD 51
R. *v.* Dunraven School Governors, ex p. B [2000] ELR 156, CA 201
R. *v.* East Sussex CC, *ex p.* D [1991] COD 374 174
R. *v.* East Sussex CC, ex p. Tandy [1998] AC 714; (1998) 1 CCLR 352,
   HL 92, 231
R. *v.* Education Committee of Blackpool BC, *ex p.* Taylor [1999] ELR 237,
   QBD 218
R. *v.* Essex CC, ex p. C [1994] ELR 273, CA; [1994] ELR 54 174
R. *v.* Essex CC, ex p. Jacobs [1997] ELR 190, QBD 54

TABLE OF CASES

R. v. Fernhill Manor School, *ex p.* A [1994] ELR 67, QBD 62, 219
R. v. Gloucester CC, *ex p.* Findlater (unreported, 14 July 2000) 29
R. v. Governing Body of K School and Independent Appeal Panel of London
  Borough of E. *See* R. (on the application of A (A Child)) *v.* Kingsmead School
  Governors
R. v. Governor of Bacon's City Technology College, *ex p.* W [1998] ELR 488,
  QBD 202
R. v. Governors of Bishop Challenor Roman Catholic Comprehensive Girls
  School, *ex p.* Choudhury [1992] 2 AC 182, HL 47
R. v. Governors of Haberdashe's Aske Hatcham Community College Trust,
  ex p. T [1995] ELR 350, QBD 107
R. v. Governors of Hasmonean High School, *ex p.* N and E [1994] ELR 343,
  CA 48
R. v. Governors of the London Oratory School, *ex p.* Regis [1989] Fam Law 67,
  QBD 215
R. v. Governors of St Gregory's Roman Catholic Aided High School and
  Appeals Committee, *ex p.* M [1995] ELR 290, QBD 214, 216
R. v. Greenwich LBC, *ex p.* Governors of John Ball Primary School (1989)
  88 LGR 589, CA 42, 45
R. v. Hackney LBC, *ex p.* GC [1996] ELR 142, CA 234
R. v. Hackney LBC, *ex p.* T [1991] COD 454 218
R. v. Harrow LBC, *ex p.* M [1997] FCR 761, QBD 220, 221
R. v. Havering LBC, *ex p.* K [1998] ELR 402, QBD 129, 175
R. v. Head Teacher and Governing Body of Crug Glas School, *ex p.* W
  [1999] ELR 484, QBD 225
R. v. Head Teacher and Independent Appeal Committee of Dunraven School,
  ex p. B [2000] ELR 156, CA 70, 76, 216, 218
R. v. Hereford and Worcester CC, *ex p.* P [1992] 2 FLR 207; [1992] 2 FCR 732,
  QBD 129, 174, 175, 223
R. v. Hillingdon LBC, *ex p.* Queensmead School [1997] ELR 331, QBD . . . 222, 231
R. v. Incorporated Froebel Educational Institute, *ex p.* L [1999] ELR 488,
  QBD 219
R. v. Independent Appeal Panel of Sheffield City Council, *ex p.* N [2000] ELR
  700, QBD 218, 219
R. v. Independent Appeal Panel of Sefton MBC, *ex p.* B [2002] EWHC
  1509 . . . . 73, 83
R. v. Islington LBC, *ex p.* GA [2000] EWHC 390 129
R. v. Kingston-upon-Thames LBC, *ex p.* Hunter [1997] ELR 223 . . . . 220, 226
R. v. Lambeth LBC, *ex p.* Campbell (1994) 26 HLR 618, QBD 31
R. v. Lancashire CC, *ex p.* M [1989] 2 FLR 279 . . . . 125, 220, 232
R. v. Lancashire CC, *ex p.* M [1995] ELR 136 218
R. v. Leicester CC Education Appeal Committee, *ex p.* Tarmohamed [1997]
  ELR 48 . . . . 54, 55
R. v. Local Commissioner for Administration for the North and East Area of
  England, *ex p.* Bradford MBC [1979] 2 All ER 881, CA 22
R. v. M, *ex p.* Board of Stoke Newington Schools [1994] ELR 131 72
R. v. Muntham House School, *ex p.* R [2000] ELR 287, QBD 62, 107, 202, 219
R. v. Neale and Another, *ex p.* S [1995] ELR 198 . . . . 213, 219

xx

R. v. Newham LBC, *ex p.* × [1995] ELR 303, QBD 202, 213, 216, 219
R. v. Northamptonshire CC, *ex p.* Weighill [1998] ELR 291, QBD 213, 218, 235
R. v. Northavon DC, *ex p.* Palmer (1993) 25 HLR 674, QBD 31
R. v. Oxfordshire CC, *ex p.* C [1996] ELR 153 222
R. v. Oxfordshire CC, *ex p.* Pittick [1996] ELR 153, QBD 231
R. v. Oxfordshire CC, *ex p.* Roast [1996] ELR 381, CA 225
R. v. Oxfordshire CC, *ex p.* Wallace [1987] 2 FLR 193, DC 232
R. v. Richmond-upon-Thames LBC, *ex p.* JC [2001] ELR 21 . . . . .29, 40, 56, 57
R. v. Rochdale MBC, *ex p.* Schemet [1994] ELR 89, QBD 175
R. v. Rotherham MBC, *ex p.* Clark [1998] ELR 152, CA 42
R. v. Rotherham MBC, *ex p.* LT [2000] ELR 76, CA 58
R. v. School Adjudicator, *ex p.* Wirral MBC [2000] ELR 620 51
R. v. Secretary of State for Education, *ex p.* Bandtock [2001] ELR 333 29
R. v. Secretary of State for Education, *ex p.* E [1992] 1 FLR 377, CA 220, 221
R. v. Secretary of State for Education, *ex p.* E [1996] ELR 312, QBD 233
R. v. Secretary of State for Education, *ex p.* E [1996] ELR 279 221
R. v. Secretary of State for Education and Science, *ex p.* Davis [1989] 2 FLR
    190, DC 234
R. v. Secretary of State for Education and Science, *ex p.* E [1992] 1 FLR 377,
    CA 230
R. v. Secretary of State for Education and Science, *ex p.* Islam [1994] ELR 11,
    QBD 38
R. v. Secretary of State for Education and Science, *ex p.* Threapleton (1988) *The
    Times,* 2 June, CO302/22, DC 29
R. v. Secretary of State for the Home Department, *ex p.* Pierson [1998] AC 539,
    HL 200
R. v. South Glamorgan Appeal Committee, *ex p.* Evans (unreported, 10 May
    1984) 47
R. v. South Gloucestershire Education Appeals Committee, *ex p.* Bryant [2001]
    ELR 53, CA 58
R. v. Southend Borough Education Appeals Committee, ex p. Southend-on-Sea
    BC [2000] Ed CR 368, QBD 59
R. v. Special Educational Needs Tribunal, *ex p.* Brophy [1997] ELR 291, QBD . .225
R. v. Special Educational Needs Tribunal, *ex p.* F [1996] ELR 213, QBD 225
R. v. Special Educational Needs Tribunal, *ex p.* F [1999] ELR 417, QBD 226
R. v. Special Educational Needs Tribunal, *ex p.* J [1997] ELR 237, QBD . . .224, 227
R. v. Special Educational Needs Tribunal, *ex p.* South Cambridgeshire CC and
    Chapman [1996] CLY 2493, QBD 224, 225
R. v. Special Educational Needs and Disability Tribunal, *ex p.* South Glamorgan
    CC [1996] ELR 326, CA 225
R. v. Staffordshire CC, *ex p.* Ashworth (1997) 9 Admin LR 373, QBD 216
R. v. Stockton-on-Tees BC, *ex p.* W [2000] ELR 93, CA .59
R. v. Surrey CC Education Committee, *ex p.* H (1984) 83 LGR 219, CA 231
R. v. TV School Adjudicator, *ex p.* Wirral MBC [2002] ELR 620, QBD 10
R. v. Wandsworth LBC, *ex p.* M [1998] ELR 424, QBD 221
R. v. Wiltshire CC, *ex p.* Razazan [1997] ELR 370, CA .58
Rhondda Cynon Taff CBC *v.* Special Educational Needs and Disability Tribunal
    and V [2001] EWHC Admin 823; [2002] ELR 290, QBD 222

TABLE OF CASES

Richardson v. Solihull MBC [1998] ELR 319 222
Robinson v. St Helen's MBC [2002] All ER (D) 388, CA 99, 101, 103
S v. Bracknell Forest BC and Special Educational Needs and Disability Tribunal
 [1999] ELR 51, QBD...223
S v. Brent LBC; T v. Oxfordshire CC, P v. Head Teacher of Elliot School and
 Secretary of State for Education and Skills (Interested Party) [2002]
 EWCA Civ 693; [2002] ELR 556, CA 39, 62
S v. Hackney LBC [2001] EWHC Admin 572; [2002] ELR 45, QBD 223, 229
S v. Special Educational Needs Tribunal [1996] 1 WLR 382, CA; *affirming*
 [1995] 1 WLR 1627, QBD 224, 225, 227,
 230, 233, 234, 235
S v. Special Educational Needs Tribunal [2002] EWHC 1047; [2003] ELR 85,
 QBD 227, 228
S v. Swansea City Council and Confrey [2000] ELR 315, QBD 145, 226
S and C v. Special Educational Needs Tribunal [1997] ELR 242,
 QBD 224, 227, 230
S, T and P v. Brent LBC [2002] EWCA Civ 691; [2002] ELR 556,
 CA 201, 202, 212,
 213, 216, 217
Sage v. South Glamorgan CC and Confrey [1998] ELR 525 227
Sayers v. Clarke Walker (Practice Note) [2002] EWCA Civ 645; [2002] 1 WLR 3095,
 CA..227, 228
School Admission Appeal Panel v. Mayor and Burgesses of Hounslow LBC
 [2002] EWCA Civ 900; [2002] 1 WLR 3147; [2002] ELR 602 ....57, 58
Secretary of State for Education and Science v. Tameside MBC [1977] AC 1014,
 HL 25, 213
Skilbeck v. Williamson and Oxfordshire CC [1999] EWHC Admin 815 228
Smith v. Havering LBC [2004] EWHC 599; [2004] ELR 629, QBD 101
South Glamorgan CC v. Long and M [1996] ELR 400,
 QBD 226, 227, 229, 230, 234
Southampton City Council v. G [2002] EWHC Admin 1516; [2002] ELR 698,
 QBD 223, 224
Special Educational Needs and Disability Tribunal DRC/03/8674 164
Special Educational Needs and Disability Tribunal 04/50116, 18 April 2004 168
Staffordshire CC v. J and J [1996] ELR 418, QBD 234
Stevens v. United Kingdom (1986) 46 DR 245 40
Sunderland City Council v. Plumpton and C [1996] ELR 283, QBD 227, 233
Sythes v. Camden LBC and Special Educational Needs Tribunal (unreported, 21
 June 1996) 229
T v. Special Educational Needs Tribunal and Wiltshire CC [2002] EWHC Admin
 1474; [2002] ELR 704, QBD 223, 229, 233
T v. Islington LBC [2001] EWHC Admin 1029; [2002] ELR 426, QBD 222, 226
W v. Gloucestershire CC [2001] EWHC Admin 481; (2001) 98(29) LSG 39,
 QBD 224
W-R v. Solihull MBC and Wall [1999] ELR 528, QBD 232
Wakefield MDC v. Dorsey [1998] EWHC Admin 96, QBD 231
Wakefield MDC v. E [2001] EWHC Admin 508; [2002] ELR 203.............232
Wandsworth LBC v. K [2003] EWHC 1424; [2003] ELR 554, QBD 223

Wardle-Heron *v.* Newham LBC and Special Educational Needs Tribunal [2002]
    EWHC Admin 2806; [2004] ELR 68, QBD 237
Wednesbury, see Associated Provincial Picture Houses Ltd *v.* Wednesbury Corp
White *v.* Ealing LBC [1998] ELR 319, CA 233, 234
Wilkin and Goldthorpe *v.* Coventry City Council [1998] ELR 345 224
X (Minors) *v.* Bedfordshire [1995] 2 AC 633, HL 97, 98, 102, 108, 236

Table of statutes

Access to Justice Act 1999
   s.6 87
Children and Young Persons Act 1969
   s.39 . . . . .192, 197
Data Protection Act 1998 . . . . .105, 161
Disability Discrimination Act
   1995 . . . . .xii, 69, 133, 148, 159,
                161, 170, 198, 205, 208
   Part III 153, 154, 156, 158,
                               161
   Part IV 12, 148, 149, 151,
                  153–155, 162, 166, 169
   s.1 . . . .149–152, 164, 165, 166, 167
   s.18 150
   s.19, 20 154
   s.28A 156, 157, 206–208
      (1), (2) 155
      (3) 156
   s.28B 206–208
      (1) 156, 207
      (2) 156, 157, 207
      (6) 157
      (7), (8) 157, 207
   s.28C 156, 157, 161, 207, 208
      (4) 158
   s.28D 160
      (2) 161
   s.28E 160
   s.28F 162, 207, 208
      (1)(a) 207
   s.28G 162, 207, 208
      (2) 207
   s.28J 163
   s.53A 149
      (8) 150
   Sched. 1 150

      para. 2 151
      para. 4, 6 152
      para. 8(1)(b) 152
   Sched. 4A 154
Education Act 1944 177
Education Act 1981 . . . .97, 99, 177, 231
Education Act 1993 . . . . .99, 177
Education Act 1994
   s.11A 4
Education Act 1996 . . .99, 105, 177, 207
   Part II, Chap. V 10
   Part IV 109
   s.7 88
   s.9 . . . . .38, 126, 223, 232, 233
   s.10 4
   s.11 . . . . .4, 226
   s.13(1) 5, 57
   s.13A 6
   s.14 . . . . .5, 88
   s.15 107
   s.19 . . . . .6, 39, 50, 92, 96, 190,
                    202, 203, 225, 231
      (1) 89
      (2) 93
      (4), (4A) 89
      (6) 90
   s.83(1) .18
   s.170 7
   s.225 10
   s.312 . . . . .110, 149
   s.313 . . . . .4, 6
   s.316 . . . . .127, 128, 208
   s.317 . . . . .12, 111
   s.319 .233
   s.321 6
   s.322A, 322B 111

TABLE OF STATUTES

s.323 118
s.324 ....6, 96, 124, 127, 129
   (5)(a)(i) 209
      (b) 12, 208
s.325 133
s.326 ....133, 134
s.329 134
s.329 134
s.329A 118, 134
s.333–336, 336ZA 133
s.351 ....4, 6
   (1) 12
s.356 ....4, 5
s.390 6
s.408 5
s.409 ....6, 12, 21
s.434(1) 12
s.444 173
   (5) 173
s.447 6
s.463(1) 3
s.482 ....2, 3
s.483(2) 18
s.484 4
s.488 4
s.495 5
s.496 ....5, 24
s.497 ....5, 24
   (1) 25
s.497A, 497B 25, 26
s.509 ....7, 171
   (1) 171, 174
   (3) 172, 176
   (4) 172
s.509A 7, 172
s.518 7
s.579(6), (7) 171
Sched. 1 93
Sched. 26 109
Sched. 27 ....109, 128, 134, 208
   para. 3 128
      (1) 125
      (3) 125, 126, 231
      (4) 126
   para. 4 ....122, 125
   para. 11(5) 225
Sched. 35A 19

Education Act 1997
   s.19 5
   s.38 ....13, 162
   s.39 13
   s.47 89
Education Act 2002 ....1, 21, 42
   Pt 10 ....3, 14
   s.49 49
   s.52 ....61, 199
   s.65 ....3, 5, 18
   s.70 ....8, 17
      (7) 17
   s.71 19
      (4) 19
   s.72 19
   s.159(1) 14
   s.161(3) 14
   s.163(1), (2) 14
   s.165(2) 14
      (3) 14, 15
   s.171 ....4, 14
   s.195 133
   s.482(1) 18
   Sched. 7 ....5, 18, 19
   Sched. 8 ....8, 17
   Sched. 9 19
   Sched. 18, para. 5, 7 133
   Sched. 22, Pt 3 49
Education (No. 2) Act 1986
   s.50 5
Education Reform Act 1988 22
   s.209, 210 4
   s.211 5
   s.218 5
Education (Schools) Act 1992 13
Human Rights Act 1998 ....21, 30, 32, 38, 42, 175, 190, 202
   s.6 ....57, 223
   s.8 96
      (3) 31
Learning and Skills Act 2000 .....3, 21
   s.1 7
      (2) 7
   s.7 ....4, 7
   s.19 8
   s.22 8
   ss.30–51 7
   s.65 19

TABLE OF STATUTES

Learning and Skills Act 2000 (*cont.*)
   s.113A(1)(b) 19
   Sched. 4 .7
Limitation Act 1980
   s.11 101
   s.33 101
Local Government Act 1966
   s.11 5
Local Government Act 1974
   s.26 22
      (4)–(7) 23
   s.31(3) 23
Race Relations Act 1976 . . . . .69, 198
   s.17 155
   s.71 6
Race Relations Amendment Act
2000 68
Sex Discrimination Act 1975
   s.22 155
   s.25 6
School Inspections Act 1996 162
   s.17, 18 .13
   s.23 13
   s.24 . . . . .7, 13
School Standards and Framework Act
1998   1, 2, 21,
                              24, 25, 41
   Part II, Chap. III 10
   Part II, Chap. IV 10
   s.1 . . . . .4, 47
   s.2 6
   s.3 4
   s.4 47
   s.5, 6 6
   s.14 22
   s.15 . . . . .13, 20, 22
      (1), (4), (6) 7
   s.16 .11, 13
   s.17 . . . . .7, 13
   s.18 13
   s.19 . . . . .5, 7, 20
   s.20 . . . . .1, 9
      (1) 61
   s.24 6
      (1) 8
   s.25 . . . . .5, 9
   s.26(1) 6, 16
      (5) 8

s.28 . . . . .1, 5, 6, 8–10, 17, 48
   (5) 18
s.29 . . . . .5, 6, 8, 20, 29
s.30 . . . . .5, 20
s.31 . . . . .1, 5, 6
s.32 5
   (1) 20
   (3) 9
s.34 . . . . .5, 20
s.38(2) 11
s.42 11
s.45 6
s.50(3), (7) 11
s.54 . . . . .1, 6
s.55 . . . . .2, 6
s.61(2A) .12
s.62 7
s.65(1)(c), (d) 12
s.67 6
s.84 . . . . .4, 52
   (1) 43
s.85 4
s.85A .44, 88
s.86 . . . . .42, 57
   (1) 42
   (2) 43
   (3)(a) 42, 95
      (c) 43
   (3A) 42, 43
   (3B) 42
   (4) 47, 55, 95
   (5) .44, 47
   (6) 49
   (8)(a) .46
s.87 . . . . .43, 50
s.88 6
   (1)(a)(ii) 12
s.89 48
s.89A(1) .44
s.90 .10, 48
   (1) 50
   (3) 51
s.92 6
s.94 . . . . .6, 12, 43
   (1), (2) 51, 94
   (5), (5A)–(5C) 52
s.95 . . . . .50, 94
   (2), (3) 50

s.96 . . . . .7, 49, 57, 94, 95	Sched. 12 11
(4), (5) 49	Sched. 16 1
s.97(5) .49	Sched. 17 . . . . .2, 11
s.98(3) .42	Sched. 24 58
s.99 48	para.12(a) 55, 56
s.100 46	(b) 56
s.101 46	Sched. 25 50
(1) .21	Special Educational Needs and
s.102 46	Disability Act 2001 . . . . .68, 99, 109,
(1), (4) 48	133, 148
s.104(7) 46	s.1 127
s.118 .112	s.2, 3 .111
s.127 4	s.8 118
Sched. 2 1	ss.323, 325, 326, 328, 329 224
para.3 2	Sched. 2 154
Sched. 5 9	Supreme Court Act 1981
Sched. 6 . . . . .8, 9, 20	s.31 26
para.3(2) 18	(3) .27
Sched. 7 . . . . .5, 9, 20, 43	(4) .31
para.8 9	(6) .28
Sched. 8 1	s.35A .181
Sched. 9 . . . . .7, 10	Trade Union and Labour Relations
Sched. 10 10	(Consolidation) Act 1992
Sched. 11 10	s.244(1) 84

Table of statutory instruments

Civil Procedure Rules 1998, SI 1998/3132
r.3.1 .... .203
    (2)(a) .... .228
r.3.9(1)(h), (i) .... .228
r.7.5(2) .... .101
PD 15, para. 4.2, 4.3 .... .181
r.18.1 .... .106
r.39.2 .... .192
Pt 52 .... 147, 225, 226, 227
r.52.15(1) .... .35
PD 52, para.15 .... .35
    para. 17.3 .... .225
r.54.3(2) .... .31
r.54.5 .... 26–28, 203
r.54.14 .... .35
r.54.12(5) .... .35
r.54.16(2)(b) .... .35
PD 54, para.8.4 .... .34
Sched. 1, RSC Ord. 15, r.6 .... .227
    RSC Ord. 55 .... 225, 226
Disability Discrimination (Meaning of Disability) Regulations 1996, SI 1996/1455 .... .150
    reg. 3, 4 .... .152
Education (Additional Secondary School Proposals) (Amendment) Regulations 2003, SI 2003/1421 .... .17
Education (Additional Secondary School Proposals) Regulations 2003, SI 2003/1200
    reg. 3 .... .17
    regs. 9–17 8
    Sched. 1 .... .17
Education (Admission Appeals Arrangements) (England) Regulations 2002, SI 2002/2899
    Sched. 1 .... .52
Education (Admission Forums) (England) Regulations 2002, SI 2002/2900 ..... .44
Education (Budget Statements) (Wales) Regulations 1999, SI 1999/440 .... .10
Education (Government of New Schools on Transition to New Framework) Regulations 1998, SI 1998/3097 .... .11

TABLE OF STATUTORY INSTRUMENTS

Education (Independent School Standard) (England) Regulations 2003, SI 2003/1910 14
Education (Infant Class Sizes) (England) Regulations 1998, SI 1998/1973 47
Education (Objection to Admission Arrangements) (Amendment) Regulations 2002, SI 2002/2901 .... 10, 51
Education (Objection to Admission Arrangements) Regulations 1999, SI 1999/125 10
    regs. 5, 6, 7 51
Education (Pupil Exclusions and Appeals) (Maintained Schools) (England) Regulations 2002, SI 2002/3178 .... 61, 63, 199
    reg. 2(2) 64
    reg. 3 63
    reg. 4(5) 63
    reg. 5(1)(c)(i) 63
        (ii) 64
        (d) 63
        (8) 73
        (9) 64
    reg. 6(3) 79
        (4) 82
        (6) 83
    reg. 7(2) 62
    reg. 7A 69
    Sched., para. 2 79
        (2)(c) 80
Education (Pupil Exclusions and Appeals) (Pupil Referral Units) (England) Regulations 2002, SI 2002/3179 .... 61, 63
    reg. 4 63
    reg. 5(5) 63
    reg. 8(2) 62
    reg. 8A 69
    Sched., para.2(2)(c) 80
Education (Pupil Exclusions) (Miscellaneous Amendments) (England) Regulations 2004, SI 2004/402 61
    reg. 2 64
        (3) 92
    reg. 4 69
Education (Pupil Information) (England) Regulations 2000, SI 2000/297 75
Education (Pupil Registration) Regulations 1995, SI 1995/2089 12
    reg. 9(1)(k) 83
Education (School Government) (Transition to a New Framework) Regulations 1998, SI 1998/2763 11
Education (School Inspection) Regulations 1997, SI 1997/1966 13
Education (School Inspection) (Wales) (Amendment) Regulations 1999, SI 1999/1440 13
Education (School Inspection) (Wales) Regulations 1998, SI 1998/1866 13

TABLE OF STATUTORY INSTRUMENTS

Education (School Organisation Committee) (England) Regulations 1999, SI 1999/700
    reg. 5(1) 8
Education (School Organisation Plans) (England) Regulations 1999, SI 1999/701 . . 9
    reg.3 16
    reg.7 16
Education (School Organisation Proposals) (England) (Amendment) Regulations 2003, SI 2003/1229 .... 8, 9, 20
Education (School Organisation Proposals) (England) Regulations 1999, SI 1999/2213 .... 8, 9, 17, 20
    reg. 5(2)(a) 18
    reg. 7 18
    reg. 10 9
Education (School Organisation Proposals) (Wales) Regulations 1999, SI 1999/1671 .... 8, 9, 21
Education (School Performance Targets) (England) Regulations 1998, SI 1998/1532 11
Education (School Performance Targets) (Wales) Regulations 1998, SI 1998/2196 11
Education (Special Educational Needs) (England) Consolidation Regulations 2001, SI 2001/3455 .... 110, 121
    regs. 6–13 119
    reg. 6(1), (3) 119
    reg. 12(5) 120
        (6)–(9) 121
    reg. 17(1) 122
        (a) 122
        (2) 122
        (a) 122
        (3), (4) 128
    reg. 18(1) 130
    reg. 19 131
    reg. 20(8), (9) 130
        (10), (13), (14) 131
    reg. 23 132
    reg. 25(2), (4) 146
    Sched. 1, Pts A, B 122
    Sched. 2 123
Education (Special Educational Needs) (Information) (England) Regulations 1999, SI 1999/2506 .... 110, 111
Education (Special Educational Needs) (Provision of Information by Local Education Authorities) (England) Regulations 2001, SI 2001/2218 ...... 110, 111
Education (Student Support) Regulations 2002 39
Financing Maintained Schools Regulations 1999, SI 1999/101 10
Learning and Skills Council for England Regulations 2003, SI 2003/507 20
    Pt 3 9
School Governance (Procedures) (England) Regulations 2003, SI 2003/1377 72

TABLE OF STATUTORY INSTRUMENTS

Special Educational Needs and Disability Tribunal (General Provisions)
    Disability Claims Procedure) Regulations 2002, SI 2002/1985 133
       reg. 44 ....151, 167
          (2) 167
       Sched. 3, para. 10 163
Special Educational Needs Tribunal Regulations 2001, SI 2001/600 133
       reg. 8 135
       reg. 12(6) 143
       reg. 15 139
       reg. 16(3) 143
       reg. 20 141
       reg. 21 142
       reg. 26 141
       reg. 30(2)(a) 143
          (4)(b) 143
       reg. 33 ....140, 186
       reg. 39 ....146, 234
       reg. 40 145
       reg. 43 135

EUROPEAN LEGISLATION

EC Treaty (Treaty of Rome)
    Art. 13 155
European Convention on Human Rights ....xii, 31, 38, 42, 229
    Art. 6 ....27, 39, 57, 202, 212
    Art. 8 ....39, 40, 46
        (1), (2) 223
    Art. 9 40
    Art. 10 40
    Art. 14 39
    Protocol 1, Art. 2 ....38, 39, 50, 96, 175, 190, 202, 215, 223

CHAPTER 1
Structure of the school system

1.1 CATEGORISATION OF SCHOOLS

The School Standards and Framework Act (SSFA) 1998 was the predominant legislation for the current categorisation of maintained schools. Recently, this has been augmented by the Education Act (EA) 2002, particularly in relation to the development of academies.

LEA-maintained school

Under SSFA 1998, s.20, new categories of LEA-maintained schools were introduced as from September 1999. The main changes were as follows:

(a) county schools became community schools;
(b) grant-maintained schools or grant-maintained special schools became foundation schools or foundation special schools;
(c) controlled schools or aided schools became voluntary controlled or voluntary aided schools;
(d) maintained special schools became community special schools.

Schedule 2 to SSFA 1998 describes the allocation of classifications, which was either: automatically by virtue of pre-existing status; or by establishment under SSFA 1998, s.28 or s.31; or by way of changing category under the procedure set out in Schedule 8.

Community schools

Community schools are in general those wholly maintained by the LEA which also employs community school staff (SSFA 1998, s.54 and Sched. 16).

Foundation schools

Foundation schools are schools which before the implementation of SSFA 1998 provisions had been grant-maintained schools. The status of the foundation school turns on the status of the grant-maintained school before it became grant maintained (SSFA 1998, Sched. 2, para. 3). Categorisation is as follows:

(a) grant-maintained schools which were formerly county or controlled schools became foundation schools;
(b) grant-maintained schools which were formerly aided or special agreement schools became voluntary aided schools;
(c) grant-maintained schools which were special schools became foundation special schools;
(d) grant-maintained schools established by promoters became foundation schools.

The maintenance and responsibility for employment in foundation schools is divided. A body of persons will be established other than the LEA, whether incorporated or not, but excluding the governing body, which will hold the land on trust for the purposes of the school. The LEA will still be wholly responsible for maintaining the foundation school but the school staff will now be employed by their school governing body (SSFA 1998, s.55 and Sched. 17).

Voluntary schools

There are two types of voluntary schools, which are controlled and aided schools. Voluntary controlled schools will be wholly maintained by the LEA, which will also employ the staff. Voluntary aided schools will be mainly but not wholly maintained by the LEA, and the voluntary aided governing bodies will be the employers of the school staff (SSFA 1998, s.55 and Sched. 17).

Special schools

Special schools are those schools specially organised for children with special educational needs (SEN). They will be approved by the Secretary of State to perform this function. They will either be maintained by the LEA or come under foundation school status.

City technology colleges

City technology colleges and city technology colleges for the arts were established under EA 1996, s.482. They were independent schools with private sponsors, which received funding from central government. They had a particular technological emphasis and the aim was to provide a wider choice of secondary school to inner city children aged 11–18. Under SSFA 1998 they were allowed to keep their status as independent schools, although there was

STRUCTURE OF THE SCHOOL SYSTEM

provision for any city technology college which did so to join the maintained sector.

Academies

The background to development of the academy system is the city technology college. Section 482 of EA 1996 was amended by the Learning and Skills Act (LSA) 2000 to allow for city academies. These were based on city technology colleges with a wider range of curriculum. The academies were introduced by the then Secretary of State in March 2000 and the first academy projects were announced in September 2000. Academies are an integral part of central government's announced strategy for raising educational standards in the most disadvantaged areas. The new academies created under EA 2002, s.65 are different in the following ways:

(a) they can be established anywhere in England;
(b) they do not have a restricted emphasis of curriculum and can offer any subject area or combination of areas;
(c) they are not limited to secondary education.

Academies receive central government funding with an emphasis on the involvement of private 'sponsors' mainly from the business sector.

Independent schools

Independent schools are defined under EA 1996, s.463(1). They are now subject to an inspection and regulation regime, under EA 2002, Part 10, which will be discussed later.

Independent schools may be referred to as 'private schools' or 'public schools'. They are wholly outside the state sector and may be run for charitable purposes or for profit. They are fee charging and do not receive public funds other than funds arising from agreements to provide for children with SEN. They are schools which are wholly responsible for their own running and management.

1.2 ADMINISTRATION AND DECISION-MAKING

There has been an increasing move away from local management of the school system by LEAs towards central government control and devolving power downwards to school governing bodies. The main organisations for the administration and decision-making in the school system are described below.

Secretary of State

The Secretary of State and central government have increasing influence on the development of education. This can be seen particularly in the new school initiatives such as the academy system, and the development of specialist schools and business schools, etc. Central government's programme for schools is based on the tenet of private sector sponsors and government funding. There has been an increase in the powers of the Secretary of State, whose main duties and powers are now as follows.

Duties

1. To promote education generally (EA 1996, s.10).
2. To provide public funds to all bodies responsible for securing educational provision (EA 1996, s.11).
3. To issue and revise a code of practice on SEN (EA 1996, s.313).
4. To make arrangements for securing sufficient facilities for training teachers for schools, further education and higher education (EA 1994, s.11A).
5. To pay each LEA a grant equal to the amount given in mandatory grants by the LEA (Education Reform Act 1988, s.209).
6. To revise the National Curriculum when she/he considers it is necessary or expedient (EA 1996, s.356).
7. To ensure that the curriculum for maintained schools is balanced and broadly based (EA 1996, s.351).
8. To issue a code of practice relating to admission arrangements for LEAs, governing bodies of maintained schools, appeal panels and adjudicators on admission to schools (SSFA 1998, ss.84 and 85).
9. To issue codes of practice often containing practical guidance to secure an effective relationship between LEAs and the schools maintained by them (SSFA 1998, s.127).
10. To make regulations imposing limits on infant class sizes and to reimburse LEAs for expenditure in this regard (SSFA 1998, ss.1 and 3).
11. To keep a register of independent schools in England (EA 2002, s.171).

Powers

1. To make grants to and appoint members of the Learning and Skills Council (LSA 2000, s.7).
2. To give education standard grants to LEAs (EA 1996, s.484).
3. To give grants for the education of travellers and displaced people (EA 1996, s.488; Education Reform Act (ERA) 1988, s.210).

4. To give grants to LEAs and governing bodies of further education institutions to provide for ethnic minorities (Local Government Act 1966, s.11; ERA 1988, s.211).
5. To give grants for teaching training (Education (No. 2) Act 1986, s.50).
6. To prescribe the staffing of schools and the qualification required for teachers (ERA 1988, s.218).
7. To direct the closure of a school requiring special measures (SSFA 1998, s.19).
8. To require the closure of a community or foundation special school in the interest of the health, safety or welfare of pupils (SSFA 1998, s.32).
9. To direct the rationalisation of school places (SSFA 1998, s.34 and Sched. 7).
10. To approve any significant change in the category of a school or its closure (SSFA 1998, ss.28–31).
11. To establish and provide money for academies (EA 2002, s.65 and Sched. 7).
12. To appoint an adjudicator for schools (SSFA 1998, s.25).
13. To determine disputes between LEAs and governing bodies (EA 1996, s.495).
14. To prevent the unreasonable exercise of functions where he/she believes that an LEA or governing body has acted or is proposing to act 'unreasonably' (EA 1996, s.496).
15. Where satisfied that an LEA or governing body has failed to discharge its duty, to give directions to enforce the performance of that duty (EA 1996, s.497).
16. To require LEAs, governing bodies and head teachers to provide such information as required by regulations (EA 1996, s.408).
17. To set attainment targets, programmes of study and assessment arrangements in relation to the National Curriculum (EA 1996, s.356).
18. To require governing bodies to set annual targets for the performance of pupils (EA 1997, s.19).

Local education authorities

The main duties and powers of LEAs are set out below.

Duties

1. To secure that it has sufficient schools to provide primary and secondary education in its area (EA 1996, s.14).
2. To 'contribute towards the spiritual, moral, mental and physical development of the community by securing that efficient primary education, secondary education and further education are available to meet the needs of the population of their area' (EA 1996, s.13(1)).

PRACTICAL EDUCATION LAW

3. To make arrangements for the education of children who may not receive this at school (EA 1996, s.19).
4. To promote high standards in primary and secondary education (SSFA 1998, s.5, inserting s.13A into EA 1996).
5. To establish a school organisation committee (SSFA 1998, s.24).
6. To produce an education development plan for education in its area (SSFA 1998, s.6).
7. To prepare a school organisation plan (SSFA 1998, s.26(1))
8. To publish proposals and carry out plans to establish, alter or close a community, foundation, voluntary or special school (SSFA 1998, ss.28, 29 and 31).
9. To give a financial budget to all maintained schools (SSFA 1998, s.45).
10. To employ all staff in community, voluntary controlled or community special schools or foundation, voluntary aided and foundation special schools (SSFA 1998, ss.54 and 55).
11. To ensure a broad and balanced curriculum in all schools in its area (EA 1996, s.351).
12. To be the admission authority for community and voluntary controlled schools (unless this is delegated to the governing body) (SSFA 1998, s.88).
13. To publish information each school year about admissions (SSFA 1998, s.92).
14. To establish a complaints procedure to deal with complaints of unreasonableness by LEA or by a governing body in relation to the curriculum, provision of information, or religious education (EA 1996, s.409).
15. To make arrangements for appeals against exclusions (SSFA 1998, s.67).
16. To make arrangements for appeals against admission (SSFA 1998, s.94).
17. To identify and be responsible for children with SEN in its area (EA 1996, s.321).
18. To have regard to the code of practice on SEN (EA 1996, s.313).
19. To make arrangements for educational provision in statements of SEN (EA 1996, s.324).
20. To prepare plans for the reduction of infant class sizes (SSFA 1998, s.2).
21. To enforce school attendance (EA 1996, s.447).
22. To secure that facilities provided by the LEA with any benefits or services ancillary to those facilities are provided without sex discrimination (Sex Discrimination Act 1975, s.25).
23. To eliminate unlawful race discrimination and to promote equality of opportunity and good relations between persons of different racial groups (Race Relations Act 1976, s.71).
24. To establish a standing advisory council on religious education (EA 1996, s.390).

STRUCTURE OF THE SCHOOL SYSTEM

Powers

1. To arrange nursery education (EA 1996, s.170).
2. To appoint some governors to maintained schools (SSFA 1998, Sched. 9).
3. To establish a school inspection service to tender for school inspections (School Inspections Act 1996, s.24).
4. To provide transport (EA 1996, ss.509 and 509A).
5. To pay the cost of children taking part in school activities (EA 1996, s.518).
6. To direct that a child be admitted to a particular school (SSFA 1998, s.96).
7. To take such steps as may be necessary to prevent the breakdown of discipline in a maintained school (SSFA 1998, s.62).
8. To intervene in maintained schools if the school has been subject to a formal warning under SSFA 1998, s.15(1) or has serious weaknesses identified in an inspection, or requires special measures identified in an inspection (SSFA 1998, s.15(4) and (6)).
9. To direct the closure of a school and to suspend the right to a delegated budget (SSFA 1998, ss.19 and 17).

Learning and Skills Council

The central Learning and Skills Council for England was created as a body corporate under LSA 2000, s.1. (An equivalent body exists for Wales with similar functions under LSA 2000, ss.30–51 and Sched. 4.) Members are appointed by the Secretary of State and must not number less than 12 or more than 16 (LSA 2000, s.1(2)).

The Learning and Skills Council is centrally government funded. It is responsible for funding school sixth forms (LSA 2000, s.7) and for the funding of post-16 SEN provision, which is made available through LEAs. The main functions of the Learning and Skills Council are as follows:

(a) securing provision of proper facilities for education and training for persons aged 16–19 years;
(b) ensuring provision of reasonable educational training for those aged over 19 years;
(c) encouraging individuals to undergo post-16 training;
(d) encouraging employers to participate in the provision of post-16 educational training;
(e) encouraging employers to contribute to the cost of post-16 educational training;
(f) core funding of school sixth forms and post-16 provision of SEN through LEAs.

The Learning and Skills Council must establish a local committee for each area of England as specified by the Secretary of State (LSA 2000, s.19). The local Learning and Skills Council members are appointed by the central Learning and Skills Council with approval of the Secretary of State. The Secretary of State will appoint the local chairperson but will take advice from the central Learning and Skills Council.

The local Learning and Skills Council will publish a local plan each year, which sets out the needs of the population and of employers for education and training and how these objectives will be met (LSA 2000, s.22). There should be liaison between the LEA and the local Learning and Skills Council and the plan of the local Learning and Skills Council is taken into account in the preparation by the LEA of its school organisation plan.

Included in the local plan will be a statement of the education and training and connected leisure-time education which the local Learning and Skills Council would like the LEA to provide for persons over the age of 19 years. The plan will make proposals as to how the finances will be provided by the Learning and Skills Council to secure such provision.

School organisation committee

Under SSFA 1998, s.24(1), every LEA must set up a school organisation committee for its area. Membership of the committee is to consist of or be drawn from or nominated by various groups with an interest in education in the area (Education (School Organisation Committee) (England) Regulations 1999, SI 1999/700, reg. 5(1)). For example, members can be drawn from the LEA, governing bodies, or the Diocesan Board of Education.

The main functions of the school organisation committee are:

1. To consider and decide on the school organisation plan as presented to it by the LEA (SSFA 1998, s.26(5)).
2. To consider proposals presented LEAs for establishment of 'additional' schools prior to submission to the Secretary of State (EA 2002, s.70 and Sched. 8; Education (Additional Secondary School Proposals) Regulations 2003, SI 2003/1200, regs. 9–17).
3. To consider and decide on proposals presented by the LEA or others for the establishment of 'non-additional schools' (SSFA 1998, s.28 and Sched. 6; Education (School Organisation Proposals) (England) Regulations 1999, SI 1999/2213, as amended by the Education (School Organisation Proposals) (England) (Amendment) Regulations 2003, SI 2003/1229 (in Wales: Education (School Organisation Proposals) (Wales) Regulations 1999, SI 1999/1671, as amended)).
4. To consider and decide on proposals by the LEA to cease to maintain these schools (SSFA 1998, s.29 and Sched. 6).

STRUCTURE OF THE SCHOOL SYSTEM

5. To consider and decide on proposals by the Secretary of State for a reduction in the number of primary and secondary schools in an LEA's area (SSFA 1998, Sched. 7, para. 8).
6. To consider and decide on proposals for 'prescribed alterations' to primary and secondary schools (SSFA 1998, s.28 and Sched. 6; Education (School Organisation Proposals) (England) Regulations 1999, SI 1999/2213, as amended by the Education (School Organisation Proposals) (England) (Amendment) Regulations 2003, SI 2003/1229 (in Wales: Education (School Organisation Proposals) (Wales) Regulations 1999, SI 1999/1671, as amended)).
7. To consider and comment on proposals submitted by the Learning and Skills Council to establish or discontinue a maintained school sixth form (School Organisation Proposals by the Learning and Skills Council for England Regulations 2003, SI 2003/507, Part 3).

Adjudicator

The adjudicator is appointed by the Secretary of State by way of his/her powers under SSFA 1998, s.25. Regulations governing the adjudicator's decision-making are made by the Secretary of State under SSFA 1998, Sched. 5

Main functions

The adjudicator's main functions are as follows:

1. Consideration of and decision on draft school organisation plans referred by a group of members of the school organisation committee (Education (School Organisation Plans) (England) Regulations 1999, SI 1999/701).
2. Consideration of and decisions on proposal to establish (non-additional) schools by LEAs and others as referred by the school organisation committee (SSFA 1998, Sched. 6; SI 1999/2213, reg. 10).
3. Consideration of and decision on proposals to cease to maintain schools as referred by a group of members of the school organisation committee or by the school organisation committee at the request of the LEA (SSFA 1998, s.20).
4. To consider and decide on proposals by the Secretary of State to reduce excessive school provision (SSFA 1998, s.32(3) and Sched. 7).
5. To decide on proposals for discontinuing sixth forms as referred by the Learning and Skills Council (School Organisation Proposals by the Learning and Skills Council for England Regulations 2003, SI 2003/507, Part 3).

PRACTICAL EDUCATION LAW

6. To consider and decide on proposed alterations to schools as referred by the school organisation committee (SSFA 1998, s.28).
7. To act as a decision maker on school admission arrangements including policies and over-subscription criteria in disputes between local admission authorities and schools and to hear objections from eligible parents (SSFA 1998, s.90; Education (Objections to Admission Arrangements) Regulations 1999, SI 1999/125, as amended by Education (Objections to Admission Arrangements) (Amendment) Regulations 2002, SI 2002/2901. See also *R. v. TV School Adjudicator, ex p. Wirral Metropolitan Borough Council* [2002] ELR 620 for guidance on jurisdiction).

Governing bodies

The introduction of Local Management of Schools (LMS) saw a devolution in schools maintained by LEAs of the power of management from LEAs down to school governing bodies (EA 1996, Part II, Chap. V, re-enacted in SSFA 1998, Part II, Chap. IV, and the Financing Maintained Schools Regulations 1999, SI 1999/101. See also the Education (Budget Statements) Wales Regulations, SI 1999/440). The majority of schools that are maintained by LEAs, being community schools, foundation schools, voluntary schools and special schools, are covered by the LMS scheme; nursery schools and pupil referral units (PRUs) are not. The LEA is required to establish a scheme, which provides for the allocation of resources to and between schools and to allocate those schools covered by the scheme a budget share. Every school covered by the scheme must have a delegated budget. The budget remains the property of the LEA until spent by the governing body or head teacher.

Since the introduction of SSFA 1998, Part II, Chap. III, responsibility for the provision of education in schools broadly rests with head teachers and governing bodies. Governing bodies are dealt with in SSFA 1998 as follows:

1. Schedule 9 sets out the constitution of governing bodies. Depending on the classification of the school, governors may be LEA governors, parent governors, partnership governors, co-opted governors, foundation governors, or staff and teacher governors. The Head Teacher is appointed to every governing body, ex officio (EA 1996, s.225; SSFA 1998, Sched. 9).
2. Schedule 10 deals with the incorporation of the governing body and its powers. It gives governing bodies powers to borrow, acquire and dispose of land and other property, contract, invest, accept gifts and do anything incidental to the conduct of the school.
3. Schedule 11 establishes the membership and proceedings of governing bodies. This includes the procedure for election or appointment of governors, what qualifications they should hold and how long they

should hold office. It deals with governors meetings and proceedings, information which is to be given as to meetings, expenses and the training and support of governors.
4. Schedule 12 establishes instruments of government (rather than articles of government for each school, which preceded the new structure under SSFA 1998) (Education (School Government) (Transition to a New Framework) Regulations 1998, SI 1998/2763; Education (Government of New Schools on Transition to New Framework) Regulations 1998, SI 1998/3097).

The main functions of governing bodies are as follows:

1. To manage the small budget delegated by the LEA. The governing body may delegate to the head teacher its power to spend delegated budgets to the extent that it is appropriate (SSFA 1998, s.50(3)). The governors will not incur any personal liability in respect of anything done in good faith in the exercise of their powers under the LMS (SSFA 1998, s.50(7)).
2. Recruitment and selection of staff subject to monitoring by the LEA. In the case of community, voluntary controlled and community special schools, the LEA remains the staff employer and determines the number of teaching and non-teaching staff that a school will employ. The LEA retains the power to appoint, suspend and dismiss teachers subject to a general duty to consult with the governing body (SSFA 1998, s.16).
3. In the case of voluntary aided, foundation and foundation special schools, it is the governing body of the school which employs the staff. The LEA will retain the power to decide the number of teachers and non-teaching staff employed by the school and its consent is required for the appointment or dismissal of teachers (SSFA 1998, Sched. 17).
4. To produce an annual report containing the details of public examinations and assessments, the continuing education and employment details of pupils leaving school, annual targets for the school year, etc. (SSFA 1998, s.42; Education (School Performance Targets) (England) Regulations 1998, SI 1998/1532; Education (School Performance Targets) (Wales) Regulations 1998, SI 1998/2196).
5. To be responsible for the conduct of maintained schools and to conduct these schools in the manner which ensures high standards of educational achievement (SSFA 1998, s.38(2)). Together with the head teacher and the LEA, the governing body must exercise their function so that they provide a 'balanced and broadly based' curriculum. This curriculum must do the following:

    (a) promote the spiritual, moral, cultural, mental and physical development of pupils at the school and of society; and

(b) prepare pupils at the school for the opportunities, responsibilities and experiences of adult life (EA 1996, s.351(1)).

The head teacher is responsible for implementation of the curriculum and must ensure that the National Curriculum is implemented.

6. To draft school complaints procedures and act as decision-making body at stage three. The LEA administers the complaints procedure and appoints a clerk to the governing body who should be the first point of contact and who will decide how the complaint progresses (EA 1996, s.409).
7. For foundation or voluntary aided schools, to act as the admission authority for the school. For community or voluntary controlled schools, the admission authority will be the LEA unless the LEA has delegated this responsibility to the governing body (SSFA 1998, s.88(1)(a)(ii)). In foundation and voluntary aided schools the governing body arranges admission appeals. In the case of community or voluntary controlled schools, the LEA will arrange any admission appeals. The governing bodies of foundation or voluntary aided schools can make joint arrangements for appeals with the LEA (SSFA 1998, s.94).
8. To keep an admission register and attendance register of pupils (EA 1996, s.434(1); Education (Pupil Registration) Regulations 1995, SI 1995/2089).
9. To make and review periodically a written whole-school behaviour policy (SSFA 1998, s.61(2)(A)).
10. To consider any representations made by a parent or pupil aged over 18 years against any exclusion, whether fixed term or permanent (SSFA 1998, s.65(1)(c), (d)).
11. To use their best endeavours to ensure that children at their school who have SEN get the appropriate special educational provision including ensuring teachers know that the child has SEN and identifying and providing for those needs (EA 1996, s.317). Governing bodies of maintained schools must admit a child whose statement of SEN names that school (EA 1996, s.324(5)(b)).
12. To comply with the statutory provisions of the Disability Discrimination Act (DDA) 1995, Part IV not to discriminate in:

    (a) school admissions;
    (b) education and associated services; and
    (c) exclusions.

The above functions apply to governors of maintained schools. This mainly includes voluntary aided and foundation schools, and where there are differences these have been indicated.

1.3 INSPECTION AND REGULATION

Maintained schools

The Education (Schools) Act 1992 created the Office for Standards In Education (Ofsted), the head of which is the Chief Inspector for Schools.

The Chief Inspector has to ensure that schools are inspected every five years in England (Education (School Inspection) Regulations 1997, SI 1997/1966) and every six years in Wales (Education (School Inspection) (Wales) Regulations 1998, SI 1998/1866, as amended by SI 1999/1440). Teams of inspectors contract with Ofsted to carry out inspections of individual schools. Contracts are awarded following submission of tenders on the basis of 'value for money'. The contractors are private companies, which are selected from a pool of qualified inspectors for each particular inspection.

LEAs may maintain a school inspection service to inspect their own or other schools on a for cost basis and subject to tendering arrangements (School Inspections Act (SIA) 1996, s.24).

In carrying out its inspection the Ofsted team considers:

(a) whether the school is fulfilling its duty to deliver the National Curriculum;
(b) the breadth and range of the whole curriculum;
(c) the management and leadership of the school;
(d) whether the school is providing 'value for money'.

There is a separate system of inspection for denominational education and collective worship in denominational schools (SIA 1996, s.23).

An Ofsted inspection usually lasts about one week but this does depend on the size of the school. The report is published. If the Ofsted team considers that a school has 'serious weaknesses' or 'requires special measures' the matter will be referred up to Her Majesty's Inspectors who work under the Chief Inspector for Schools. If the inspectors agree with the Ofsted decisions, they will monitor the school regularly and the governing body together with the LEA will be required to draw up action plans (SIA 1996, ss.17 and 18).

If a school requiring special measures fails to improve, various events may occur. The Secretary of State may appoint additional governors or direct the school to close. Alternatively, the LEA may intervene and it may appoint additional governors or suspend the school's delegated budget (SSFA 1998, ss.15–18).

The Chief Inspector for Schools can also review the way in which LEAs are performing any of their functions which relate to pupils of compulsory school age (EA 1997, ss.38–39). Inspection of LEAs includes both investigating the officers of the authority and interviewing the schools. If, following investigation problems are identified, the LEA can be required to draw up an action plan for improvement, and in a similar way to 'failing schools', Her Majesty's Inspectors may take 'special measures' to improve the LEA.

Inspection and regulation of independent schools

Under EA 2002, Part 10, a new regime was established for the regulation of independent schools.

An independent school must be a 'registered school', that is a school which is entered in the register of independent schools in England or Wales (EA 2002, s.171). The register is maintained by the Secretary of State in England and the National Assembly in Wales. It is a criminal offence for a 'proprietor' to conduct an independent school which is not a 'registered school'. (Under EA 2002, s.159(1) this offence is liable on summary conviction to either a fine or imprisonment for six months or both.)

On application for registration, the registration authority notifies the Chief Inspector for Schools who must arrange to inspect the school and report back to what extent the school meets and is likely to be able to continue to meet the 'independent school standards' (Education (Independent School Standard) (England) Regulations 2003, SI 2003/1910). If, following inspection, the Chief Inspector for Schools confirms that the school meets and is likely to be able to continue to meet the 'independent school standards' the registration authority must consider his report and other evidence and make a determination. If the registration authority determines that the school does meet the standards and is likely to be able to continue to meet the standards, the registration authority is under a duty to enter the school in the register (EA 2002, s.161(3)).

The registration authority may at any time require the Chief Inspector to inspect any registered school (EA 2002, s.163(1) and (2)).

In addition to inspection, an independent school is required to provide the registration authority with prescribed information within three months of admission of pupils, by way of an annual return every school year, and where a proprietor has ceased to use a person's services because that person is unsuitable to work with children, this must be reported to the Secretary of State.

If, following an inspection, the registration authority is satisfied that any one or more of the independent school standards is not being met, it has two courses of action open to it:

(a) if there is a risk of serious harm to the welfare of pupils at the school, then the school can be removed from the register of independent schools (EA 2002, s.165(2)); or

(b) a notice can be served on the proprietor by identifying the relevant independent school standards which are not being met and requiring the proprietor to submit an action plan by a specified date (EA 2002, s.165(3)). If the action plan is not submitted or is rejected, the registration authority can remove the school from the register or make an order requiring further action.

The proprietor has a right of appeal to the Care Standards Tribunal against the decision to remove the school from the register, against an order or against a refusal to vary or revoke an order.

CHAPTER 2

Planning and policy decisions and remedies

It is not possible to give more than an overview of the structure for the taking of decisions on school provisions and the main routes that may be available for challenge. This chapter is written from the perspective of advising parents/carers of children at school.

2.1 SCHOOL PROVISION: PLANNING AND POLICY DECISIONS

School organisation plan

Section 26(1) of the School Standards and Framework Act (SSFA) 1998 requires the Local Education Authority (LEA) to prepare a school organisation plan. This is a statement, which sets out how the LEA proposes to exercise its function for a five-year period to meet the provision of primary and secondary education suitable to the requirements of pupils of compulsory school age in its area. The plan will include the facilities the LEA expects to have available outside its area. The contents of the plan are set out in regulations (Education (School Organisation Plans) (England) Regulations 1999, SI 1999/701, reg. 3) and will include the provisions made for pupils with special educational needs (SEN); how the LEA will secure the raising of standards and improve outcomes for all pupils; how it will achieve greater diversity in the type of schools and greater community coherence, etc.

The draft plan is sent to a wide range of interested parties in the area of the LEA and adjoining authorities. There is two months allowed for objections after which within one month, the plan must be sent with any objections made or any revisions in the light of objections, to the school organisation committee (SI 1999/701, reg. 7).

The school organisation plan requires the approval of the school organisation committee or the adjudicator. The school organisation committee can do the following:

(a)   approve the plan without modification;

(b) prepare its own plan for publication by the LEA as its approved plan; or
(c) refer the draft plan to the adjudicator.

Establishment of schools by the local education authority

As part of its planning, the LEA may make a decision that in order to provide education within its area, it needs to establish a new community or foundation school, or maintained nursery school. The procedure to be followed will depend on whether this is an 'additional' or 'non-additional' school. The definition of what is an 'additional school' is set out in Education Act (EA) 2002, s.70(7). It is a school that does not replace a secondary school which is a community, foundation or voluntary school or an academy and which has been or is to be discontinued.

Opening of additional schools

Where the LEA decides that to fulfil its statutory duty to secure that there are sufficient schools to provide education in its area it needs to open an 'additional school', it must follow the procedures set out in EA 2002, s.70 and Sched. 8.

The LEA must issue a notice inviting proposals from others as to the establishment of the school. The notice will identify a possible site for the school; specify a date by which proposals must be submitted, and include other prescribed matters (Education (Additional Secondary School Proposals) Regulations 2003, SI 2003/1200, reg. 3 and Sched. 1, as amended by the Education (Additional Secondary School Proposals) (Amendments) Regulations 2003, SI 2003/1421).

Proposals must be submitted before the date specified in the notice and must contain prescribed information. After receiving such proposals, the LEA is obliged to publish them and may publish its own proposals. The proposals are then considered and commented on by the school organisation committee prior to submission and consideration by the Secretary of State. In general, once a proposal has been approved it has to be implemented unless the Secretary of State lifts the obligation to do so.

Opening of 'non-additional' schools

The setting up by an LEA of new community or foundation schools or maintained nursery schools which are not additional schools is covered by SSFA 1998, s.28 and the Education (School Organisation Proposals) (England) Regulations 1999, SI 1999/2213. The regulations contain detailed provisions relating to the publication of proposals and the information those proposals should contain. Briefly, the scheme is as follows:

PRACTICAL EDUCATION LAW

1. Proposals must be posted in at least one conspicuous place in the area which would be served by the new school and published in at least one newspaper circulating in that area (reg. 5(2)(a)).
2. There must be consultation by the LEA prior to publishing proposals (SSFA 1998, s.28(5)). The consultation must be with relevant parties including the school which is subject to the proposals; any LEA likely to be affected; any school in the LEA area or outside likely to be affected; parents and teachers.
3. Two months are allowed for objections (reg. 7).
4. A copy of the published proposals goes to the school organisation committee or, in Wales, the Secretary of State, together with any objections within one month of the closing time for objections.
5. The school organisation committee can do the following:
    (a) reject the proposal;
    (b) approve it without modification so long as it is satisfied there are adequate financial arrangements;
    (c) approve it with modification so long as it is satisfied there are adequate financial arrangements;
    (d) refer it to the adjudicator (SSFA 1998, Sched. 6, para. 3(2)).
6. The LEA has a duty to implement the proposals approved by the school organisation committee or the adjudicator.
7. The same procedures for 'additional' and 'non-additional' schools will apply if the LEA determines to establish a special school.

Establishment of academies

Academies are the responsibility of the Secretary of State under EA 2002, s.65 and Sched. 7.

The procedure for the establishment of academies is far less complicated than that for the establishment of other schools. The pivotal requirement is an agreement between the Secretary of State and the person who undertakes to establish and maintain the school under EA 2002, s.482(1). The Secretary of State must consult with the LEA in whose area the school is to be situated prior to entering into the agreement.

The agreement entered into by the Secretary of State requires that he/she is satisfied that the academy will make no charge for admission and any other requirements as are specified in the particular agreement. If the Secretary of State is so satisfied then he/she may make payments both in respect of capital and current expenditure (EA 1996, s.83(1), as amended by EA 2002, s.65). The Secretary of State can make payments in relation to current expenditure either for an indefinite period or for a period of not less than seven years (EA 1996, s.483(2), as amended).

There are provisions relating to land when academies are established (EA 1996, Sched. 35A, as amended by EA 2002, Sched. 7).

Establishment of schools by direction of Secretary of State

The Secretary of State can direct an LEA to establish new schools under EA 2002, s.71. This direction would be made if the Secretary of State were of the opinion that the provision of primary or secondary education in the area of the LEA was or was likely to become insufficient. The Secretary of State has default powers under EA 2002, s.71(4) to publish his/her own proposals to establish the necessary schools if the LEA has not complied with the direction.

Establishment of sixth forms

The decision to establish maintained school sixth forms comes under the auspices of the Learning and Skills Council (EA 2002, s.72 and Sched. 9). The Learning and Skills Council has the power to make proposals regarding the establishment of sixth forms as long as one of three preconditions are met. The preconditions are as follows:

1. The proposals must be made with a view to meeting recommendations made in the report of an area inspector under the Learning and Skills Act (LSA) 2000, s.65.
2. The proposals must be made with a view to meeting one or more of the relevant objectives as set out in LSA 2000, s.113A(1)(b). These are:
   (a) an improvement in the educational or training achievements of those who are above compulsory school age but under 19 years;
   (b) an increase in the number of such persons who participate in education or training which is suitable to the requirements of a person in that age group; or
   (c) an expansion in the range of educational or training opportunities suitable to the requirements of such people.
3. The proposals are made in addition to any proposals relating to education or training other than in schools. The combined proposals must be made with a view to promoting one of the relevant objectives as set out above.

When exercising these powers the Learning and Skills Council must take account of statutory guidance. The Learning and Skills Council should exercise its powers in collaboration with other partners such as schools and LEAs.

The procedure for publishing and developing the proposals by the Learning and Skills Council is set out in the School Organisation Proposals by the Learning and Skills Council for England Regulations 2003, SI 2003/507. There is a wide-ranging duty to consult, which includes consultation with the LEA; adjoining LEAs; governing bodies of schools and further education colleges likely to be affected; school organisation committee; Diocesan Boards and other such persons as the Learning and Skills Council considers appropriate. The decision on whether to proceed is made by the Secretary of State, who can modify, agree or reject proposals.

Decision to cease to maintain schools

In considering its plan for education in its area, the LEA may decide that it wishes to cease to maintain a community, foundation or voluntary school or maintained nursery school. If it takes such a decision it must publish a formal proposal under SSFA 1998, s.29. The procedures regarding consultation, publication, representation, approval and implementation which are set out in SSFA 1998, s.29 and Sched. 6, follow the same stages as for the establishment of additional schools which are described above.

Section 30 of SSFA 1998 deals with closure by a governing body of a voluntary or independent school.

The Secretary of State can decide to direct an LEA to close a school without formal proposals under SSFA 1998, s.19. This is specific to a school which is causing concern and which is subject to a warning notice by the LEA under SSFA 1998, s.15. Such warning notices will be issued referring to the safety of pupils or staff at a school where there has been a breakdown of discipline or where a breakdown of discipline is threatened.

The Secretary of State has also the power to direct the LEA to discontinue a school if he/she considers that this must be done in the interest of the health, safety or welfare of a community or foundation special school (SSFA 1998, s.32(1)). In addition, the Secretary of State can direct that the LEA make proposals to close the school where the Secretary of State is of the opinion that the provision for primary or secondary education in maintained schools is excessive (SSFA 1998, s.34 and Sched. 7). Where an LEA does not comply with the direction then the Secretary of State can make proposals for the reduction of the surplus places. These proposals require the approval of the school organisation committee or the relevant adjudicator. There is provision for the making of objections and the holding of a local enquiry.

Prescribed alterations

The LEA may consider that it needs to make alterations to its school provision. What amounts to prescribed alterations is specified in the Education (School Organisation Proposals) (England) Regulations 1999, SI 1999/2213 (as amended by the Education (School Organisation Proposals) (England)

(Amendment) Regulations 2003, SI 2003/1229; the equivalent regulations for Wales are the Education (School Organisation Proposals) (Wales) Regulations 1999, SI 1999/1671). Prescribed alterations are defined as follows:

(a) an enlargement, other than a temporary enlargement, of premises of a school which would increase the capacity of the school by more than 30 pupils plus 25 per cent of the previous capacity or 200 pupils, whichever is the less;
(b) the making permanent of a temporary enlargement;
(c) the increase other than a temporary increase of pupils in any relevant age group by 27 or more;
(d) the alteration of the age range of the school involving an extensional reduction for a full school year or more;
(e) the establishment or discontinuance of provision reserved for children with SEN;
(f) the introduction of admission arrangements which allow maintained schools to make provision for selection by ability under SSFA 1998, s.101(1);
(g) changes from single sex to mixed, or vice versa;
(h) transfer of the school to a new site or discontinuance of a site where the school occupies more than one site.

The procedure where the LEA proposes a prescribed alteration is similar to that for establishment of a new school, which is set out previously in this chapter on p. 17.

The Schools Standards and Framework Act 1998 and subsequent legislation in particular LSA 2000 and EA 2002, have seen the establishment of a structure of additional statutory decision-making bodies such as the school organisation committee, the relevant adjudicators, the Learning and Skills Council and the inspection regime for independent schools. Being set up under statute, the new bodies would be acceptable to administrative law requirements and requirements of the Human Rights Act (HRA) 1998.

2.2 CHALLENGES TO PLANNING AND POLICY DECISIONS: THE MAIN REMEDIES

The purpose of this section is to give an overview of the main remedies which may lie against decisions in the school reorganisation process. Before deciding to pursue one of the main remedies outlined in this chapter, an adviser must bear in mind whether it is appropriate to proceed by way of the complaints procedure of the governing body of the school concerned or that of the LEA. Under EA 1996, s.409, the LEA is required to establish a local procedure to deal with complaints about the curriculum and related matters. The general principles on which complaints procedures should be based are set out in Annexe A of DfEE Circular 1/89 'Education Reform Act 1988: The local arrangements for the consideration of complaints'. Most LEAs will now have a much more sophisticated complaints procedure than the principles require and a copy should be requested from the LEA prior to advising a client on the most appropriate remedy.

Additionally, LEAs have statutory powers under SSFA 1998, ss.14–15 to intervene in cases where schools are giving cause for concern. Issue of a warning notice under s.15 may follow an inspection if a school is identified as having 'serious weakness' and a parent can request an LEA to use this power if he/she is concerned about the functioning of school and considering that changes in the organisation of LEA's school system may need to be made.

Commissioner for local administration

A complaint may have been made to the Local Government Ombudsman following exhaustion of the complaints procedure of the LEA. The Local Government Ombudsman's powers are derived from the Local Government Act (LGA) 1974, s.26. The powers of the Local Government Ombudsman are to investigate a complaint made in writing from a member of the public or on behalf of a member of the public where it is alleged that the person has suffered an injustice as a result of maladministration in connection with an action taken by or on behalf of an authority in exercise of its administrative functions.

What amounts to maladministration?

A definition of what amounts to maladministration was set out in *R.* v. *Local Commissioner for Administration for the North and East Area of England ex p Bradford Metropolitan Borough Council* [1979] 2 All ER 881, CA, at 898. The description was as follows:

> bias, neglect, inattention, delay, incompetence, inaptitude, perversity, turpitude, arbitrariness and so on.

The Ombudsman is limited in that he/she can only deal with the way in which a decision was reached or a discretion exercised. It is not within the Ombudsman's powers to look at the merits of a decision or exercise of discretion. As long as a decision or the discretion was exercised in accordance with proper procedures, the Ombudsman cannot investigate on the basis that the complainant does not like the result. The complainant does not have to specify any particular piece of maladministration in the complaint as long as there is a general reference to what the complainant considers to be the defect.

PLANNING AND POLICY DECISIONS AND REMEDIES

Limits on the Ombudsman's powers

1. The Ombudsman can investigate complaints against LEAs and the appeal committees, but schools are excluded.
2. The Ombudsman will require the LEA to be given an opportunity to deal with the complaint first using its complaints procedure (LGA 1974, s.26(5)).
3. The Ombudsman may not investigate when the complaint was not made within twelve months of the day the complainant first knew of the matters alleged in the complaint. There is a discretion to investigate in special circumstances outside this time limit when it is proper to do so (LGA 1974, s.26(4)).
4. Where the complainant has a right of appeal to the tribunal or to the minister or where there may be a remedy by way of court action, the Ombudsman may choose not to investigate the complaint. The Ombudsman can investigate if he/she considers that it is not reasonable to expect the complainant to exercise these rights (LGA 1974, s.26(6)).
5. Where the Ombudsman is of the opinion that what is complained of affects all or most of the inhabitants of the LEA's area he/she should not investigate the complaint (LGA 1974, s.26(7)).
6. Where the subject matter of the complaint has already been considered by the court, then the Ombudsman cannot revisit the subject matter (*R. v. Commissioner for Local Adminstration ex p. H* [1999] ELR 314, CA).

Procedure

A complaint should be initiated in writing on a complaint form which is available from the office of the Commission for Local Administration. If the complaint is one that may lead to court proceedings it will be necessary to explain in detail why a decision has been taken not to initiate court proceedings at this stage.

The initial investigation will usually involve correspondence between the Ombudsman, the LEA and the complainant. There will follow an examination of the LEA's files and interviews with the relevant LEA officers. In certain cases, the Ombudsman may decide to interview the complainant.

A draft report is always sent to the LEA for comment. To ensure anonymity the name of the complainant will be altered.

If the Ombudsman makes a finding of maladministration he/she can recommend that certain action be taken by the LEA. Compensation will be recommended only if the Ombudsman makes a finding that the prejudice suffered by the complainant has been sufficient to amount to injustice (*R. v. Commissioner for Local Adminstration ex p. S* [1999] ELR 103, QBD). The Ombudsman can recommend that the LEA pay the complainant's legal costs but there is no legal obligation on the LEA to do so (LGA 1974, s.31(3)).

Funding

For a complainant entitled to funding from the Legal Services Commission (LSC), complaints will be dealt with under the Legal Help Scheme. A complaint to the Ombudsman will not be covered by a public funding certificate. The proposed introduction by the LSC of the fixed fee scheme may mean that pursuing a complaint to the Ombudsman will involve costs in excess of the allocated basic fixed fee limit, not taking into account the exceptional cases regime.

Ombudsman or judicial review?

Cases which raise issues of maladministration may also be cases which could be susceptible to issue of a judicial review claim. Careful consideration will need to be given as to whether the client's grievance is best pursued by complaint to the Ombudsman or by issue of a judicial review claim. The Ombudsman will not have jurisdiction to consider matters already dealt with by the court, although, whether this applies to cases abandoned before the permission stage of judicial review is reached is not clear.

In a limited number of cases it may be possible to make a complaint to the Ombudsman and then to pursue a judicial review claim. Given the three-month time limit on the issue of a judicial review claim this is not likely to be possible in most cases as the Ombudsman's investigations usually take months to complete.

It will be up to the adviser to determine which will be the appropriate remedy. Factors that will need to be taken into account are: costs (complaint to the Ombudsman is obviously much cheaper than issue of a judicial review claim); urgency (it may be possible to obtain interim relief from the court for an urgent hearing); whether the LEA is likely to require a court order to ensure it responds appropriately; whether the issue is still a live issue or is a complaint in respect of past defects, etc.

Secretary of State for Education

The powers of the Secretary of State to intervene in the exercise by LEAs; governing bodies and funding authorities of their functions are set out in EA 1996, ss.496 and 497, as amended by SSFA 1998.

Acting or proposing to act unreasonably

The Secretary of State is given powers to intervene if he/she is satisfied that one of the bodies set out above is acting or proposing to act unreasonably. There is no requirement that a complaint be made and he/she can make directions that appear expedient. Even where a body has a discretion, the

Secretary of State can substitute his/her own opinion and has far wider powers than those of the court.

The question of what is 'unreasonable' was considered in the case of *Secretary of State for Education and Science* v. *Tameside Metropolitan Borough Council* [1977] AC 1014. The case concerned proposals made by the Secretary of State that all the LEA's schools should become comprehensive. The Conservative council opposed the proposals and the Secretary of State issued a direction that the proposals be implemented. When the LEA continued to refuse, the Secretary of State made an application to court for a mandatory order. The House of Lords decided that the LEA was entitled to have a policy, and the Secretary of State was not entitled to make the LEA abandon its policy merely because the Secretary of State disagreed. In taking his decision the Secretary of State had failed properly to consider the proposals by the LEA for dealing with selection and to take into account that there was considerable local support for the LEA's own proposals.

Default powers

Where the Secretary of State is satisfied that the LEA, governing body or funding authority has failed to discharge any duty imposed on it by or for the purposes of EA 1996, he/she may make an order under EA 1996, s.497(1) as follows:

(a) declaring the body to be in default in respect of that duty; and
(b) giving such directions for the purpose of enforcing the performance of the duty as appeared to him or her to be expedient.

There is no requirement for a complaint to be made before the power can be exercised. The Secretary of State is not required to investigate and can limit him/herself to the making of a direction. It is usual for the Secretary of State to request a written explanation from the body, and this may be all that is required to satisfy his/her concerns.

The School Standards and Framework Act 1998 added specific default powers by introducing EA 1996, ss.497A and 497B, which applied to intervention by the Secretary of State in the provision of education to registered pupils and those of compulsory school age. The threshold for failure as set out under s.497A is lower than that under s.497. Under s.497A, if the Secretary of State is satisfied that a body is failing to perform any function to which the section applies to an adequate standard or at all, the Secretary of State can intervene. The requirement is based on the opinion of the Secretary of State. The powers of the Secretary of State include:

(a) a power to direct that the function in question be performed on behalf of the LEA by a third party;

(b) to require the LEA to enter into a contract or other arrangement with that third party containing such terms as the Secretary of State specifies in a direction;
(c) a direction that the function be performed by the Secretary of State or a person nominated by him or her and that the body shall comply with any instructions of the Secretary of State or his/her nominee in relation to the exercise of the function.

The Secretary of State can give other directions as he/she thinks expedient for the purposes of securing that the function in question is performed to an adequate standard.

Section 497B contains the necessary consequential provisions to ensure that directions under s.497A are effective. Additionally, there are powers under s.497B to authorise persons to enter LEA premises and to inspect and copy any documents and records which the person considers relevant, and the LEA/school is obliged to give the person authorised by the Secretary of State assistance in connection with the exercise of his/her functions.

Complaint to Secretary of State or court?

The powers given to the Secretary of State are wide. The court will consider whether a complaint to the Secretary of State should have been pursued as an alternative to a judicial review claim. One practical consideration is that complaints to the Secretary of State can take a considerable length of time, and a delay of two years or more in reaching a decision is not unknown. There is also no requirement on the Secretary of State to consult or provide feedback. It is often the case that a much more urgent solution to a problem is required in an education case and this may justify the bypassing of the Secretary of State. Certainly, courts have not failed to intervene in cases of urgency or complexity on the basis that an application should instead have been made to the Secretary of State.

Funding

Funding for a client entitled to assistance from the LSC will be under the Legal Help Scheme. Again, under the proposed fixed fee scheme a complicated complaint to the Secretary of State would be likely to exceed a basic fixed fee limit and require an exceptional case application.

2.3 JUDICIAL REVIEW

The making of a claim for judicial review is covered by the Supreme Court Act 1981, s.31 and Civil Procedure Rules 1998, rule 54.5 to which there is a pre-action protocol setting out what should be contained in the letter before claim and time limits. When considering the appropriateness of a judicial review claim, it must always be borne in mind that judicial review is a discretionary remedy and that relief may be refused because the court is satisfied that the LEA or other body is trying to put things right or is concerned about the expense to the defendant in complying with the court order. Additionally, in claims alleging procedural defects, the court may be limited to sending the matter back to the decision-making body to reconsider or take the decision in the procedurally correct way.

Basic requirements

Is there an alternative remedy?

Judicial review is only available when alternative remedies have been exhausted or are not appropriate. In education cases an adviser must consider the availability of other potential remedies. These include appeal panels, complaints procedures, complaint to the Local Government Ombudsman, the Secretary of State, the Special Educational Needs and Disability Tribunal (SENDIST), etc. Only if none of these is available can a judicial review claim be considered.

Who can bring a judicial review claim?

A judicial review remedy is available to any legal person, and possibly an unincorporated body, who has 'sufficient interest' (Supreme Court Act 1981, s.31(3)) to challenge the decision of a public body or a body carrying out statutory functions, on the basis that the body has acted unlawfully. Courts usually apply liberal rules of standing. In the case of school reorganisation, parents, children, promoters of a proposed reorganisation, objectors to proposals and people making representations on proposals would all have standing. Recently, issues as to the availability of public funding, which are dealt with later, have become relevant to who brings a judicial review claim. In some cases, statutory rights are vested in parents and it is they who should bring the challenge, not the child. This is particularly the case in relation to admission and to statutory appeals from a decision of SENDIST.

Time limits

Under the provisions of CPR, rule 54.5 any application for judicial review should be made promptly and in any event within three months of the decision to be challenged. There has been recent judicial review consideration of whether the requirement of promptness was compatible with Article 6 of ECHR and European Community Law (*R. (on the application of Burkett)* v.

Hammersmith and Fulham London Borough Council [2002] 1 WLR 1593; *R. (on the application of Elliot)* v. *Electoral Commission* [2003] EWHC 395; *R. (on the application of Young)* v. *Oxford City Council* [2002] EWCA Civ 990). There is no definitive guidance on the point but the predominant view of the court is that the requirement of promptness in bringing a judicial review claim remains. An adviser therefore should aim to issue any judicial review claim as soon as is practicable after the decision to be challenged and within the three-month time limit.

Undue delay

The court has a discretion to allow claims issued outside the time limits under CPR, rule 54.5 but this is only done in exceptional circumstances and should not be relied upon. Under Supreme Court Act 1981, s.31(6), the court may refuse to grant permission or any relief sought on the application if:

> ... it considers that the granting of relief sought will be likely to cause substantial hardship to or substantially prejudice the likes of any person or would be detrimental to good administration.

The court therefore has the sanction of refusing relief for failure to comply with time limits. It is likely that the defendant will raise the issue of delay in his/her acknowledgement of service to ensure that the matter is before the court.

Timing of bringing a challenge

Judicial review claims in the education setting will raise the question of the stage at which it is appropriate for a judicial review claim to be issued and against which body. A simple example would be in the exclusion field where consideration should be given as to whether a claim should be brought against the school's unlawful exclusion or whether this could be corrected by appeal to the governing body or appeal panel. In the area of school organisation the situation is far more complex. Advisers will need to consider whether a claim should be issued: against the LEA for failing to lawfully consult; against the decision of the school organisation committee; or to challenge a decision made by an adjudicator, or the Secretary of State. Broadly, challengeable defects in school reorganisation will fall into two categories:

(a) where statutory consultation did not on the face of it comply with statutory requirements or where either no proposals complying with statute or the wrong proposals were used;

(b) the *Wednesbury* 'unreasonable' challenge. This is a far more difficult claim to bring than a procedural defect claim. It is far more likely that a later decision maker could correct a flaw by a wider consideration of proposals.

The guidance from the court is somewhat contradictory, although later cases indicate that a challenge should be brought as early as possible. In *R.* v. *Secretary of State for Education and Science ex p. Threapleton* (1988) *The Times*, 2 June, CO302/88, a judicial review challenge to the decision of the Secretary of State was allowed even when the grounds of the decision were available at an earlier stage. In the case of *R.* v. *Secretary of State for Education ex p. Bandtock* [2001] ELR 333 (see also *Nichol* v. *Gateshead Metropolitan Borough Council* (1988) 87 LGR 435 and *R.* v. *Gloucester County Council ex p. Findlater* (unreported, 14 July 2000)), the question of timing was further considered. The case concerned the failure of the LEA to comply with its statutory duty to consult on reorganisation proposals because the notice of proposals was ambiguous. The court made *obiter* comments that if proposals were unlawful, then they should be challenged at the time they were made rather than awaiting the decision of the Secretary of State. A similar view was taken in the case of *R. (on the application of Louden)* v. *Bury School Organisation Committee* [2002] EWHC 2749 which concerned the challenge to the decision of a school organisation committee based on the invalidity of an LEA's decision to trigger the mechanism for closure under SSFA 1998, s.29.

Funding – who applies?

Decisions in the field of school admissions have indicated that it will be an abuse of process to issue a judicial review claim in the name of the child in order to qualify for public funding and to avoid costs orders (see, in particular, the case of *R.* v. *Richmond London Borough Council ex p. JC* [2001] ELR 21), which raised the issue of whether the view in respect of public funding applications had a wider applicability in the education field beyond admission cases).

More recent court decisions seem to indicate that the decision in the *Richmond* case may be limited to school admission disputes. The case of *R. (on the application of Boulton and Another)* v. *Leeds School Organisation Committee* [2002] EWCA Civ 884, is one case in which the court indicated that, at least so far as school organisation disputes were concerned, it was usually the parents who had the main interest in bringing the case. It could be an abuse of process to bring the case in the name of the child where this was done to obtain public funding and to avoid costs orders. However, clear evidence of such abuse would need to be before the court. In the *Boulton* case there was no evidence of such abuse, as the applicants had been chosen from a random group. If the intention had been to put forward claimants eligible for public funding, there were a number of other parents who would have qualified as they were in receipt of state benefits.

In most education disputes, it will be the parent who has the primary interest in the decision. Courts are likely to look carefully at pre-existing practice and to require an explanation as to why proceedings have been brought in the name of the child rather than the parent. The defendants will be sure to raise the point in their Acknowledgement of Service at the pre-permission stage. Once permission is granted it is unlikely that the court will exercise its discretion to refuse relief in a well-founded claim, although adverse comments may be made.

What relief can be granted?

The court may order various forms of relief:

1. *A declaration*. This is a determination by the court of the respective rights and obligations of the parties or, on some occasions, a setting out of the error into which the decision maker has fallen. A declaration will be granted only where one of the other remedies of quashing order, mandatory order or order of prohibition could have been granted. A declaration can be sought instead of one of these orders. A declaration of incompatibility with HRA 1998 may also be sought within a judicial review claim.
2. *A quashing order*. The court can take a decision to quash a decision or order itself or may remit the matter back and direct the relevant body or tribunal to reach a conclusion in accordance with the court's findings.
3. *A mandatory order*. This is an order that requires the performance of a specific act or duty. There are certain limitations on the entitlement to claim a mandatory order as follows:

    (a) an absolute duty must exist, as distinct from a mere discretion or a duty arising only upon the defendant being satisfied regarding certain facts;

    (b) the defendant must have already decided, having considered all the issues necessary, that a duty is owed to the claimant to do what the claimant requests;

    (c) where only two decisions were possible and, of those two, the one made by the defendant was held to be perverse by the court, this will leave only one lawful option open. in these circumstances, the court will remit the matter back to the body to reconsider in accordance with the law. The court will not substitute its own order for that of the deciding body.

In many cases courts are reluctant to grant mandatory orders and will prefer to make a declaration.
4. *A prohibiting order.* This prevents the decision maker from acting or continuing to act in a certain way. As with mandatory orders, the courts are reluctant to make prohibiting orders and will often grant declarations.
5. *An injunction.* An injunction, like a declaration, will be granted only if the court could have made a quashing order, mandatory order or prohibiting order. An injunction can be claimed instead of one of these orders and is often claimed as interim relief in emergency judicial review claims. An injunction can be made in an emergency situation prior to the granting of permission.
6. *Damages.* A judicial review claim may include a claim for damages but may not seek damages alone (CPR, rule 54.3(2)). An award of damages is discretionary, and a court may only make an award if it is satisfied that if the claim had been brought as a private law action the claimant could or would have been awarded damages. If the claim for judicial review has been successful, the course usually taken by the court is to order at the end of the substantive hearing that the damages can proceed as if commenced by a private action and stand adjourned, mostly to the Queen's Bench Division, but sometimes to the county court, for an assessment of damages hearing. It is not usual for the judicial review court to hear the damages claim or to assess quantum itself. (On the question of damages, see *R.* v. *Northavon District Council ex p. Palmer* (1993) 25 HLR 674, QBD; *O'Rourke* v. *Camden London Borough Council* [1998] AC 188, HL; *O'Rourke* v. *United Kingdom* (unreported, 26 June 2001); *R. (on the application of Morris)* v. *Newham London Borough Council* [2002] EWHC Admin 1262; and *R.* v. *Lambeth London Borough Council ex p. Campbell* (1994) 26 HLR 618.)
7. *Damages in HRA 1998 cases.* The court's ability to award damages for breaches of ECHR rights is limited by the requirements of HRA 1998, s.8(3). The court will only have the power to award damages for breaches of ECHR rights if the combination of other remedies which the claimant has been awarded is insufficient to compensate the claimant properly in respect of the breaches. The same general requirement for the award of damages in judicial review proceedings under Supreme Court Act 1981, s.31(4) will apply to damages awarded for ECHR breaches. (For cases on HRA 1998 damages, see *R. (on the application of KB)* v. *Mental Health Review Tribunal* [2003] EWHC Admin 193, [2003] 3 WLR 185; *Anufijeva* v. *Southwark London Borough Council* [2003] EWCA Civ 1406; and *R. (on the application of Bernard)* v. *Enfield London Borough Council* [2002] EWHC Admin 2282, [2003] HRLR 4.)

Judicial review procedure

Judicial review procedure was updated to come into force at the same time as commencement of HRA 1998 on 2 October 2000. Claims are now dealt with by the Administrative Court, which is based in the Royal Courts of Justice. As part of the updating of procedure a pre-action protocol was introduced, which has been in force since 4 March 2002.

Pre-action protocol

The basis of the pre-action protocol is that the claimant should send a detailed letter before claim to the defendant and give the defendant time to respond before proceedings are lodged.

Contents of letter before claim

A pro-forma letter is annexed to the pre-action protocol itself at Annexe A. In summary, the letter before claim must deal with the following matters:

- a clear outline of the facts on which the claim is based;
- the date and details of the decision or act or admission which is being challenged;
- reasons as to why the decision is wrong;
- the action that the defendant is expected to take and the timescale for the taking of such action;
- details of any information which is being sought, including any more detail in respect of the decision under challenge;
- the claimant's details and those of the claimant's legal adviser;
- the address for reply and service of court documents;
- details of any interested parties which are known to the claimant;
- proposed reply date.

Note also the persons to whom the letter before claim should be addressed. It would be expected that a defendant should respond within 14 days. Failure to do so will be taken into account by the court if there is no good reason. If the defendant cannot respond with the time limit, the defendant should provide an interim response giving reasons why a full response cannot be made and request for a reasonable extension of time. A standard format for the defendant's responses is also annexed to the protocol at Annex B.

When deciding on extending time for the defendant's response the claimant should bear in mind the following:

(a) the three-month time limit for any judicial review claim;
(b) whether it is reasonable to grant an extension. If an extension could reasonably be granted and the claim still be made within the judicial review time limits then this should be done. If a claim is issued

unreasonably then the court can apply sanctions (Protocol, Annex B, para. 14).

The protocol at para. 6 sets out two cases when an extension would not be appropriate.

1. When the defendant does not have the legal power to alter the decision under challenge. An example would be a tribunal which no longer has the jurisdiction in respect of the case that was before it. In the case of SENDIST then a statutory appeal rather than a judicial review would be the way to proceed.
2. The protocol will not be appropriate in urgent cases and/or where emergency interim relief is being sought. Most education cases will not come under the 'urgent cases' regime and should follow the pre-action protocol. Urgent applications may be applicable in education cases involving unlawful exclusions and in some admission cases, but these will be rare. The urgent case procedure is outlined at para. 7 of the protocol and in guidance from the Administrative Court (*Practice Statement (Administrative Court: Administration of Justice)* [2002] 1 WLR 810, Scott Baker J, 1 February 2002). Basically, an urgency application will require completion of a Form N463, which sets out the need for urgency, the timescale within which permission applications should be considered and the date by which the substantive hearing should take place. If an interim injunction is sought, the claimant must also provide a draft order and the grounds for seeking an injunction. Prior to the issue of proceedings the defendant must be served with the Form N463, the claim form, the draft order and the grounds for the application.

Commencement of proceedings

If it has not been possible to resolve matters by way of pre-action protocol letters, an application is commenced by filing with the Administrative Court office two copies of a paginated and indexed bundle. The index must also indicate what is essential reading for the court. The current fee payable on the issue of proceedings is £50.

Permission applications are now dealt with initially on the papers. The paginated bundle lodged at court must contain the following:

- Form N461, being a claim form and including grounds of claim;
- any written evidence in support of the claim or application to extend time (usually by way of a witness statement);
- a copy of any order that the claimant seeks to have quashed;
- if the judicial review claim relates to a decision of the court or tribunal, an approved copy of the court or tribunal's reasons for reaching the decision;

- a copy of any documents on which the claimant proposes to rely;
- copies of any relevant statutory material;
- a notice of issue of public funding/notice of acting;
- in the case of a person without capacity, the certificate of a solicitor as to the appointment of a litigation friend.

The claim form must be served on the defendant and any interested party within seven days of date of issue. Although there is no explicit requirement to serve documents filed with the claim form, it is good practice that these documents should also be served. The court will not serve these documents and will require a certificate of service completed by the solicitor to confirm service has been made.

Acknowledgement of service

The defendant or interested party who wishes to take part in judicial review proceedings must file and serve an acknowledgement of service by way of form N462. The acknowledgement must be filed not more than 21 days after service of the claim form and must be served on the claimant not later than seven days after it is filed with the court. The defendant may serve evidence with the acknowledgement of service to assist the court in reaching a decision. In urgent cases, time limits for filing the acknowledgement of service may be abridged.

Permission

The court must consider at the permission stage whether there is an arguable case for review. The court will also look at whether the claimant has sufficient interest in the matter of the claim, whether the claimant has standing, and questions of delay.

The practice is for the court to consider the permission application on the papers (CPR Practice Direction 54, para. 8.4). Where permission is granted the court may also give directions including the order of a stay of proceedings to which the claim relates or the making of an injunction. Where the court makes a decision on the papers to refuse permission, or to grant permission subject to conditions or on certain grounds only, it will serve its reasons for that decision at the same time as serving the order.

In a case where the court is not sure whether permission should be granted on the papers, then it has the power to adjourn the permission application to open court for a hearing at which the defendant and other interested parties may or can be required to attend.

Renewal of applications

If a claim is refused on the papers or there is only a conditional grant of permission, the claimant may request that the claim be reconsidered at an oral hearing. The Administrative Court office will serve with the order a form to be completed and filed requesting an oral hearing. This form must be returned within seven days of the service of the order and reasons (CPR, rule 54.12(5)). When completing this form, the claimant is required to set out the grounds for the renewal in the light of the reasons given by the court when refusing permission on the papers (*Practice Statement*, Scott Baker J, 1 February 2002).

The oral hearing of the renewed application is treated as a new application. The test is the same as that applied on the paper application, although it is sensible to prepare a skeleton argument, which addresses the original reasons for refusal.

Refusal of permission – oral hearing

If, following an oral hearing, permission is refused then the claimant may apply to the Court of Appeal for permission to appeal against refusal (CPR, rule 52.15(1)). The application for permission to appeal must be made within seven days of the judge's refusal of permission. Permission to appeal is made by way of completing an appellant's notice under Form N161. CPR Practice Direction 52, para. 15 deals with the documents to be filed with the application for permission to appeal and procedural aspects.

Post-permission procedure

On the grant of permission currently an additional fee of £180 becomes payable. This fee must be paid within seven days of service on the claimant of the order granting permission.

The defendant or interested party who intends to contest the claim must serve evidence and detailed grounds for defending within 35 days from service of the order granting permission (CPR, rule 54.14). Time limits for service of the defendant's evidence can be abridged by the court.

Following receipt of the defendant's evidence and detailed grounds, there is an obligation on the claimant's legal representatives to reconsider the merits of the application and to withdraw the application from the court list if there are no reasonable prospects of success.

If it is decided that the claim should proceed, where the claimant wishes to reply to evidence filed by the defendant or to update the court on the current circumstances, permission of the court will be required for the filing of additional grounds or evidence (CPR, rule 54.16(2)(b)). The claimant must give notice to the defendant and the court not less than seven clear days before the hearing. It is usual for this to be done by consent. If it is intended to rely on additional evidence, a copy of the evidence should be sent to the defendant and any interested party with a request for consent. If the defendant and/or interested party will not consent, then any application as regards additional evidence or change in grounds should be made returnable at the substantive hearing.

Substantive hearing

Once the case is ready for a substantive hearing, it will enter the warned list and all parties will be informed. The claimant must file and serve a skeleton argument and a bundle of documents for the hearing not less than 21 working days prior to the date of the hearing. Defendants and interested parties wishing to make representations at the hearing must file and serve a skeleton argument not less than 14 working days before the hearing date.

The hearing is generally before a single judge in the Administrative Court, and one bundle is required to be lodged. If the hearing is before a Division Court then two bundles will need to be lodged.

Settlement and consent orders

Claims frequently settle before a substantive hearing. If all parties agree on the final order that should be made, they can submit a draft of the terms of the proposed agreed order and two copies signed by all parties to the court. This should be accompanied by a short statement of reasons why the proposed order has been agreed.

Costs

Costs will generally follow the event. Ordinarily, if permission is granted, costs will be reserved to the full application. If the matter is settled prior to the granting of permission, it is unusual for the claimant to be awarded costs even if it was necessary to issue the application. If the substantive matter is agreed between parties, then a consent order withdrawing the matter from the court list can contain a provision that the costs issue be dealt with by way of paper submissions to the court.

Public funding

If a client is eligible for LSC funding, an application for public funding can be made for judicial review proceedings. In considering a grant of funding, the LSC will consider the following:

PLANNING AND POLICY DECISIONS AND REMEDIES

(a) whether permission has been granted;
(b) whether judicial review is available;
(c) whether all other appeals and procedures have been exhausted;
(d) if the defendant public authority has been given a reasonable opportunity to respond to the challenge and deal with the issues raised;
(e) the prospects of success;
(f) whether the likely benefits of the proceedings justify the cost.

Guidance on what will be considered is set out in the *LSC Manual*, Funding Code: Decision Making Guidance, Section 16.

Where permission has been granted, it is easier to obtain public funding or an extension of public funding to cover proceedings. There was formerly a presumption that if permission was granted public funding would follow if the proceedings were of overwhelming importance to the client, raised human rights issues or could be shown to have a wider public interest. This presumption no longer applies, although the threshold for the granting of public funding is still lower in cases where there is a permission order in favour of the claimant.

The LSC will look closely at applications for the funding of judicial review proceedings. It is therefore essential that in the public funding application, the matters set out above are properly addressed. The LSC recently published proposals to limit funding for judicial review and to amend the Funding Code for damages in education claims. These had been shelved at the time of publication but practitioners should look out for future proposals.

Possible judicial review challenges in planning and policy field

Traditionally, judicial review claims challenging the exercise of statutory rights to plan education resources have not been successful. There are possible areas of challenge, which are listed below, but extreme caution should be exercised before a judicial review claim is issued. Considerable research will need to be done into the viability of such a claim and the possibility of success:

(a) failure by an LEA to comply with its obligations as to consultation, in particular in relation to closure of schools and/or prescribed alterations;
(b) misconstruction of the statutory guidance by an LEA, a school organisation committee or an adjudicator;
(c) failure of the LEA to comply with obligations as to the provision of information on published proposals;
(d) failure by the LEA to comply with obligations as to providing information to the school organisation committee or Secretary of State;
(e) consequences of a flaw by the LEA on decisions taken at second tier by a school organisation committee or adjudicator;

(f) the problems of bias in decisions by school organisation committees given the constitution of those committees;
(g) decisions as regards establishing new schools (see *R.* v. *Secretary of State for Education and Science ex p. Islam* [1994] ELR 11 for a successful challenge by promoters wishing to establish a voluntary aided school).

2.4 CLAIMS FOR BREACHES OF HUMAN RIGHTS

The scope of this book allows for no more than a mention of rights arising under the ECHR which may be relevant in the education law field. Claims for breaches of ECHR rights are most often claims within judicial review proceedings. It should be borne in mind that there are different rules of standing for ECHR breach claims and different time limits.

The ECHR and HRA 1998 set out the test for 'standing' in the terms that the person seeking to claim a breach must be a 'victim' of the act or decision that is complained of. Broadly, a claimant for judicial review would be covered for a claim of breach of ECHR rights. There is one noticeable exception in that the Convention does not allow applications to be made by groups. A pressure group would not itself be able to be a party for a claim for a breach, and it would be necessary to select a 'test claimant'.

The time limit for bringing a claim of breach of ECHR rights is 12 months from the alleged breach. If the claim forms part of a judicial review claim then the judicial review time limits, being shorter, will prevail.

Article 2 of First Protocol to the European Convention on Human Rights

Article 2 of the First Protocol to ECHR provides for education in the following way:

> no person shall be denied the right to education. In the exercise of any functions which it assumes in relation to education and teaching, the State shall respect the right of parents to ensure such education and teaching in conformity with their own religious and philosophical convictions.

The United Kingdom has entered a reservation in respect of the second sentence of Article 2 which limits the scope of that sentence as follows:

> only so far as it is compatible with the provision of efficient instruction and training and the avoidance of unreasonable public expenditure.

The reservation reflects the wording of EA 1996, s.9.

The result of Article 2 is to give a conditional right to education (*A* v. *Head Teacher and Governors of Lord Grey School* [2004] EWCA Civ 382; see also for discussion of EA 1996, s.19). There is no obligation on the state to establish or to subsidise education of any particular type or any particular level. The precedent case on interpretation of Article 2 of the First Protocol is the *Belgian Linguistic* case ((No. 2) 23 July 1968, (A/6) (1979–80) 1 EHRR 252, ECHR), which provides guidance on the scope of the first sentence of Article 2.

The right set out in the second sentence of Article 2 of the First Protocol has been considered in a number of cases before the European Court. The view overall that the court has taken is that there is no obligation on the state to subsidise any particular form of education in order to respect the religious and philosophical beliefs of parents. It is sufficient for the state to show respect for those convictions within the existing education system.

Article 14

Where there is 'discrimination' in relation to enjoyment of an ECHR right, then there is arguably an infringement of ECHR, Article 14 (*R. (on the application of Douglas)* v. *North Tyneside Metropolitan Borough Council* [2003] EWCA 1847, regarding loan arrangements under the Education (Student Support) Regulations 2002 for tertiary and higher education). Article 14 was considered with Article 2 of the first protocol in the *Belgian Linguistic* case.

Article 14 of ECHR provides a right of freedom from discrimination. It cannot be the subject of a freestanding claim and must be pleaded with breach of another ECHR right.

Article 6

Article 6 ensures the right to a fair trial. The accepted view of the interpretation of Article 6 is that the right to education is not a civil right within the meaning of Article 6, except possibly in the field of exclusions (*S and Others* v. *Brent London Borough Council and Others* [2002] ELR 556). Admission panels are likely not to be covered but even if they are, it has been held that the arrangements for admission do comply with the requirements of Article 6 (*R. (on the application of B)* v. *Head Teacher of Alperton Community School and Others* [2001] ELR 359, QBD).

Article 8

Article 8 enshrines the respect for private and family life. Although Article 8 has a broad scope, the courts have considered whether it would be appropriate in a number of education settings. They have held that breach of Article 8 rights cannot be relied upon in the following areas:

(a) school admissions (*R. (on the application of the Mayor and Burgesses of Hounslow London Borough Council)* v. *School Admission Appeal Panel for Hounslow London Borough Council* [2002] ELR 402; *R. (on the application of O)* v. *St James Roman Catholic Primary School Appeal Panel* [2001] ELR 469 and *R.* v. *Richmond upon Thames LBC ex p. JC* [2001] ELR 21);
(b) choice of school;
(c) corporal punishment and sex education (*R (on the application of Williamson)* v. *Secretary of State for Education* [2003] ELR 176);
(d) exclusion from a school.

Article 8 may have some limited applicability in the planning and school reorganisation field, in particular, if the closure or plans for prescribed alterations led to an infringement of SEN provision which affected pupils with statements of SEN.

Article 9

Article 9 enshrines the right to freedom of thought, conscience and religion. In exercising its functions, the state must respect the rights of parents to ensure that education conforms with their own religious and philosophical convictions (*R. (on the application of Begum)* v. *Head Teacher and Governors of Denbigh High School* [2005] EWCA Civ 199 and *R. (on the application of Williamson)* v. *Secretary of State for Education and Others* [2005] UKHL 15).

Article 10

Article 10 governs the right to freedom of expression. Its scope has been considered in reference to school uniform and it would, in general, seem that Article 10 will not cover how a person dresses unless the individual dresses in a particular way to express ideas or opinions (*Stevens* v. *United Kingdom* (1986) 46 DR 245 at para. 2).

CHAPTER 3
Admissions

3.1 INTRODUCTION

This chapter needs to be considered in conjunction with the school structure and SEN chapters (see Chapters 1, 7 and 8). It sets out the main parts of a complex legislative system, in which parents often operate under the mistaken belief that they have the right to choose the school that their child attends. The starting point from which many of the potential issues for the practitioner will flow is understanding that the parent's right is to express a preference for the school at which they wish their child to be educated.

All aspects of education create considerable social and emotional tension for pupils and their parents, but the intense feeling generated around school admission arrangements on an individual and community basis can be huge. Expectations of what can be achieved through the utilisation of legal remedies are often unrealistic and may need to be carefully managed.

3.2 WHO IS THE CLIENT?

In admission cases the statutory right to express a preference for the school which a child attends vests in the parent/carer. Any appeal rights are those of the parent and therefore in advising on the appeal process and any consequential judicial review issues the client will be the parent/carer. Similarly, in issues concerning the admissions adjudicator, the parent(s) will be the client.

Whilst it is not impossible for a particular issue to arise which would result in the child being the appropriate person to pursue a judicial review claim, that is likely to be a rare occurrence.

3.3 THE STATUTORY FRAMEWORK

The main legislative framework is set out in:

- School Standards and Framework Act (SSFA) 1998;

- Education Act (EA) 2002;
- Human Rights Act (HRA) 1998;
- European Convention on Human Rights (ECHR);
- the Schools Admissions Code of Practice (DfES/0031/2003);
- the Admission Appeals Code of Practice (DfES/0030/2003);
- voluminous secondary legislation, referred to below where appropriate, but generally offering a level of detail outside the scope of this chapter.

Parental preference

Section 86 of SSFA 1998 provides a right to parents to express a preference as to the school at which they wish their child to be educated and a mandatory duty to comply with parental preference is imposed on the LEA and the school's governing body subject to specific exceptions.

All LEAs are under a duty to make arrangements for enabling the parents of children resident within their area of responsibility to express a preference as to the school they wish their child to attend and to give reasons for that preference (SSFA, s.86(1)).

Whilst parents cannot be compelled to exercise their right to express such a preference, admission arrangements allocating pupil places in a manner which fails to offer the opportunity to express a preference will be unlawful (*R* v. *Rotherham Metropolitan Borough Council ex p. Clark* [1998] ELR 152).

The mandatory duty to comply with an expression of parental preference, save on the specific grounds set out in the statute, is absolute in respect of school age children and qualified in respect of children of below or above compulsory school age (SSFA 1998, s.86(3A and 3B), s.98(3); *R* v. *Cleveland County Council ex p. Commission for Racial Equality* [1994] ELR 44, (1993) 1 SCR 597, CA).

The parent has a right to express a preference for any maintained school, notwithstanding that the school may be maintained by a neighbouring LEA (*R.* v. *Greenwich London Borough Council ex p. Governors of John Bull Primary School* (1989) 88 LGR 589, at 599 and also 602).

However, the issue of individual LEAs' financial resources may become relevant, particularly in relation to transfer of funds between authorities (*B* v. *Harrow London Borough Council* (No. 1) [2000] ELR 109, HL).

Exceptions to obligations to comply with parental preference

Children of compulsory school age

Exceptions are made:

(a) where it would prejudice the provision of efficient education or efficient use of resources (SSFA 1998, s.86(3)(a));

ADMISSIONS

(b) if compliance with the preference would be incompatible with admission arrangements based on permitted selection of pupils (SSFA 1998, s.86(2) and (3)(c));
(c) where a child has been permanently excluded from two or more schools and less than two years has elapsed since the last exclusion (SSFA 1998, ss.86(2) and 87).

Failure to comply with the express parental preference generates a right of appeal to an independent admission appeal panel (AAP) (SSFA 1998, s.94 and Sched. 7).

Children under compulsory school age

No s.86(2) right to express a preference arises, unless specific admission arrangements for the school in question provide such a right for school, not nursery education.

Children over compulsory school age

No duty to admit such young persons arises where relevant selection arrangements are based on ability and aptitude (SSFA 1998, s.86(3A)).

The Codes of Practice on admission arrangements

The Schools Admissions Code of Practice has statutory force pursuant to SSFA 1998, s.84(1) and the Secretary of State is obliged to issue practical guidance under SSFA 1998, s.84(1). The current Code on admission arrangements applies to school admissions from September 2004 onwards (DfES/0031/2003). A further Code of Practice gives guidance on admission appeals (DfES/0030/2003).

The purpose of admission arrangements is set out in the School Admissions Code as being:

(a) to exist for the benefit of parents and children;
(b) to be as simple as possible;
(c) to ensure that the parent's expressed preferences are complied with insofar as possible;
(d) to ensure that admission criteria are fair, objective, clear and for the benefit of all children;
(e) to provide easy access to information for parents;
(f) to comply with the legal requirements;
(g) to co-ordinate arrangements between authorities.

Admission forums

In order to promote the objectives above, LEAs are obliged to set up local admission forums to advise them on 'admissions' (SSFA 1998, s.85A) and to consider:

(a) how well existing arrangements are working and how to improve them;
(b) how accessible and comprehensive is the information provided by the authority to parents in respect of arrangements;
(c) how effective is the co-ordination of arrangements with other authorities;
(d) how to promote agreement on admissions issues;
(e) how to monitor admission of children to schools outside the usual round of admissions;
(f) how to promote arrangements for vulnerable groups, e.g. children with SEN, excluded children and looked after children.

Membership of such forums is prescribed by regulation (Education (Admission Forums) (England) Regulations 2002, SI 2002/2900) and can include, in addition to members of the LEA, nominated members put forward by community groups and those who represent local interests.

Note: The admission provisions of SSFA 1998 do not apply to special schools. A wholly separate set of admission arrangements relate to children with SEN, which are considered in Chapter 7.

3.4 ADMISSION ARRANGEMENTS

Admission numbers

Admission authorities have to set the number of pupils to be admitted into each relevant year group in any academic year (SSFA 1998, s.89A(1)). The number set provides the minimum number of pupils to be admitted to the school in the relevant year group, calculated in accordance with Department for Education and Skills (DfES) guidance 'Assessing Net Capacity in Schools' (DFES/0739/2001 rev) as updated in August 2002. The School Admissions Code of Practice makes clear that until the standard number is reached children must be admitted. Thereafter children should be admitted beyond that number only where exceptional circumstances apply (para. A47 and SSFA 1998, s.86(5)).

Where a school is undersubscribed or has places available, it is obliged to admit any pupil whose parent expresses a preference for the school, unless any of the exceptions set out below apply.

Where a school is oversubscribed, it is lawful to operate admission criteria, as a means of selecting pupils for admission on a fair and objective basis.

Admission criteria

The LEA or school is entitled to have any lawful admission criteria it wishes. However, the guidance makes clear that admission criteria must be objective, fair, and compatible with disability and equal opportunities legislation (*R* v. *Greenwich London Borough Council ex p. Governors of John Ball School* [1990] 88 LGR 589; School Admissions Code of Practice, para. 3.4).

Below are some examples of lawful and unlawful admission criteria, following which there is some consideration of the most likely issues in respect of admission criteria, which may arise in advising the client.

Lawful admission criteria

These are listed but not exclusively defined in the School Admissions Code of Practice (para. 3.5):

- siblings of pupils attending the school;
- distance from the school, measured by objective distance measurement criteria;
- catchment areas;
- feeder primary or nursery schools;
- ability in schools where selection is permitted;
- medical or social grounds;
- looked after children should be given priority (paras. 3.14–3.15);
- ease of access by public transport.

Unlawful admission criteria

The following admission criteria are defined by case law and the School Admissions Code of Practice (paras. 3.5, 3.12, 3.14, 3.16, 7.29) as unlawful:

- admission by lot/ballot;
- order by date of application received/length of time on waiting list;
- requirement to sign home–school contract;
- limiting number of pupils with SEN without statements;
- discriminatory criteria on grounds of race, sex or disability, parental occupation or employment, or home facilities;
- limit on number of pupils with poor behaviour;
- performance at interview.

Specific points

Although a *sibling* link criterion is clearly lawful, guidance does indicate that application of a sibling criterion may discriminate against ethnic minority groups (School Admissions Code of Practice, para. 3.12). However, the courts have held that the education of siblings together is important and needs to be considered within the operation of ECHR, Article 8 (*R. (on the application of K)* v. *Newham London Borough Council* [2002] ELR 390 at para. 39).

Nevertheless, parents often assume that the attendance of one child at a school automatically guarantees the admission of subsequent children. This is not the case, as demonstrated graphically in the infant class size cases considered below.

Catchment areas are a notorious breeding ground for discontent. A school's catchment area cannot be defined by an LEA's geographical boundary (see SSFA 1998, s.86(8)(a)). The courts have been concerned with a number of cases in which catchment areas were drawn up after the admission applications had been received. Despite historic guidance reinforced in the current School Admissions Code of Practice regarding the need for the published information to be clear and to allow parents to make an informed decision about the likelihood of successfully obtaining a place, ex post facto catchment areas have not been historically considered automatically unlawful (*R.* v. *Bradford Metropolitan Borough Council ex p. Sikander Ali* [1994] ELR 299).

The Code of Practice now states that, where catchment areas are used, a map should be provided, which indicates the geographical limits within which parents have been successful in obtaining places in the past admission rounds.

A *distance* criterion differs from a catchment area in that it provides for a measured distance from home to school to be determinative of priority for admissions. The question is then how is it measured? The School Admissions Code of Practice makes clear that the measurement test should be clear and obvious, and emphasises the need to take into account the shortest walking distance in determining the nearest route. The guidance also identifies the need to consider the position of children who live at two addresses (para. 3.6).

Schools able to set lawful *ability/aptitude* criteria are defined by statute as:

- grammar schools (SSFA 1998, s.104(7));
- schools whose authorised admission arrangements allow for selection of pupils of compulsory school age by ability or aptitude (SSFA 1998, ss.100, 101);
- schools whose authorised admission arrangements allow for selection by aptitude for particular subjects (SSFA 1998, s.102).

See below for a fuller consideration of the role of schools whose admission criteria allow for parental preference to be displaced by its selection process. The adjudicator has considered objections to the percentage of pupils which individual schools can accept by selective admission on a number of occasions. His role is defined below.

No *interviews* with either parents or children should play any part in an admission process, except to enable consideration of whether the child may be suitable to board at a school (School Admissions Code of Practice, para. 3.16).

It is normally unacceptable to refuse to admit a child because of previous behaviour and/or perceived behavioural SEN, unless the school can establish that:

(a) the application is outside the normal year of entry;
(b) admission would be prejudicial to the provision of efficient education/ efficient use of resources; and/or
(c) the school has a high level of pupils with challenging behaviour, or the individual pupil is particularly challenging; and
(d) the school is subject to review and serious concerns have been raised by Ofsted, or is a newly opened or fresh start school, or 25 per cent or less of the pupils are achieving five or more GCSE grades A–C.

Other issues and concerns arise in relation to pupils with SEN which are considered in Chapters 7 and 8.

Exceptions to the duty to comply with parental preference

As we have already seen, where a school is undersubscribed it must admit any child whose parent expresses a preference for the school unless one or more of the exceptions considered below is established.

(a) Prejudice to efficient education or efficient use of resources

All schools must admit up to their designated standard admissions number (SSFA 1998, s.86(5)), before any prejudice can be established. Once that number has been reached, by way of the school becoming oversubscribed, prejudice may be established and, in particular, may be established by reason of measures which might need to be taken to ensure compliance with the duty to limit infant class sizes to 30 (SSFA 1998, ss.1, 4 and 86(4)), and the Education (Infant Class Sizes) (England) Regulations 1998, SI 1998/1973).

Once a school is oversubscribed, compliance with the preference of all applicants would inevitably prejudice proper education at the school through overcrowding and/or prejudice the efficient use of the school's resources (see *R. v. Governors of Bishop Challenor Roman Catholic Comprehensive Girls School, ex p. Choudhury* [1992] 2 AC 182 at 193 per Lord Browne-Wilkinson).

However, the school standard admissions number is the minimum number of pupils that must be admitted by the school, assuming there is the demand for places. In order to establish prejudice, the school has to provide factual and subjective evidence that such prejudice exists or that prejudice to the provision of efficient education or efficient use of resources will result if there is compliance with parental preference. As a result, the 'two-stage test' has developed (see *R. v. South Glamorgan Appeal Committee ex p. Evans* (unreported, 10 May 1984); *R* v. *Brighouse School Appeal Committee* ex p. *G and B* [1997] ELR 39).

The two-stage test, as set out by Sedley J in *Brighouse*, requires the school to demonstrate at the appellate stage of the admissions process, that prejudice will in fact arise through compliance with individual parental preference. Only if the appeal committee is satisfied that such prejudice will arise can it reject the appeal. If the AAP is satisfied that prejudice will arise if a further child is admitted to the school, the AAP must go on to conduct a balancing exercise in considering whether the degree of prejudice established overrides the parental appeal.

A school's contention that admission of a particular child will prejudice the provision of efficient education has been held to be permissible in cases where, for example, the school could not make adequate provision for a child's SEN, the result of which might be a disruption of the education of other pupils (*R.* v. *Governors of Hasmonean High School ex p. N and E* [1994] ELR 343, CA).

(b) Incompatibility with selection on the grounds of ability or aptitude

Maintained schools, including community foundation or voluntary aided schools (but not special schools), can operate a partial selection process, whereby a specific proportion of their pupil population may be admitted on the grounds of ability or aptitude or may be designated as grammar schools, where all pupils are admitted on the basis of their ability (SSFA 1998, s.99).

Partial selection is now restricted in respect of ability to cases where there are pre-existing arrangements dating from at least the academic year 1997/1998, where selection is designed to secure pupil bonding within the various year groups, or where the selection is in connection with the school's sixth form.

Selection by aptitude is permitted where there are pre-existing arrangements identical to those in relation to ability, or where the school has a recognised specialism in modern foreign languages, the performing arts, the visual arts, physical education or sport, design and technology, or information technology. The selective admissions in any age group cannot exceed 10 per cent of the total admissions (SSFA 1998, s.102(1) and (4)).

The School Admissions Code of Practice deals with this subject in para. 5 and Annex A70. It should be noted that the introduction of selection by aptitude does not constitute a prescribed alteration to the character of the school. Therefore, there is no statutory requirement to publish proposals and/or to undertake consultation. However, the introduction of selective arrangement by ability does constitute a prescribed alteration (see SSFA 1998, s.28). Therefore, both consultation and the reference of objections to the admissions adjudicator are obligatory (SSFA 1998, ss.89 and 90, and para. 5 of the School Admissions Code).

Complex arrangements are set out in relation to grammar schools and their continuance, which are outside the scope of this chapter's consideration.

Note: incompability with special arrangements to preserve religious character is no longer a lawful exception (EA 2002, s.49 and Sched. 22, Part 3).

Co-ordinated admission arrangements:

With permission from the Secretary of State, two or more maintained schools may agree to co-ordinated admission arrangements, enabling them to have standard application forms and a common admissions timetable for all schools in a particular sector e.g. primary schools. Once those co-ordinated admission arrangements have been approved by the Secretary of State, they will take precedence over the general duty to give effect to parental preference (SSFA 1998, s.86(6), and see Schools Admissions Code, Chapter 6, paras. 3.9–3.12].

Additional powers

Authorities have power to direct the governing body of a specified school to admit a child to that school, provided the school is within the LEA's area of responsibility, is a reasonable distance from the child's home, and is a school from which the child has not been permanently excluded (SSFA 1998, s.96).

Once a direction is given, the governing body of the specified school must admit the child (SSFA 1998, s.96(5)). However, before such a direction is given, the LEA must consult with the governing body of the proposed specified school and the parent of the child concerned, take a positive decision to give a direction, serve written notice of its decision on the governing body of the school and its head teacher and allow a period of 15 days, beginning with the date of service of the notice, for the school's governing body to refer the proposed direction to the Secretary of State.

The LEA must defer issuing a direction until the Secretary of State has made a determination. The Secretary of State has power to determine whether the school must admit the child and/or may specify that the child be admitted to an alternative school either within the area of the responsible LEA or that of a different LEA. Neither the LEA nor the Secretary of State may specify that a child be admitted to a school, if this would result in prejudicing the provision of efficient education or the efficient use of resources (SSFA 1998, ss.96(4) and 97(5)).

Permanently excluded children

Note that the two strikes rule disengages the statutory obligation to give effect to parental preference. Where a child has been permanently excluded from two or more schools, with at least one of the relevant exclusions taking effect after 1 September 1997 (SSFA 1998, s.95(2) and (3)) the duty to give effect to parental preference does not apply for a period of two years beginning on the date when the head teacher of the child's school took the decision to exclude him or her (SSFA 1998, s.87).

Whilst a school can admit children in those circumstances if it chooses to do so, no right of appeal will arise if admission to a particular school is refused. If the LEA, as the admission authority for community voluntary controlled schools, decided to admit a child to a particular school in those circumstances, the governing body of the school may appeal against that decision and the decision of the appeal panel is binding on both the LEA and the governing body (SSFA 1998, s.95 and Sched. 25).

In *R. (on the Application of T)* v. *Head Teacher of Wembley High School* [2001] EWHC Admin 299, [2001] ELR 359 at para. 62, it was held that the provisions of s.87 do not infringe the right not to be denied education contained in Article 2 of the First Protocol of ECHR, on the basis that the LEA retains an obligation to ensure suitable education for the child in question and will be required to make education available pursuant to EA 1996, s.19 and, in any event, the operation of s.87 simply disengages the obligation to comply with parental preference.

3.5 THE ADJUDICATOR

Powers of adjudicator

Adjudicators have responsibility for determining disputes between local admission authorities and schools about admission arrangements and policies and oversubscription criteria (SSFA 1998, s.90(1)).

Adjudicators are also able to hear objections from groups of parents (10 or more), whose eligibility is defined by regulation, to hear objections about selective admission arrangements, and when and if an admission authority has arranged for a standard admission number lower than the one set by application of the criteria set out in the net capacity formula.

Where the adjudicator has a power to determine issues, the existence of that remedy will almost certainly need to be pursued prior to consideration of any application for judicial review.

The adjudicator is able to consider disputes, notwithstanding the consultation exercise which an admission authority must undertake in deciding what admission arrangements/criteria are appropriate for its area and in respect of particular schools. Where a school or group of parents wishes to lodge an objection, the objection must be lodged within six weeks of the decision in respect of which the objection was raised, although the adjudicator can extend this time limit if he/she is satisfied it was not reasonably practical for the objector to lodge the objection within the six-week period (Education

(Objections to Admission Arrangements) Regulations 1999, SI 1999/125, as amended by SI 2002/2901, regs 5–6).

Provided the objection concerns matters which are within the adjudicator's jurisdiction, it must be determined by him or her. The courts have held that the adjudicator has unobstructed power to reach decisions which are different from, possibly substantively different from, the original decision taken by the admission authority (*R. v. School adjudicator ex p. Wirral Metropolitan Borough Council* [2000] ELR 620).

Note that the adjudicator has no jurisdiction to determine any objection concerning criteria for admission to a school relating to a person's religion, religious denomination or religious practice (SI 1999/125, reg. 7). In those circumstances the adjudicator must refer the matter to the Secretary of State and must, if asked to do so, provide his/her advice to the Secretary of State in respect of the referred objection (SSFA 1998, s.90(3))

Adjudicator's procedure

The adjudicator has to have statutory regard to the School Admissions Code of Practice, but otherwise has broad discretion on the type of procedure to be followed, provided he/she adheres to the public law principles of natural justice and fairness. The adjudicator is obliged to give reasons for his/her decision (*R v. Downes ex p. Wandsworth London Borough Council* [2000] ELR 425).

Where there is dissatisfaction with the decision of an adjudicator, it is possible to seek judicial review. However, as the adjudicator's function is to provide a complete review of the original decision, taking into account all the evidence provided to him or her and to provide reasons which deal with the substantive issues raised, a successful challenge to the adjudicator's decision is likely to be a rare occurrence. The courts consider the adjudicator to be a specialist well placed to determine the local and educational issues which may arise in relation to admission arrangements.

3.6 STATUTORY APPEALS

There are two different bases for appeal:

(a) against a decision of an LEA allocating a child to a specific school; and/or
(b) against a decision of a governing body to refuse to admit a child.

The responsibility for arranging appeals is that of the LEA in relation to community voluntary controlled schools. The governing body has a corresponding responsibility to make the necessary arrangements for appeals in relation to foundation or voluntary aided schools (SSFA 1998, s.94(1) and (2)).

Arrangements for appeals

There are detailed arrangements set out within the statute as to the appeal process and the composition of AAPs, supported by the School Admissions Appeals Code of Practice issued by the Secretary of State (SSFA 1998, ss.84, 94(5), (5A), (5B), (5C), and the Admission Appeals Arrangements (England) Regulations 2002, SI 2002/2899, Sched. 1).

Composition of the admission appeal panel

An AAP should consist of three or five members, including at least one appointed from each type of prescribed person. Prescribed persons are defined as follows:

(a) persons eligible to be lay members (i.e. persons without personal experience of the provision of education, or of the management of a school, except as a school governor); and
(b) persons who have experience of education, are acquainted with education in the area, or are parents of a pupil registered at a school.

Disqualified persons are prescribed as follows:

(a) any member of the LEA, employee of the LEA, or employee or governor of the school in question;
(b) any person whose past connection with the school or authority might reasonably raise doubts about his/her ability to act impartially.
(c) any person who has been involved in any question considering whether the child concerned should be reinstated at a school from which he/she has been permanently excluded.

Preparatory procedural issues

The School Admissions Appeals Code of Practice gives guidance that the admission authority should supply the clerk of the AAP with relevant documentation for the hearing at least five working days before the date set for the hearing, which should be circulated to parents. This documentation should comprise a written statement summarising the admission arrangements for the school, a written statement summarising the reasons for the decision, including where appropriate information supporting the assertion of prejudice to the provision of efficient education or efficient use of resources, and copies of any information or documents which are to be considered by the panel at the hearing, including anything submitted by the parent (School Admissions Appeals Code of Practice, para. 4.30). Failure to circulate information in this way may raise procedural unfairness points.

Preparation for hearing

Advisers to parents should consider what they are seeking to achieve, e.g. to show that it will not prejudice the efficient provision of education if the child in question is admitted to the school. Advisers may wish to consider the following:

1. Obtain a copy of the admissions policy to check whether the admission policy has been properly applied, e.g. criteria such as distance, siblings.
2. What evidence can be put forward to undermine the 'prejudice' argument? The client should provide information on issues such as numbers in the current years above and below the year under consideration. Do they exceed the standard number? If so, it may be possible to demonstrate that no subjective or genuine prejudice has been caused in the past. If, however, the school is able to establish prejudice, the appeal will need to focus on satisfying the second stage of the two-stage test and outweighing the prejudice caused by admission by the strength of the appeal.
3. Consider the physical characteristics of the school: whether it has large classrooms, external play areas, or whether children are taught in corridors or in cramped, difficult conditions.
4. Provide a detailed written appeal document setting out the basis of the appeal and attaching as much documentary evidence as possible:

    (a) medical evidence relating to the child, the parent's incapacity to provide transport, the conditions of siblings;
    (b) transport difficulties, i.e. difficulties in accessing public transport, the parent's inability to drive; distance to other schools and information regarding routes;
    (c) social and emotional issues;
    (d) details of any children of the family with SEN.

If a report or document is not currently available, it should be made clear that it will be provided as soon as possible. Reports produced at the last minute may create procedural difficulties, which can undermine the presentation of the appeal.

Conduct and procedure at the hearing

The procedure is informal but will be conducted efficiently and in a purposeful manner. The AAP will have a clerk available to record the proceedings and to give legal advice. The clerk, however, does not have to be legally qualified, although guidance suggests he/she should be. The clerk has to provide neutral and non-partisan advice.

Parents must be given an opportunity to present their case, although there is no requirement to attend, and to ask questions of the admission authority representative. Children do not generally attend but clearly may do so if appropriate.

Parents are entitled to be represented, although admission appeal panels are infamously disapproving of legal representation. If fresh evidence is introduced by the LEA on the day of the appeal, it may be necessary to seek an adjournment, and refusal to grant an adjournment in those circumstances may be procedurally unfair. If the LEA is unexpectedly legally represented on the day, the unrepresented parent may wish to have the hearing adjourned to seek legal advice.

The panel is obliged to indicate to parents if it is minded to disbelieve any aspect of their case and to give them the opportunity of dealing specifically with the points concerning the panel (*R. v. Birmingham City Council EAC ex p. B* [1999] ELR 305).

The order of procedure is likely to be:

1. The school/LEA presents evidence on why prejudice will be caused if the child is admitted.
2. The parent/representative asks questions.
3. The panel asks questions.
4. The parents present their appeal; witnesses may give any evidence.
5. Questions are raised by the school/LEA.
6. Questions are raised by the panel.
7. The school/LEA presents a summing up.
8. The parents present a summing up.

Reaching a decision: the two-stage process

The panel must take account of all relevant factors in determining first whether prejudice has been established by the school and second, whether the parental appeal outweighs that prejudice (*R. v. Essex County Council ex p. Jacobs* [1997] ELR 190).

A common method of dealing with multiple appeals in respect of the same school is for the appeals to be heard on a group and/or individual basis before the same AAP. The procedure for a multiple appeal is likely to involve the admission authority making its case in relation to prejudice once only.

If the panel then concludes that prejudice has been established it will go on to hear each individual parental appeal prior to considering collectively the strength of the various appeals having heard them all. In *R. v. Leicester County Council Education Appeal Committee ex p. Tarmohamed* [1997] ELR 48, Sedley J indicated that the starting point must be: would prejudice be created if all the children were admitted? If the answer is no, then all the appeals will succeed.

However, if the answer is yes, the next step is to decide which of the appeals heard raises a sufficiently strong case to counterbalance the creation of prejudice. If the number of potentially successful appeals exceeds the number of children who can be admitted to the school without serious and significant disruption, then those potentially successful appeals should be ranked in order of priority to determine which should be admitted to the school. It was held that only at the latter stage is a comparison between the various appeals appropriate.

The School Admission Appeals Code of Practice suggests the AAP should first determine how many children could be admitted to the school before 'breaking point' and then allow appeals up to that number. Following *Tarmohamed* the parents are not entitled to comment on the relative strengths of each other's appeals through this process. The admission authority is required to present the same argument on prejudice in each case. Its failure to do so may result in unfairness (*R. (on the Application of C)* v. *Governing Body of Cardinal Newman High School* [2001] EWHC Admin. 299, [2001] ELR 359).

Infant class size appeals:

The AAP's approach to infant class sizes does not involve consideration of the two-stage test. Once the admission authority has decided there is class size prejudice, there is no escape in balancing particular parental considerations against that prejudice, assuming proper application of lawful admission criteria.

Any measures which are required to be taken to assure compliance with the infant class size limit of 30 children per class may constitute prejudice to the provision of efficient education, or the efficient use of resources. The AAP's remit on hearing infant class size appeals allows for an appeal to be upheld only where an AAP is satisfied:

(a) that the decision was not one which a reasonable admission authority would make in the circumstances of the case; or
(b) that the child would have been offered a place if the admission arrangements had been properly implemented (SSFA 1998, s.86(4) and Sched. 24, para. 12).

The Court of Appeal has held that on appeal under Sched. 24, para. 12(a) that parents need to:

> make a particular case which is so compelling that the decision not to admit the child is shown to be perverse. A local education authority opposing an appeal will need to explain their admission arrangements, explain their particular problems in relation to the school in question, and show that, unfortunate though it may be, it was objectively fair not to admit the child in question . . . As to the panel, their task is not simply to rubber stamp the local education authority's decision, but they can only uphold the appeal if they conclude that it was perverse in the light of the

admission arrangement to refuse to admit the particular child. Their task is not to take again the original decision.

(*Hounslow* case at para. 63, per May LJ)

The comments made were consistent with those made by the Court of Appeal in *R.* v. *Richmond-upon-Thames LBC ex p. JC* at para. 41 per Kennedy LJ).

Schedule 24, para. 12(b) allows AAPs to correct an error of an LEA in the implementation of the admission arrangements which has resulted in the child being denied a place at the school. However, following the Court of Appeal decision in *Hounslow* 'the error should be discernible without recourse to additional material', although in the *Richmond* case, Ward LJ took a different view and considered that fresh evidence should be admissible under para. 12(b) as well as para. 12(a).

3.7 REMEDIES: JUDICIAL REVIEW

The following types of claims are possible:

1. A claim may be brought by parent(s) against a decision of the admission appeal panel ('AAP').
2. The maintaining LEA or school governing body may also seek to challenge a decision of the AAP.
3. A parent and/or the LEA may seek to challenge a school's refusal to admit a child notwithstanding an appeal being allowed by the AAP.
4. A parent and/or the LEA may seek to challenge a school's refusal to admit a child where that school is named in Part IV of a child's statement of SEN. Similarly, a school's governing body may seek to challenge an LEA's decision to name a school in Part IV of a child's statement of SEN.

Note: An application for judicial review will not generally be considered by the court unless *all* other remedies have been exhausted.

Preliminary considerations

The application of judicial review principles in admissions appeal challenges are illustrated by the cases set out below. However, certain preliminary points should be noted.

The parties

Any review sought in respect of a child must be brought by the parent(s) (*R.* v. *London Borough of Richmond ex p. JC* [2001] ELR 21, CA): in this case it was held that whilst a child might have sufficient interest to mount a challenge, and whilst in some exceptional circumstances it might be appropriate for the child to seek permission to apply for judicial review, normally the only reason why the application was made in the name of the child was to obtain public funding and to protect the parent's position in relation to costs. The Court of Appeal held this was an abuse and that permission to apply for judicial review on that basis could be refused (per Kennedy LJ at para. 31, Ward LJ concurring at para. 69).

Note that:

1. The defendant to any application will be the AAP and/or the LEA or school governing body.
2. Were a challenge to be brought by an LEA to a decision of an AAP, the defendant would be the AAP, with the child's parent(s) included as an interested party.
3. If a school governing body seeks to challenge a decision of an AAP, the AAP and/or LEA will be defendants to the claim, with the parents as interested parties. That will also be the position if the governing body of the school seeks to challenge an LEA direction to the governing body to admit a child (see EA 1996, s.13(1) and SSFA 1998, s.96).

Whilst judicial review proceedings must be brought promptly and in any event within three months, particularly stringent application of the requirement for promptness has been shown by the court on a number of occasions in admission cases (see, e.g. *R. (on the application of South Gloucestershire LEA)* v. *South Gloucestershire Schools Appeal Panel* [2001] EWHC Admin 732, [2002] ELR 309, per Stanley Burnton J at paras. 69–72).

Article 6 ECHR has been held not to apply to AAPs as the parental right to express a preference under SSFA 1998, s.86 has been held not to be a civil right (*R* v. *Richmond-upon-Thames LBC ex p. JC* (above) at para. 59; *R (on the application of B)* v. *Head Teacher of Alperton Community School and Others* [2001] EWHC Admin 229, [2001] ELR 359; *R (on the Application of C)* v. *Governing Body of Cardinal Newman High School* [2001] EWHC Admin 229, [2001] ELR 359 at para. 43). However, both LEAs and AAPs are public authorities within HRA 1998, s.6 and must take account of and give effect to ECHR rights both in school admission arrangements and in considering the impact of oversubscription criteria (*School Admission Appeal Panel* v. *Mayor and Burgesses of Hounslow London Borough Council* [2002] ELR 602 at para. 62; see also *R. (on the application of K)* v. *Newham London Borough Council* ([2002] EWHC Admin 405, [2002] ELR 390).

Examples of judicial review challenges to the admission process

Challenges to the legality of admission criteria, to be implemented when a school is oversubscribed, generally arise in the following areas:

(a) the basis on which distance criteria have been created;
(b) definition of catchment areas (for example, some children may as a result not reside in any school's catchment area (*R. v. Bradford Metropolitan Borough Council ex p. Sikander Ali* [1994] 2 ELR 299). It has been held that it is not unlawful to deny a place to a child living outside an oversubscribed school's catchment area where that child has been offered a place within another school (*R. v. Wiltshire County Council ex p. Razazan* [1997] ELR 370, CA). Drawing catchment areas which in part effectively follow a particular LEA boundary has been held not to be unlawful (*R. v. Rotherham Metropolitan Borough Council ex p. LT* [2000] ELR 76, CA); *Razazan* above; but note that in *ex p. LT* the Court of Appeal acknowledged that there might be circumstances where drawing of a catchment area close to the LEA boundary could give rise to a challenge to the catchment area or to the LEA's published admissions policy). However distance criteria or catchment areas are defined they must be intelligible and clear. The more complex the definition, the more likely the criterion may be open to successful challenge (see the *South Gloucestershire LEA* case (above) and contrast with *R. v. South Gloucestershire Education Appeals Committee ex p. Bryant* [2001] ELR 53, CA);
(c) the operation of a criterion which gives preference to siblings, or which fails to give sufficient priority to siblings (see *South Gloucestershire LEA* and *Hounslow* cases above);
(d) application of specific criteria established to maintain a school's particular religious ethos.

Procedural challenges may also be made to the admissions process published and implemented by the LEA or school's governing body, for example where there has been a failure to provide a mechanism which positively enables the parent to express a preference, or where admission criteria are so complex and contradictory as to be unintelligible.

Procedural challenges to the appeal process itself might include, for example, a challenge against the composition of the panel, where it appears that a member of the appeal panel belongs to one of the category of persons disqualified from appointment (SSFA 1998, s.94 and Sched. 24).

It is clearly unlawful for an LEA to take any step to affect the composition of the panel in a manner which may be perceived as reflecting the LEA's interest (*South Gloucestershire LEA* case, and see *R. (on the application of L) v. Independent Appeal Panel of St. Edward's College* [2001] EWHC Admin 108, [2001] ELR 452, for consideration of whether an individual panel member was in a disqualified category).

It should be noted that the substitution of members after the start of a hearing is not permitted (*R. v. Camden London Borough Council ex p. S* (1990) 89 LGR 513). However, if a member dies after the commencement of an appeal, or becomes too ill to continue, the AAP may continue to hear and determine the appeal, as long as the total panel numbers do not fall below three, and at least one of each type of member is included.

Infant class size challenges

The parent appealing an infant class size prejudice decision faces an uphill task, although occasionally cases have been successful (*R.* v. *Southend Borough Education Appeals Committee ex p. Southend-on-Sea Borough Council* [2000] Ed CR 368, QBD, a case in which an LEA was held to have acted unreasonably in refusing to accept compelling evidence in respect of the address at which a child was residing and in failing to inform parents of the possibility of submitting evidence in relation to 'exceptional medical circumstances'; *South Gloucestershire LEA* case as above).

Failure to give reasons

The AAP decision letter must give sufficient information to enable parents to know why they have or have not been successful in their appeal. It has been held that a pro-forma letter which contains 'a ritual incantation of the two stage test' is inadequate (*R.* v. *Birmingham City Council ex p. Education Appeals Committee ex p. B* [1999] ELR 305 at 312, per Scott Baker J). The letter must specifically mention material findings of fact, which it was required to determine, and whether the decision was made in accordance with the admission criteria or on some other basis, and if so what that basis was (*McKeown* v. *Appeal Committee and Governors of Cardinal Heenan High School and Leeds City Council* [1998] ELR 578, QBD).

It should be noted that even where parents have been offered a place at a school it is possible for that offer to be lawfully withdrawn (*R.* v. *Beatrix Potter School ex p. K* [1997] ELR 468). The extent to which certain circumstances may create a claim based on legitimate expectation has been considered by the court on a number of occasions, generally unsuccessfully (see *R.* v. *Stockton-on-Tees Borough Council ex p. W* [2000] ELR 93, CA; *R.* v. *Birmingham City Council ex p. L* [2000] ELR 543).

CHAPTER 4

School exclusions

4.1 INTRODUCTION

School exclusion is an area which is often extremely emotive and highly charged. An adviser to the parent or guardian and the pupil is often presented with a family under enormous stress. The parties' relationship with the school is usually strained and feelings may be running high. It is also not uncommon for the pupil's relationship with the parent to deteriorate during this stressful process. The parent is often feeling angry and disappointed with the pupil or the school. Some parents are at a complete loss and have tremendous difficulty coping with the uncertainty of their child's future schooling. The young person often feels deeply wronged and rejected by the school, is likely to feel alienated from his/her peers, isolated and may be very anxious about the future. The client will be worried about a number of issues, including feeling concerned that the pupil's school record will be blemished and the effect this may have on his/her future prospects. The client could also be anxious that the pupil may not return to full-time schooling quickly. If the pupil is approaching or is already in Year 10 or 11, there will be added concern that he/she is missing vital GCSE coursework and that his/her chances of obtaining the optimum number of qualifications are under serious threat. In certain parts of the country where there is a shortage of school places, parents have the added worry that their child may not easily secure a place in another mainstream school if a permanent exclusion is upheld or if reinstatement is refused.

The adviser to the parent and pupil should bear all of these factors in mind. Time is of the essence in obtaining instructions, advising on the merits and assisting the clients to make decisions which are in the best interest of the young person.

4.2 WHO IS THE CLIENT?

Although it is the pupil who is most directly affected by the exclusion process and who is the subject of a decision to exclude, the statutory framework vests the appeal right in the parent and not the pupil. Clearly, to obtain the most accurate understanding of the alleged incidents which precipitated the exclusion, an adviser needs to obtain instructions from the pupil if he/she has sufficient understanding and capacity. Where a young person is old enough to give instructions, it is good practice to see him or her with the parent or guardian in order to give advice on the proceedings so that the pupil understands the process. If it appears that the pupil has difficulty giving instructions in the presence of the parent or guardian, consideration should also be given to seeing him or her separately from the parent.

4.3 THE STATUTORY FRAMEWORK

Legislation

Section 52 of Education Act (EA) 2002 is the primary legislative provision. It provides:

(1) The head teacher of a maintained school may exclude a pupil from the school for a fixed period or permanently.
(2) The teacher in charge of a pupil referral unit may exclude a pupil from the unit for a fixed period or permanently.

The section also provides that regulations will make provision for appeal procedures. These are currently:

- Education (Pupil Exclusions and Appeals) (Maintained Schools) (England) Regulations 2002, SI 2002/3178, which regulate procedures for maintained schools;
- Education (Pupil Exclusions and Appeals) (Pupil Referral Units) (England) Regulations 2002, SI 2002/3179, which govern appeal procedures for pupil referral units (PRUs): SI 2002/3129 largely reflects SI 2002/3178;
- Education (Pupil Exclusions) (Miscellaneous Amendments) (England) Regulations 2004, SI 2004/402.

Maintained schools are community mainstream schools, community special schools, foundation mainstream schools, foundation special schools, or voluntary schools (School Standards and Framework Act (SSFA) 1998, s.20(1)).

DfES guidance

The original Secretary of State guidance, DfEE Circular 10/99 'Social Inclusion: Pupil Support' on pupil attendance, behaviour, exclusion and re-integration was implemented in September 1999 by the Labour government in a bid to promote social inclusion and as part of its political agenda of reducing the number of exclusions.

Numerous amendments by way of DfES letters were subsequently made to Chapter 6 and Annex D of the guidance which dealt with exclusions.

DfES Circular 0087/2004 'Improving Behaviour and Attendance: Guidance on Exclusion from Schools and Pupil Referral Units' (revised with updated Chapter 6 and Annex D) came into effect on 20 January 2003 and consolidated those changes whilst also revising the guidance significantly.

Further revised guidance was implemented on 22 March 2004 through DfES Circular 0354/2004 'Improving Behaviour and Attendance: Guidance on Exclusion from Schools and Pupil Referral Units'. Minor amendments were made to the said guidance on 22 July 2004 and 8 October 2004.

Regulation 7(2) of SI 2002/3178 places a mandatory duty upon head teachers, governing bodies, LEAs and independent appeal panels (IAPs) to have regard to the guidance when considering exclusions from maintained schools. The mirror provision for PRUs is in SI 2002/3179, reg. 8(2).

Although the Court of Appeal observed, *obiter*, in *S* v. *Brent London Borough Council*; *T* v. *Oxfordshire County Council*; *P* v. *Head Teacher of Elliot School and others and Secretary of State for Education and Skills (Interested Party)* [2002] EWCA Civ 693, CA that the guidance must not be 'slavishly followed', it is accepted that parties in the exclusion process must at least take it into account.

The guidance is extremely detailed and comprehensive. It consists of eight parts:

1. Promoting positive behaviour and early intervention
2. Removing pupils from a school site and exclusion
3. Procedures for excluding a pupil: role of the head teacher
4. Responsibilities of the governing body
5. Independent appeal panel
6. Police involvement and parallel criminal proceedings
7. LEA responsibility to provide full-time education and reintegrate permanently excluded pupils
8. Arrangements for money to follow pupils who have been permanently excluded from school.

Independent schools

This statutory framework applies only to maintained schools. Exclusion from private schools is governed by contract law (*R.* v. *Fernhill Manor School ex p. A* [1994] ELR 67, QBD; *R.* v. *Muntham House School ex p. R* [2000] ELR 287). Private schools frequently include in their terms and conditions of contract a term giving them the right to withdraw a school place, and it would not seriously be disputed that they have an implied right to do so. Such implied terms

SCHOOL EXCLUSIONS

do not necessarily include any sort of appeal mechanism or right of independent review. Parent advisers can, however, argue that an implied term of any contract is that the school should act reasonably.

Case law

There is a body of case law which establishes that public law principles must be adhered to during the decision-making process. Further references are made below and in Appendix K.

4.4 TYPES OF EXCLUSION

Head teachers of schools and teachers in charge of PRUs can either exclude for a fixed-term period or permanently. Such exclusions are regulated in SI 2002/3178 for schools and SI 2002/3179 for PRUs.

Fixed-term exclusions

The maximum number of days that a head teacher can exclude a pupil in any academic year is 45 (this is prescribed by SI 2002/3178, reg. 3 in the case of schools, and by SI 2002/3179, reg. 4 in the case of PRUs). Paragraph 25 of the guidance confirms that this limit applies to the pupil and not the institution. Any previous exclusions therefore follow the pupil if he/she moves schools.

Details of exclusions should be provided to the LEA. Parents can make representations to the governing body which usually appoints a three- or five-member committee to deal with disciplinary matters (see 4.7).

Regulation 5(1)(c)(i) of SI 2002/3178 requires the governing body to meet where the decision to exclude results in the young person being excluded for more than 15 days in any particular school term. The parents must be informed of the date of the meeting and their right to make representations.

Where the pupil is excluded for more than five but less than 16 days in a term, reg. 5(1)(d) makes provision for a parent or guardian to request a meeting with the governing body. Where such a request is made, the governing body has to convene a meeting within 50 school days of the request.

Where a decision to exclude results in an aggregate total exclusion of five days or less in one term, the parent can only make written representations. The governing body does not have to meet to consider the exclusion. The head teacher is required, however, to report those exclusions to the LEA and governors once a term (SI 2002/3178, reg. 4(5); SI 2002/3179, reg. 5(5)).

Permanent exclusions

When a decision to exclude permanently is taken, the governing body has to meet to consider the decision to exclude. The LEA also has the power to send a representative to the meeting. While the appeal process is pursued, the young person's name remains on the school roll. If the decision to exclude is upheld by the governors and the subsequent IAP, the pupil's name is then removed from the school roll and it is the responsibility of the LEA to make educational provision for the pupil. The school continues to receive funding for the pupil until the 'relevant date' which is either the date when the appeal is finally decided or, if there is no appeal, the last date for lodging the appeal or the date when the parent advises the LEA that no appeal is to be pursued (SI 2004/402, reg. 2).

Lunchtime exclusions

Regulation 2(2) of SI 2002/3178 provides that an exclusion between the morning and afternoon is the equivalent to half a school day. This gave legal recognition for the first time to this type of exclusion which has been used for many years and which is known as a lunchtime exclusion. Because it is specified as a half-day exclusion, this means that it can no longer be used as an indefinite disciplinary measure and without any regulation. Indefinite exclusions are unlawful as the statutory framework enables head teachers to exclude only for a fixed-term period or permanently.

The guidance provides at para. 32 that lunchtime exclusions should not be used over a prolonged period of time. Practitioners have found that they are often used for pupils with emotional and behavioural difficulties by schools which do not have the funding to provide adequate staff supervision and where the child does not have a statement of SEN with sufficient learning support assistant hours. The guidance recognises that these exclusions are sometimes used by schools instead of approaching the LEA or otherwise resolving the long-term problem.

Lunchtime exclusions can cause enormous disruption and stress to parents who are expected to collect the child on a daily basis. Where parents are unable to co-operate, the school has a duty of care towards the child and cannot require the child to leave the premises regardless of any consequences. Further information is provided to schools in para. 33 of the guidance.

Excluding pupils due to sit public examinations

Regulation 5(1)(c)(ii) of SI 2002/3178 requires the governing body to meet where an exclusion will result in a pupil missing a public examination. This applies irrespective of the length of the exclusion. Regulation 5(9) requires the committee to take steps to consider the exclusion prior to the dates of the examination.

4.5 REMOVALS

The guidance permits a head teacher or teacher in charge of a PRU to remove a pupil from the school on two grounds which do not amount to a exclusion and which do not attract any right of review or appeal.

Criminal accusation

Paragraphs 8(b) and 23 of the guidance permit a head teacher to require a pupil to receive educational provision off-site where he/she has been accused of a serious criminal offence that took place outside the school. Paragraph 23 suggests that this could arise where there are compelling reasons for removal pending the outcome of a police investigation; parental consent is not required.

Health and safety

Paragraph 8(c) of the guidance permits a head teacher to remove a pupil who poses an immediate and serious risk to the health and safety of other pupils or staff on medical grounds. Paragraph 24 suggests that the head teacher should consult the parents and a health professional as appropriate; it envisages that the provision can be invoked where the pupil has a diagnosed illness, such as a notifiable disease which poses an immediate and serious risk to the health and safety of other pupils and staff. The removal should be for the shortest time possible.

4.6 THE DECISION TO EXCLUDE

When to exclude

Paragraph 9 of the guidance provides:

> A decision to exclude a pupil should be taken only:
> (a) in response to serious breaches of the school's behaviour policy; and
> (b) if allowing the pupil to remain in school would seriously harm the education or welfare of the pupil or others in the school.

When to exclude permanently

Paragraph 11 provides:

> A decision to exclude a child permanently is a serious one. It will usually be the final step in a process for dealing with disciplinary offences following a wide range of other strategies, which have been tried without success. It is an acknowledgement by the school that it has exhausted all available strategies for dealing with the child and should normally be used as a last resort.

The guidance then advises that in exceptional situations it may be justifiable to impose a permanent exclusion for a first or 'one off' offence. Paragraph 12 provides that the likely scenarios might include:

(a) serious, actual or threatened violence against another pupil or member of staff
(b) sexual abuse or assault
(c) supplying an illegal drug
(d) carrying an offensive weapon.

Who can exclude

Paragraph 10 provides:

> Only the head teacher or teacher in charge of a PRU (or, in the absence of the head teacher or teacher in charge, the most senior teacher who is acting in that role) can exclude a pupil.

An adviser to a parent should always establish which member of staff took the decision to exclude. For practical reasons, if the head teacher is absent from school, disciplinary decisions must reasonably pass to another senior member of staff.

Early intervention and alternatives to exclusion

Part 1 of the guidance reflects the government's social inclusion policy by placing emphasis upon early intervention and steps that should be taken by schools to identify pupils at risk of exclusion. These include engaging with parents, implementing proactive strategies, considering assessment of SEN, placement in a special school and liaising with relevant agencies.

There is a specific section on alternatives to exclusion, namely:

- restorative justice;
- mediation;
- internal seclusion;
- a managed move.

Managed move

A managed move entails an agreement between the school and parent to move the pupil to an alternative school. It is important that parents are in full agreement with a managed move and do not feel pressurised due to fear of unsuccessfully challenging the decision to exclude or concern about the pupil's record being tainted with a permanent exclusion.

Where, on the evidence presented by the school and by the pupil's own admission, a serious incident occurred which will be difficult to challenge successfully, it may be advisable for the parent and pupil to consider a managed move at an early stage. It is still important for the parent's adviser to be satisfied that appropriate preventative measures were taken by the school, as the parent will be effectively accepting that the decision of the school to exclude is correct. Parents often find that, in these circumstances, the process of transferring the pupil to a new school is less traumatic and acrimonious. It is open to a parent to request a managed move. If, however, the school refuses to co-operate and decides to proceed with the exclusion process, the parent has no option but to challenge the exclusion or to accept it.

Steps preceding exclusion

The guidance emphasises that exclusion should be a last resort. The governors of a school have a legal duty to maintain and publicise the school's discipline policy.

If acting for the parent, it is essential to obtain a copy of the policy. Schools often include it in the school prospectus. Alternatively, it may be sent to parents in the home–school agreement when the child starts at the school.

The discipline policy should clearly explain the standard of behaviour expected of pupils and the sanctions which are likely to be imposed for certain offences. It should indicate which offences carry the sanction of fixed-term or permanent exclusion, and the likely length of fixed-term exclusions. The policy usually provides details of any reporting scheme operated by the school for initial or low-level misbehaviour. The policy should provide a coherent framework for regulating discipline and make it clear to pupils what sanctions are likely to be imposed for certain types of misdemeanour. It also serves the purpose of promoting consistency of treatment between pupils so that discipline is seen to be administered fairly and so that pupils and parents are fully aware of the consequences of misbehaviour.

If it appears that a school is, for example, seeking to impose a permanent exclusion for an offence which, according to the discipline policy, should attract a fixed-term exclusion, this is a matter which should be raised before the governing body or subsequent IAP.

Vulnerable pupils

African-Caribbean pupils (para. 49 of guidance)

Statistics show that African-Caribbean boys are seven times more likely to be excluded than their counterparts. The issue of the disproportionately high numbers of excluded boys of African-Caribbean origin has dogged their community for over three decades. Consequently, the Race Relations Amendment Act 2000 places a requirement on maintained schools to have regard to the need to eliminate unlawful racial discrimination. This extends to the area of exclusions. Schools should take active steps to monitor decisions to exclude in order to ensure that they do not discriminate during the decision-making process. The duties are set out in the Code of Practice on the duty to promote race equality, and there is also a guide 'The duty to promote race equality: a guide for schools'; both are published by the Commission for Racial Equality and are referred to in the main guidance on exclusions.

Pupils with special educational needs (paras. 42–45 of guidance)

Pupils with SEN are four times more likely to be excluded than their counterparts. The original Circular 10/99 made provision that pupils with statements of SEN should only be excluded in exceptional circumstances and that steps should be taken to avoid exclusion when it was apparent that a placement was at risk. Despite this provision being in place since 1999, disproportionate numbers of pupils with SEN continue to be excluded.

The revised circular places even greater emphasis on the requirement to avoid exclusion of pupils with SEN. Paragraph 43 provides:

> Other than in the most exceptional circumstances, schools should avoid permanently excluding pupils with statements. They should also make every effort to avoid excluding pupils who are being supported at School Action or School Action Plus under the Special Educational Needs Code of Practice, including those who are at School Action Plus who are being assessed for a statement.

Disabled pupils (para. 46 of guidance)

Under the Special Educational Needs and Disability Act (SENDA) 2001, schools are prohibited from discriminating against pupils on disability grounds. There is therefore a requirement on schools to ensure that decisions to exclude have not been made in a discriminatory manner. Schools must now comply with a Code of Practice issued by the Disability Rights Commission (DRC).

Paragraph 47 outlines that permanent exclusions involving allegations of disability discrimination will be heard by the IAP; fixed-term exclusions of this nature will be heard by the Special Educational Needs and Disability Tribunal (SENDIST).

Children in public care (para. 51 of guidance)

The guidance recognises that children in care are at particular risk of underachieving. It advises schools to take measures to avoid exclusion and to involve social services where there are difficulties. It also advises schools that a number of individuals may be involved in the child's life in conjunction with the local authority; thus all relevant parties should be included in any exclusion proceedings.

Before taking the decision to exclude

The head teacher, or teacher in charge of a PRU, should properly investigate the alleged incident and ensure that the decision is taken fairly and openly. This should entail obtaining statements from all relevant parties. The accused pupil should be given an opportunity to state his/her version of events. Any relevant background to the incident should also be taken into account. If, for example, there has been a history of incidents between pupils, this may be a relevant factor. If the accused pupil raises issues of harassment based on disability, race, sexual orientation or gender, the school should take such allegations seriously and consider the prospective exclusion incident in the context of any such history.

Paragraph 17 of the guidance provides:

> Exclusion should not be imposed in the heat of the moment, unless there is an immediate threat to the safety of others in the school or the pupil concerned. Before deciding whether to exclude a pupil, either permanently or for a fixed period, the head teacher should:
>
> (a) ensure that an appropriate investigation has been carried out
> (b) consider all the evidence available to support the allegations, taking into account the school's behaviour and equal opportunities policies, and where applicable, the Race Relations Act 1976 as amended and the Disability Discrimination Act 1995 as amended
> (c) allow the pupil to give his/her version of events
> (d) check whether the incident may have been provoked, for example by bullying, homophobic bullying, or by racial or sexual harassment
> (e) if necessary, consult others, but not anyone who may later have a role in reviewing the head teacher's decision, for example a member of the governing body.

Burden of proof

Regulation 7A of SI 2002/3138 and SI 2002/3139, reg. 8A (as inserted by SI 2004/402, reg. 4) require head teachers, teachers in charge of PRUs, governing bodies and IAPs to apply the ordinary civil burden of the balance of probabilities. This effectively overturned the important *Dunraven* case (*R v. Head Teacher and Independent Appeal Committee of Dunraven School ex p. B* [2000] ELR 156, CA) which required a 'distinct' balance of probabilities standard for exclusions involving serious offences.

The head teacher should therefore only take a decision to exclude if, on the balance of probabilities he/she is satisfied that the pupil is culpable.

Paragraph 18 of the guidance provides a sliding scale approach, however, to serious offences by providing:

> However, the more serious the allegation, the more convincing the evidence substantiating the allegation needs to be. This is not the same as requiring the criminal standard to be applied, but it does mean that when investigating the more serious allegations head teachers will need to gather and take account of a wider range of evidence (extending in some instances to evidence of the pupil's past behaviour) in determining whether it is more probable than not that the pupil has committed the offence.

This provision is also reflected in para. 40 in respect of the governing body's deliberations, and in para. 120 in respect of IAP deliberations.

Parallel criminal proceedings

Part 6 of the guidance provides advice to head teachers, governors and IAPs on how to handle exclusions where there are parallel criminal proceedings. When this situation occurs, difficulties may arise because the head teacher can be restricted in obtaining evidence due to parallel police investigations. The pupil and prospective witnesses may also be in a position where tactical decisions have to made on the degree of disclosure which should be made within exclusion proceedings when criminal proceedings are outstanding. The school and appeal panel may feel that the outcome of police investigations or a prosecution is vital to the exclusion procedure. A major difficulty is the time-scale of criminal proceedings or investigations and the consequent impact on the ability of the school or appeal panel to consider the exclusion expeditiously and in the best interests of all affected parties. Part 5 of the guidance provides advice on the factors which should be taken into account by the head teacher when deciding whether or not to make a decision to exclude in these circumstances. Whilst the governing body does not have power to adjourn the exclusion meeting, the IAP does. Guidance is therefore provided on the factors that should be taken into account by the appeal panel when reaching a decision. These include the likely impact on the proceedings if the panel awaits a decision by the Crown Prosecution Service as to whether the pupil is to be formally charged; the likely availability of witnesses and documents; the likely impact of delay if the hearing were adjourned and the likelihood of injustice to the excluded pupil.

Responsibilities flowing from the decision to exclude

Responsibilities are owed to the pupil, the parent, the governing body and the LEA. Unless otherwise stated, a teacher in charge of a PRU must take the same steps as a head teacher with the exception that there may be no equivalent to a governing body, requiring the LEA to make arrangements for consideration of representations.

Responsibilities to the pupil

During fixed-term exclusions, the school remains responsible for making educational provision. Arrangements must be made by the school to set and mark work. It is a common complaint of parents that schools frequently fail to comply with this requirement. If necessary, a letter should be sent to the head teacher and chair of the governing body on the parent's behalf. It may also be effective to inform the LEA of any difficulties.

Responsibilities to the parent

The head teacher is required to inform the parent or carer immediately. A decision letter with full reasons for the exclusion should be sent within one school day. The guidance is very specific about the mandatory contents of the decision letter. Model letters are appended to Part 3 of the guidance. They include a precedent for a fixed-term exclusion and a precedent for a permanent exclusion. These letters provide the contact details for the Advisory Centre for Education.

It is essential that the decision letter should confirm the nature of the exclusion and, if for a fixed term, its length. Full reasons for the exclusion must be provided to enable the parent to prepare representations adequately. The parent is otherwise in a position to argue breach of natural justice and to challenge the head teacher's failure to give reasons. The letter must also inform the parent of any entitlement to make representations to the governing body. In the case of a fixed-term exclusion from a PRU, the LEA has to make arrangements to consider representations from a parent, and those arrangements must be specified in the letter from the PRU to the parent.

Responsibilities to the governing body and local education authority

The head teacher must inform the governing body and LEA of the following exclusions by way of report within one school day:

(a) permanent exclusion;

(b) fixed-term exclusions which result in the pupil being excluded for more than five school days or 10 lunchtimes in the term in question;
(c) exclusions which will cause the pupil to miss a public examination.

The teacher in charge of a PRU must report this information to the LEA.

There is a less stringent reporting requirement for fixed-term exclusions which amount to five or fewer school days, or 10 or fewer lunchtimes in a term. The head teacher is only required to report these to the governing body and LEA once a term.

When reporting exclusions, the head teacher is required to give details of the pupil, the reason for and length of the exclusion, the pupil's SEN status if applicable, and whether the pupil is in care.

4.7 ROLE OF THE GOVERNING BODY

The governing body

As the School Governance (Procedures) (England) Regulations 2003, SI 2003/1377 enable, but do not require, schools to appoint discipline committees, the guidance (and this chapter) therefore refers to the governing body discharging the functions and duties placed upon the governors to deal with exclusions.

In practice, the governing body will usually appoint a sub-committee of the board of governors of a maintained school to deal with disciplinary matters (PRUs may not necessarily have a governing body).

The sub-committee has the specific role of reviewing the decision of the head teacher to exclude. Depending on the nature of the exclusion, the review may entail considering written representations from the parent or it may entail considering oral representations from the parties. By law, the governing body has a duty to review the head teacher's decision objectively and should not simply rubber-stamp decisions. It has to decide whether the school can satisfy the required burden of proof.

Constitution

It is essential that the governing body should be impartial and be seen to be impartial. The committee usually comprises either three or five members, who must not be directly connected to the pupil or the incident in question.

In *R v. M ex p. Board of Stoke Newington School* [1994] ELR 131, a successful challenge was brought to a decision of a governing body on the ground that the committee was unfairly constituted. The pupil's head of year sat on the committee despite having personal knowledge of a number of incidents which were relied upon for the decision to exclude.

When does the governing body have to meet?

Paragraph 76 provides that where the exclusion results in a cumulative total of five or fewer days in a term, the governing body does not have to meet but can consider written representations from the parent.

Where a fixed-term exclusion results in a cumulative total of between six and 15 days, the parent has a right to request a meeting with the governing body and the meeting must take place within 50 school days of the request.

A prompt meeting has to take place to consider permanent exclusions, fixed-term exclusions which bring the exclusion total to more than 15 days in one term, and exclusions which will result in the pupil missing a public examination. Regulation 5(8) of SI 2002/3178 requires the governing body to meet between the sixth and fifteenth school day after notification of the decision to exclude in these circumstances. Paragraph 78 of the guidance provides, however, that even if the governing body fails to comply with this time-scale, it is still required to meet and consider the exclusion. The decision of the governing body is not invalidated purely on account of meeting out of time.

If, however, the governing body does not meet for a significantly prolonged period, it may be open to the parent to seek a challenge on the grounds that the time lapse has caused undue prejudice to a fair consideration of the facts.

Where the exclusion is for a fixed term, the parent is usually concerned to ensure that a meeting takes place as soon as possible in order to challenge the exclusion before it comes to an end. Strong representations should be made to the clerk to the governing body for an early meeting date.

Where the exclusion will result in the pupil missing a public examination, the governing body must either meet before the date of the examination or, in exceptional circumstances, the chair of the governing body can meet alone with the parent. Even if the exclusion is upheld, however, *R v. Independent Appeal Panel of Sefton Metropolitan Borough Council, ex p. B* [2002] EWHC 1509 determined that the school must make arrangements for the pupil to return as a visitor for the purpose of sitting the examination.

4.8 PREPARING FOR THE GOVERNING BODY MEETING

When the parent receives the decision letter and has an entitlement to make oral representations to the governing body, he/she will have to decide whether or not to exercise that right.

Meeting date

The clerk to the governing body has to inform the parent of the proposed date for the meeting. This is open to negotiation. If the suggested date is inconvenient, the parent must inform the clerk. It is advisable for the parent to suggest convenient dates which fall within the period when the discipline committee is required to meet.

The parent is entitled to have a representative, and the clerk must take account of the representative's availability. It has been known for schools to refuse to rearrange meetings and to proceed with the meeting in the knowledge that the parent is unable to attend and has requested a postponement. It may be open to a parent to seek a judicial review in these circumstances on grounds of breach of natural justice. Arguably, such action on the part of the school is sufficiently serious to warrant a challenge in the Administrative Court on the grounds of fundamental flaw in procedure. However, the Court of Appeal in *R. (DR)* v. *Head Teacher and Governing Body and Independent Appeal Panel of W City Council*; *R.* v. *Governing Body of K School and Independent Appeal Panel of London Borough of E* [2003] ELR 104 held that parents should use the statutory remedy of appealing to the IAP, and only exceptionally seek court relief.

Evidence to support the parent's case

The exclusion letter must inform the parent of the reasons for the exclusion. This is usually insufficient to enable the parent to prepare fully. It is usual practice for the head teacher to compile a report which includes the decision letter, witness statements, relevant extracts from the pupil's school file and evidence of agreements made following any previous disciplinary matters. If the pupil has SEN, the head teacher may include documentation which outlines additional provision and the special needs history.

The report is sent to the parent by the clerk before the meeting. It is imperative for parent advisers to obtain both the parent's and, where appropriate, the excluded pupil's instructions on the school's documentation.

Evidence from the excluded pupil

One should consider whether it may be appropriate at any time to obtain instructions from the pupil without the parent being present. The adviser should be mindful that it is sometimes difficult for the pupil to give instructions in the parent's presence; a judgement should be made on how best to take instructions.

It is often extremely helpful to take a detailed statement from the pupil in which he/she provides a response to the alleged incidents, relevant background information, assurances for future behaviour, and all other pertinent information. Where appropriate, a statement should also be prepared on behalf of the parent. This may be particularly useful where the parent wishes to advise the governing body of any issues of historical relevance. The advantage in preparing statements is that the governing body has an opportunity to gain some insight into the parent and pupil's defence before the meeting when it will also be considering the school's case. Some practitioners feel that this helps to level the playing field to some extent. The majority of exclusions are upheld by governing bodies and parents often feel that they have a better chance of making an impression if the governing body is given advance knowledge of their case before the meeting.

Witnesses

Early consideration must be given to contacting witnesses for the pupil. This usually involves taking instructions from the excluded pupil on who his/her likely witnesses might be. If it appears that other pupils might be prepared to provide statements, it is essential to obtain their parents' addresses and to write to them seeking written consent for their child to provide a statement for the purposes of the governing body meeting. Alternatively, the client can consider a direct approach to the parents.

School record

The exclusion letter should, as a matter of good practice, advise the client of his/her right to inspect the child's school records. Parents and guardian have a legal entitlement to inspect the school record and to have a photocopy of the file or extracts from it (Education (Pupil Information) (England) Regulations 2000, SI 2000/297). An early decision should be taken on whether the parent's adviser will write to the school requesting a copy of the file or whether the parent will attend the school in person.

It is sometimes useful to peruse the school file as it often gives a more rounded picture of the pupil's history at the school. It may be important to demonstrate if the pupil has had achievements and periods of good behaviour in order to provide the governing body with a more balanced picture.

Expert reports

Depending on the nature of the allegations against the pupil, it may be necessary to consider instructing an independent expert such as an educational psychologist. If there are issues of unmet SEN, this is particularly pertinent.

If the child is already a patient of a therapist or medical practitioners, it may be worthwhile obtaining an updated report if this will assist in clarifying any issues which arise within the exclusion proceedings.

Challenging the decision

The adviser must consider whether the decision to exclude has been made in a manner which complies with legislation and guidance. Who made the decision to exclude and did they have the requisite authority?

Has the school complied with the procedure which is clearly set out in the guidance? If not, is the omission of a significant nature and should representations or a letter before claim be sent in advance of the meeting of the discipline committee? Subject to the response, consideration might be given to pursuing a judicial review of the head teacher's decision, bearing in mind the limitations imposed by the Court of Appeal in *R. (DR)* (above).

The school's evidence should be scrutinised closely. Are there inconsistencies between statements? Has the school complied with its discipline policy? What action has the school taken in similar circumstances in the past? Has the school failed to act upon obvious matters such as indications of unmet SEN? Is there an apparent history of bullying and what, if any, steps has the school taken in line with its anti-bullying policy? How were other pupils who were involved in the same incident disciplined?

The issue of anonymised statements is often a thorny one. The head teacher may wish to rely on such statements on the grounds that there is a likely risk to the safety of the authors. It is important to establish the reasons for the anonymity and, if appropriate, to seek to challenge them before the hearing. The challenges and response should be raised at the outset of the governing body hearing if it is the case that the excluded pupil will be prejudiced and unable to present a full defence as a result of not knowing the identity of the witnesses. *R. v. Head Teacher and Independent Appeal Committee of Dunraven School ex p. B* [2000] ELR 156 established that the excluded pupil must be given an opportunity to present a full defence and that if he/she is unable to do so because of anonymised witness statements, the decision-maker should attach less weight to those statements.

4.9 THE GOVERNING BODY MEETING

Local education authority advice

Paragraph 81 provides that the LEA is entitled to send an officer to the governing body meeting to provide advice on whether or not the exclusion should be upheld. The officer can provide assistance by, for example, advising on resources which may be available within the LEA to meet any apparent needs of the pupil. It can also be of assistance for the officer to provide guidance on LEA policies for addressing the behaviour in question and the approaches taken by other schools in the area.

The governing body should consider the advice of the LEA officer but is not required to follow the suggested decision.

In practice, due to limited resources, it is not always possible for the LEA to provide an officer for every governing body meeting within the authority. Some LEAs have a policy of prioritising permanent exclusions as is suggested in the guidance.

At the meeting

The governing body is required to consider the head teacher's reasons for the exclusion. It has to decide whether, on the balance of probabilities, the excluded pupil is responsible for the alleged incident, and whether the sanction of exclusion is concordant with the school's discipline policy, and is consequently a reasonable response.

Paragraph 80 of the guidance suggests a 'sliding scale' burden of proof where the exclusion is based on an alleged serious incident. The governing body must be satisfied that the head teacher made the decision to exclude on sufficiently convincing evidence and therefore in accordance with paragraph 18 of the guidance.

Procedure

The chair or clerk should open the meeting by outlining the procedure which is to be followed. The head teacher then usually addresses the meeting by outlining to the governing body, LEA officer and parent the reasons for the exclusion and the evidence which has been considered as the basis for the decision. The head teacher should demonstrate that a fair and reasonable investigation was undertaken and give the reasons why he/she believes, on the balance of probabilities, that the incidents occurred and that the exclusion is the last resort or is reasonable. The head teacher may call witnesses, such as staff members, to give evidence.

Where the head teacher is relying on anonymised statements, the governing body should ideally first satisfy itself that there are justified grounds for the school submitting anonymised evidence. Second, it should decide whether there will be unfairness to the excluded pupil if the statements are admitted. Third, the governing body should consider the cogency of the evidence and decide what weight to attach to it, given, in particular, the heightened requirement for evidence supporting particularly serious allegations.

Where the exclusion is based on the pupil's record and irretrievable breakdown in the relationship with the school, the head teacher has to demonstrate that adequate strategies were put in place, including a pastoral support plan; that sufficient time was given for the strategies or programmes to work; that the misbehaviour continued; that the school has exhausted all available options; and that it is no longer in a position to accommodate the pupil.

The head teacher usually prepares a report for the meeting which is circulated to the governing body and parent in advance. If documentation is not provided to the parent until a very late stage, such as the day before or the day of the meeting itself, the parent can reasonably request a short adjournment in order to have adequate time to consider the evidence.

Once the head teacher has presented his/her case, there is an opportunity for the parent and governing body to cross-examine. It is very important to question any part of the evidence which appears weak, to ask for further details where necessary, and to establish clearly whether all possible alternatives to exclusion have been fully explored.

The parent then has an opportunity to present his/her case and may rely on documentation, oral submissions and witnesses. Where the pupil is denying liability, the parent will be seeking to establish that there is insufficient evidence to support the head teacher's finding. The parent may also seek to argue that the decision to exclude is not in accordance with the school's discipline policy and, finally, that exclusion is disproportionate and not a reasonable response. If, for example the pupil has unmet SEN, it may be appropriate to argue that the school should have taken further steps to address the pupil's difficulties and that the exclusion is therefore unreasonable.

The guidance provides that the governing body should normally allow the excluded pupil to attend the meeting (para. 80). Advisers have to consider very carefully exactly how much of the meeting should be attended by the pupil. It can be very demoralising for a pupil to listen to negative discussions about him or her. Thought should be given to establishing at the outset of the meeting exactly when and for how long the pupil should join the meeting.

Where a pupil accepts responsibility for an incident, and the parent is arguing extenuating circumstances or that the sanction is disproportionate, it may be important to consider allowing the pupil an opportunity to express remorse and to provide assurances to the head teacher and governing body.

After presenting his/her case, the parent and his/her witnesses are questioned by the head teacher, governing body and LEA officer. The head teacher is given an opportunity to sum up, followed by the parent's summing up.

The decision

The governing body then has to deliberate on the evidence. It can be assisted by its clerk but it has to make its decision unaided. This means that none of the parties should confer with the governing body once the meeting has concluded. Challenges have been made to governing body decisions when, for example, parents have observed staff entering the room where the governing body is deliberating.

The governing body should inform the parent, head teacher and LEA of its decision within one school day of the meeting (para. 86 of the guidance). If the committee decides to reinstate the pupil, it cannot attach any conditions to the reinstatement.

Paragraph 79 of the guidance makes clear that the governing body's role is to review the decision; it cannot increase the severity of the exclusion. Paragraph 85 also makes clear that the governing body does not have power to overturn the exclusion but refuse to direct reinstatement; that power is only available to the IAP.

If the governing body upholds the exclusion, its decision letter must provide the reasons for its conclusion. It must also notify the parent of his/her right to appeal to the IAP, and give details of the person and address to which the appeal should be sent and the date by which it must be lodged.

Paragraph 87 sets out the required contents of the decision letter, namely, the reason for the decision, the right of appeal and name and address of the person to whom the notice of appeal must be sent, the date by which the notice should be lodged, and that the notice must set out the grounds of the appeal and can include a claim of disability discrimination.

Model decision letters are appended to Part 4 of the guidance.

4.10 ROLE OF THE INDEPENDENT APPEAL PANEL

The IAP has a quasi-judicial appellate function. It has to consider whether the decision of the governing body was reasonable. In so doing, it has to examine the original decision of the head teacher or teacher in charge of a PRU, the parent's representations to the governing body, the LEA advice at the governing body meeting and the reasons given by the governing body in reaching its decision.

Where the appeal involves any allegations of racial or disability discrimination, the IAP has to determine whether or not the discrimination took place.

Regulation 6(3) of SI 2002/3178 provides that:

> in making any decision on an appeal pursuant to arrangements made under paragraph (1), an appeal panel shall have regard both to the interests of the excluded pupil and to the interests of other pupils and persons working at the school (including persons working at the school voluntarily).

As the IAP is at arm's length from the school, parents often feel that they have a better chance of having a more objective consideration of their appeal. The IAP is assisted by a clerk; para. 99 provides that LEAs are required to provide training to panel members.

An important function of the panel is to conduct its business in a completely neutral manner and to bring independence of thought to the proceedings.

Constitution of the independent appeal panel

Concerns exist regarding the independence of panels due to constitution requirements which are specified in para. 2 of the Schedule to SI 2002/3178.

This specifies that an IAP must be constituted from three categories of members: head teachers, lay members and governors of a maintained school. A three-member panel must be constituted with one person from each category. A five-member panel must be constituted with two head teachers, two governors and one lay member. The regulations further provide that head teacher panel members will usually be appointed from within the same LEA as the excluding school. There is provision for 'small LEAs' to recruit head teacher panel members from outside authorities; however, no definition of 'small' is given. Current practice for many London LEAs is that professional panel members are drawn from the same authority as the excluding school. They are therefore likely to have some acquaintance with the head teacher whose decision is under challenge.

Consideration should be given to ascertaining the identity of the head teacher members before the hearing and checking what, if any, personal knowledge of or involvement with the school such members may have. If there are reasonable concerns as to such members' ability to act independently, their inclusion on the panel should be challenged at the outset of the hearing, if not before.

Under amended SI 2002/3178, and SI 2002/3179, Sched., para. 2(2)(c) teachers and head teachers may sit as governor panel members provided they have not served in such positions during the preceding five years.

4.11 PREPARATORY PROCEDURAL ISSUES

An appeal to the IAP must be lodged within 15 school days of the date on which the parent is notified of the decision. If the decision is communicated by first-class post, notice is deemed to have been given two working days after the date on which the decision was posted (para. 87(c) of the guidance).

A notice of appeal has to be submitted to the relevant person, usually the clerk to the IAP. It should be signed either by the parent or by the parent's representative. The grounds of appeal do not have to be particularly detailed as the parent has a further opportunity to submit additional information to the panel, including written submissions. They should state that the parent challenges the governing body decision and, as a minimum, provide brief reasons. These may include assertions that the school failed to establish to the required standard of proof that the excluded pupil was responsible for the incidents, or that the exclusion is disproportionate and has not been used as a last resort. If preferred, or where time permits, the parent can provide detailed grounds.

The LEA has responsibility for arranging appeal hearings before the IAP. It maintains a pool of panel members and convenes panels of three or five members for each appeal.

On receiving an appeal, the clerk to the IAP liaises with the parent or his/her representative to agree a hearing date. The clerk should advise the parent of the latest date by which any further documentary material must be submitted. Once the clerk has received materials, steps are taken to compile an appeal bundle. This usually contains documents which were submitted to the governing body by both the school and parent, the governing body decision letter, the parent's notice of appeal, and any further documents submitted to the clerk by the parent, school and governing body subsequent to the parent serving notice of appeal. The clerk is required to circulate the appeal bundle to the IAP, governing body and parent five working days before the hearing (para. 107).

Paragraph 105 of the guidance also provides that the clerk should ascertain whether an alleged victim wishes to make representations at the hearing, in person or in writing.

4.12 PREPARING FOR THE APPEAL TO THE INDEPENDENT APPEAL PANEL

Very similar steps should be taken as when preparing for the governing body meeting (see 4.8 above). The adviser will need to scrutinise the governing body decision letter and look closely at the reasoning. He/she will have exercised this function already when the notice of appeal was completed.

A decision will need to be taken on whether a further statement should be prepared for the IAP and what other evidence should be obtained. It may be suitable to rely purely on oral evidence at the hearing if a detailed statement was already submitted to the governing body.

An adviser will need to consider whether expert reports or other professional advice should be sought, and consider whether more information should be obtained from the school file.

A decision has to be taken about witnesses. In addition to the parent, excluded pupil and other potential pupil witnesses, an adviser should consider whether to request the attendance of any school or LEA staff. If the excluded pupil has SEN, it may be advisable that the SEN Co-ordinator, or any other professional such as the Educational Welfare Officer or therapists who have been involved with the pupil and who may be important to your client's appeal, should be requested to attend the hearing.

It is possible for the parent's adviser to ask the clerk to the IAP to make requests on his/her behalf for employees of the authority to attend. The IAP does not have the power to issue witness summonses.

The crux of the parent's preparation will be an aim to establish that the school failed to justify the exclusion before the governing body. If the decision letter appears flawed in its reasoning, this is another ground of challenge.

In relation to the governing body decision or the head teacher's decision, SI 2002/3178, reg. 6(4) provides:

> An appeal panel shall not determine that a pupil is to be reinstated merely because of a failure to comply with any procedural requirement imposed by or under these Regulations.

Nevertheless, if it appears that major procedural deficiencies have occurred, this should be included in the parent's case.

4.13 THE INDEPENDENT APPEAL PANEL HEARING

Preliminary issues such as the use of anonymised statements should ideally be raised by parties at the outset of the hearing (see 4.8 above regarding preparation for the governing body meeting).

Paragraph 120 of the guidance outlines the applicable standard of proof, which is the ordinary civil balance of probabilities subject to a heightened requirement where 'the more serious the allegation, the more convincing the evidence substantiating the allegation needs to be'. This corresponds with paras. 18 and 80 which place the same requirements on the head teacher when making the decision to exclude, and the governing body when considering representations on the exclusion.

The chair or clerk to the panel outlines the procedure which is to be followed for the hearing. The governing body usually addresses the panel first with the reasons for reaching its decision. Frequently it delegates this function to the head teacher who outlines the reasons for making the original decision. A representative from the governing body may also give evidence outlining the reasons why the governing body concluded that the permanent exclusion was justified.

The parent then has an opportunity to cross-examine the school. Members of the IAP can also ask questions.

The parent then presents his/her case and is subsequently questioned by the school and IAP.

The LEA representative may also make a contribution and be questioned by the parties.

After the parties have presented their cases and answered questions, the school is given an opportunity to sum up and the hearing concludes with the parent's summing up.

The decision is usually reserved and parties have to be notified within two working days of the hearing (para. 133 of the guidance).

The decision

Paragraph 132 of the guidance provides that the decision of the IAP is binding on all parties and cannot be revisited by the IAP; this clearly has an impact where parties consider a judicial review of the IAP decision.

Dismissing the appeal

When the IAP upholds the decision to exclude permanently, this has the effect of enabling the school to remove the pupil's name from the school roll lawfully (Education (Pupil Registration) Regulations 1995, SI 1995/2089, reg. 9(1)(k)). The school has no further responsibility for educating the pupil and does not have to continue providing schoolwork. The pupil becomes the responsibility of the LEA, which should take immediate steps to liaise with the parent to discuss future educational provision.

If the pupil is due to sit public examinations, he/she should be allowed to return to the school as a visitor for that purpose. This is notwithstanding the decision of the panel to uphold the permanent exclusion. The court in *R.* v. *Independent Appeal Panel of Sefton MBC ex p. B* [2002] ELR 676 held that this did not have the effect of overturning the exclusion. If a school refuses to confirm arrangements for the pupil's admission within a reasonable timescale of the examinations, the pupil's remedy is judicial review.

Allowing the appeal and reinstating

When the IAP decides that the school has failed to justify the decision to permanently exclude, it can allow the appeal and order the school to reinstate the pupil. It does not have power to attach any conditions to reinstatement but can direct that the reinstatement should take place at a specified future date. The main purpose for this is often to give parties an opportunity to plan the pupil's reintegration.

Allowing the appeal and not reinstating

Regulation 6(6) of SI 2002/3138 enables the IAP to:

> decide that because of exceptional circumstances or for other reasons it is not practical to give a direction requiring his reinstatement, but that it would otherwise have been appropriate to give such a direction.

Paragraph 129 of the guidance provides examples of circumstances where the IAP may decide that reinstatement is inappropriate even though the panel determines that the exclusion should not have taken place. These include 'where there has been an irretrievable breakdown in relations between pupil and teachers; between the parents and the school; or between the pupil and other pupils involved in the exclusion or appeal process'.

In carrying out its balancing function of weighing up the interests of the pupil and those of other parties at the school, the IAP can decide that the pupil should not be reinstated.

To reach such a judgment, the IAP has to decide whether it is satisfied from the evidence provided by the parties that a state of affairs envisaged by para. 129 exists. Proceedings before the IAP do not necessarily give the parent an opportunity to make representations in advance on this as the main remit of the appeal hearing is for the IAP to establish whether the permanent exclusion decision is justified.

Paragraph 130 of the guidance provides that in the decision letter, the IAP should provide details of the circumstances that made it decide not to direct reinstatement. It is, however, clearly too late at this stage for the parent to make submissions if an opportunity was not provided at the hearing.

Advisers need to bear this in mind when preparing the appeal and try to identify the issues which could be relied upon by the IAP to make a decision under para. 129. A very common issue is that of threatened industrial action by teaching staff. Where health and safety issues have been raised by the school, it would be prudent to make submissions in this regard.

Reinstatement

There have been numerous occasions when teaching staff at schools have threatened to strike if an excluded pupil is reinstated to mainstream classes, due to a refusal on the part of staff to teach the pupil. In the case of *P* v. *NASUWT* [2003] ELR 357, HL it was held that industrial action of this nature is lawful as it concerns a dispute about terms and conditions of employment and is thus afforded immunity (Trade Union and Labour Relations (Consolidation) Act 1992, s.244(1)). This has sometimes arisen when staff have health and safety concerns. In response, the school in question may make alternative arrangements for the pupil which deny him/her the opportunity to return to mainstream classes. Alternatives have included one-to-one tuition in total isolation from other pupils, or placement within a unit.

The House of Lords in *Re L (a Minor) by his father and Litigation Friend* [2003] ELR 309, HL held that it is lawful for the head teacher to take the threat of industrial action into account and to make consequent special arrangements for the reinstated pupil. The appellant challenged the refusal of the school to reinstate him into mainstream classes, requiring him instead to receive his tuition in isolation. The court held that once the school resumed responsibilities and obligations towards the pupil, the school–pupil relationship was reinstated and that the arrangements made by the school were good enough to amount to reinstatement.

The court also held that it is necessary to consider whether the school has acted in good faith and whether the arrangements are bona fide or in fact a sham. In an earlier related appeal *R. (C)* v. *Governors of B School* [2001] ELR 285 the Court of Appeal determined that the head teacher and governors of a school have to act proportionately to the threat of industrial action and that the school must ensure the least derogation from the pupil's full reintegration into the school. These issues were taken no further in *Re L* and are arguably still live. Parent advisers must therefore examine the proposed arrangements closely if the pupil is put in this position. Advisers should consider asking for evidence of the ballot by staff and steps taken by the head teacher to address their concerns; evidence of meetings between the head teacher and staff and steps taken by the head teacher to provide information about any changes in circumstances such as increased levels of support for the pupil. In *Re L* the appellant was a Year 11 pupil who only had a few more months of compulsory education. If acting for a younger pupil, it would be a reasonable requirement of the head teacher to review the pupil's and teaching staff's positions periodically. If for example the pupil is allowed partial reintegration into the school, his/her performance should be reviewed and thought should be given to extending the reintegration if there has been satisfactory progress, no further complaints about the pupil and real evidence that staff concerns are no longer justified. If these factors exist, there could be an argument that continued refusal to reintegrate fully indicates bad faith.

The adviser must also ensure that the pupil is given access to the full National Curriculum when any special arrangements are made following reinstatement. If the school is unlawfully failing to comply with the National Curriculum requirements, there is an argument that it is in breach of its statutory duty.

Discrimination claims

Where there are claims by a parent of disability or race discrimination within the appeal, there is a specific requirement on the IAP to determine whether or not such discrimination occurred. These areas of law are extremely complex; thus advisers may wish to raise questions about the training which the LEA has provided to panel members in advance of the appeal hearing.

4.14 FURTHER REMEDIES

Complaints

A parent can make a complaint to the chair of the governing body if dissatisfied with the manner in which the head teacher or governing body has conducted an exclusion. Many parents lack confidence in internal school complaint procedures. The Local Government ombudsman does not have jurisdiction to investigate complaints about internal school affairs.

If dissatisfied with the manner in which an IAP has conducted an appeal, a parent can make a complaint to the LEA through its internal complaints procedure. Most LEAs have a two- or three-tier procedure. The parent should complain promptly.

Local Government Ombudsman

Once the internal complaint has been concluded, if still dissatisfied and if the complaint is of maladministration, the parent can complain to the Ombudsman who will ask the LEA to provide a response to the parent's complaint and investigate further. The complaint must be made within one year of the alleged maladministration. If, however, the allegations have already been the subject of judicial review proceedings, the Ombudsman may not have jurisdiction to consider the complaint.

Judicial review

This remedy against decisions of the governing body has been restricted as a result of the *Kingsmead* case (*R. (DR)* v. *Head Teacher and Governing Body of S School and Independent Appeal Panel of W City Council; R. (AM)* v. *Governing Body of K School and Independent Appeal Committee of London Borough of E* [2002] EWCA Civ 1822, [2003] ELR 104). In the past, practitioners advised parents on the option of judicial review where there was a strong argument that the governing body had acted unlawfully. The Court of Appeal in this case, however, held that a parent should usually challenge a governing body decision through a statutory appeal and only in rare circumstances should a challenge to the governing body be brought by way of judicial review. The court indicated that legal proceedings could be contemplated if there was a real need for court guidance or interim relief, or if the governors had acted 'quite improperly'. Since this decision, some attempted applications to court have been criticised on the basis that the parent should have pursued the appeal to the IAP.

Challenges to the decision of the IAP can be brought through judicial review if there are the established public law grounds for challenge. Time is of the essence, and therefore proceedings must be launched without delay as the pupil is already likely to have been out of school for a number of weeks. The court will not look favourably upon applications which are not brought promptly. Practitioners must remember that an action can be out of time even if it is brought within three months. In *R (on the application of A)* v. *Head Teacher of North Westminster Community School* [2003] ELR 378, the High Court held that it is appropriate to issue proceedings at the beginning of the three-month period rather than the end.

4.15 LEGAL HELP/PUBLIC FUNDING

Legal Help

Legal Help is available for eligible applicants. The applicant is usually the parent or guardian as the form should usually be signed by a person who is over the age of 16 years. In circumstances where there is no acting parent or guardian, and the adviser is satisfied that the pupil has sufficient capacity and understanding to give instructions, then the pupil can apply. The adviser must complete the section of the form which explains why an application has been accepted from a person under 16. This may arise, for example, when acting for a young person in care where it is not appropriate to ask his/her social worker to apply for Legal Help.

Legal Help covers the cost of advising the client, preparing for the appeal hearing and obtaining expert reports where required and justified. It does not cover the cost of representation at the hearing. In exceptional cases, applications can be made to the LSC under Access to Justice Act 1999, s.6 for funding. The criteria are very narrow. In summary the adviser is required to demonstrate that, but for the funding, the client will be unable to present an appeal. Some practitioners have found that applications have been refused on the grounds that the adviser can make written legal submissions on behalf of the client. The LSC has also taken the view that IAPs are specifically trained to deal with appellants who are acting in person. Where, however, there is a strong argument that the client will need an advocate for detailed cross-examination or because he/she is particularly vulnerable or disadvantaged, there may be more scope for succeeding with such applications.

Public funding

This is available for the pupil, and therefore the pupil's means, as opposed to the parent's or guardian's, are taken into account. The Funding Code acknowledges that public funding for exclusion cases should usually be in the name of the child. It does, however, make provision for considering a refusal of an application in the child's name should it become apparent that the parents are particularly affluent.

Public funding will be necessary where there is an arguable case for pursuing judicial review proceedings. Advisers without the Specialist Quality Mark may find it useful to obtain counsel's written advice in support of an application for public funding. The LSCs has been known to refuse applications even where the merits do not appear to be in doubt.

CHAPTER 5

Pupils out of school

5.1 INTRODUCTION

A common problem presented to education advisers is the issue of pupils out of school. This problem can arise for a number of reasons. Excluded pupils are often out of school for a considerable period of time before a new school place is identified; a high percentage of excluded children never return to mainstream school. Pupils may also be out of school due to sickness or other reason, such as school phobia. Pupils with statements of SEN whose placements break down are likely to spend significant periods of time out of school while arrangements are made for their return. Time is always of the essence in either securing a pupil's return to school or arranging interim provision. The longer a pupil is out of school, the more difficult he/she is likely to find the demands of reintegrating.

Admission forums (SSFA 1998, s.85A) have responsibility for ensuring that effective local planning for the provision of school places takes place. These forums must also consider the position of excluded pupils and the availability of school places. They are encouraged to formulate and apply protocols to enable excluded pupils to find new schools outside the normal admission round. Admission Authorities must have regard to advice provided by the Admission Forum.

5.2 THE STATUTORY FRAMEWORK FOR EDUCATIONAL PROVISION

Duty to educate

Section 14 of EA 1996 places a duty upon LEAs to ensure that there are sufficient schools for the provision of primary and secondary education in their area.

There is a corresponding duty on parents under EA 1996, s.7 to ensure that a child of compulsory school age receives efficient full-time education suitable to his/her age, ability, aptitude and any SEN, either at school or otherwise.

When children are out of school

Section 19(1) of EA 1996 (as amended by EA 1997, s.47) provides:

> Each LEA shall make arrangements for the provision of suitable education at school or otherwise than at school for those children of compulsory school age who, by reason of illness, exclusion from school or otherwise, may not for any period receive suitable education unless such arrangements are made for them.

Originally, s.19(1) specified 'full-time or part-time' education, but these words were removed by amendment.

Section 19(4) specifies:

> a local education authority may make arrangements for the provision of education otherwise than at school for those young persons who, by reason of illness, exclusion from school or otherwise, may not for any period receive suitable education unless such arrangements are made for them.

This section provides for young people over compulsory school age but under the age of 18.

Section 19(4A) of EA 1996 provides:

> in determining what arrangements to make under subsection (1) or (4) in the case of any child or young person, a local education authority shall have regard to any guidance given from time to time by the Secretary of State.

When is s.19 engaged?

Where a child is excluded or is out of school by reason of illness, the duty on the LEA is indisputable. Where, however, the pupil is out of school for another reason, there may be difficulty in establishing whether s.19 is engaged and thus that the LEA has a duty to make provision.

In *R. (on the application of G)* v. *Westminster County Council* [2004] ELR 135, the Court of Appeal held that the parent has to establish 'unavoidable cause' for the pupil's lack of schooling and that it was not reasonably possible for the pupil to attend the previous school. G argued that he was unable to attend school due to bullying. The court held that persistent bullying might make it reasonable for a parent to withdraw a child, but held on the facts that G was not the victim of bullying and there had at all times been a place at the school which was suitable for G.

Whether or not there is unavoidable cause in any particular case will depend upon the facts of that case.

PRACTICAL EDUCATION LAW

5.3 GUIDANCE

The applicable guidance is as follows:

- DfES Circular 0354/2004, 'Improving behaviour and attendance: guidance on exclusion from schools and PRUs', Chapter 7: LEA responsibility to provide full time education and reintegrate permanently excluded pupils;
- DfEE Circular 11/99, 'Social inclusion: the LEA role in pupil support', Chapter 4 (Chapter 5 of Circular 11/99 was replaced by Chapter 7 of Circular 0354/2004 referred to above on 22 March 2004);
- DfEE Circular 1/98, 'LEA behaviour support plans'.

Circular 11/99 and Education Act 1996, s.19

Guidance on, *inter alia*, the implementation of s.19 is provided in DfEE Circular 11/99, which came into effect in July 1999.

The guidance confirms the statutory definition of 'suitable education' as:

efficient education suitable to the age, ability, aptitude and to any SEN the child or young person may have.

This mirrors EA 1996, s.19(6).

Chapter 4 details that LEAs should have behaviour support plans to cover arrangements for the education of children otherwise than at school, and direct reference is made to the related guidance in DfEE Circular 1/98, 'Behaviour support plans'.

Circular 1/98

Paragraph 4 advises that the requirement for LEAs to have behaviour support plans is to ensure that LEAs have a comprehensive strategy for addressing pupil behaviour and discipline problems.

Paragraph 76 provides that LEAs need to include details of their procedures for assessing the needs of pupil out of school, including for interim provision and also for finding a suitable long-term placement. They should also provide information about the support which is to be offered to assist reintegration of excluded pupils into mainstream or special schools and transitional arrangements.

Paragraph 173 also advises, for example, that if a pupil is not ready for early reintegration to school, a reintegration plan needs to map out how that pupil will be prepared for eventual reintegration to a new school.

Circular 0354/2004, Chapter 7: Exclusions guidance

The guidance on exclusions was revised on 22 March 2004 and the new Circular 0354/2004 amended DfES Circular 87/03.

A new Chapter 7 was included entitled 'LEA responsibility to provide full time education and reintegrate permanently excluded pupils'. It draws on Circulars 11/99 and 1/98 and replaces Chapter 5 of the former, thereby consolidating good practice.

The chapter focuses on the responsibilities of LEAs:

(a) to provide a suitable full time education for permanently excluded pupils; and
(b) to reintegrate those pupils as quickly as possible, where practical into a suitable mainstream school.

Throughout the guidance, an emphasis is placed upon the importance of reintegrating pupils into mainstream schools where this is compatible with the pupil.

Paragraph 160 highlights the importance of reintegration. The assumption is clear that permanently excluded pupils can, in some cases, reintegrate immediately; those who cannot may need a fixed period of time in alternative provision to assist their return to mainstream school.

Paragraph 172 provides that schools should plan to educate pupils outside mainstream schools long term only where there are significant problems which are better addressed in a specialist environment.

How much provision?

The requirement to provide full-time education to pupils excluded for more than 15 days was introduced in Chapter 4 of Circular 11/99.

Chapter 7 of Circular 0354/2004 provides guidance on the meaning of full-time education by reference to the key stage applicable to the pupil, and states that the educational provision must comprise the following number of hours:

Key Stage 1:	21 hours
Key Stage 2:	23.5 hours
Key Stage 3/4:	24 hours
Key Stage 4 (Yr 11):	25 hours

It further clarifies that the pupil's timetable can differ from that of a mainstream school in that the provision can be made by the pupil attending different venues. LEAs are to endeavour, where possible, to ensure that the National Curriculum is provided.

Paragraph 158 gives examples of the range of provision that should be considered by LEAs: schools, pupil referral units (PRUs), voluntary or community organisations, private sector providers, further education colleges or work experience placements, or IT provision. The LEA is required to monitor provision supplied by other agencies as it remains responsible for the pupil's educational provision.

Paragraph 156 specifies a prompt timescale for LEAs to start taking steps to arrange full-time provision. Planning should begin from the sixteenth school day following the head teacher's decision to exclude; prior to that, the LEA and school should work together to facilitate that planning.

5.4 SCHOOL'S DUTY TO EXCLUDED PUPILS

Where a pupil is excluded permanently or for a fixed term, the school is under a duty to set and mark work pending the pupil's return to school or the outcome of the governing body discipline committee meeting. If a permanent exclusion is upheld and the parent appeals to the IAP, the school remains responsible for providing and setting work pending the outcome of the appeal. Regulation 2(3) of the Education (Pupil Exclusions) (Miscellaneous Amendments) (England) Regulations 2004, SI 2004/402 provides that the pupil's funds remain with the school until the outcome of the IAP appeal, or the parent notifies the LEA that he/she does not intend to appeal.

Parents often complain, however, that no work or an inadequate amount of work is set by schools. Representations should be made immediately to the head teacher and, if necessary, the chair of the governing body and the LEA. This is also the type of problem that should be addressed by the LEA through the reintegration panel or its reintegration officers where a pupil is permanently excluded.

The redress may be more difficult where a short fixed-term exclusion is in issue. If the school delays in setting work, the pupil may not get the benefit of representations, as the fixed-term exclusion may end before the dispute is resolved.

5.5 DIFFERENT MODES OF PROVISION

Individual tuition

Chapter 7 of Circular 0354/2004 is silent in this regard, whereas the superseded Chapter 5 of 11/99 gave specific guidance.

Case law is sparse on the number of hours of home tuition that should be provided. In *R* v. *East Sussex County Council ex p. Tandy* (1998) 1 CCLR 552, HL the court held that s.19 imposes a target duty towards individual pupils and would not determine the specific number of hours of home tuition the LEA should provide.

Pupil referral units

The statutory framework for the creation of PRUs comprises EA 1996, s.19(2) and Sched. 1. It is also clarified that PRUs are legally both a type of school and education otherwise than at school.

PRUs are run by management committees, permit dual registration of a pupil with a school, and are headed by a teacher in charge.

Paragraph 6.7 of Circular 11/99 provides, significantly, that

> Pupils should be admitted to a PRU based on clear criteria and each pupil should have targets for reintegration into mainstream or special school, further education or employment.

Furthermore, paragraph 173(a) of Chapter 7 provides:

> LEAs need to ensure that pupils who could be reintegrated successfully into a mainstream school are not left long term in a PRU due to a lack of planning or unwillingness on the part of local schools to take excluded pupils ...

In practice, many pupils remain in PRUs long-term, partly due to the shortage of school places, in inner city areas in particular. There is often a serious issue as to the quality of provision made to individual pupils. Where a pupil has SEN, it is all the more important that parents should investigate and consider the provision carefully. Where appropriate, they should consider challenging the provision if it is unsuitable for the pupil's requirements.

Paragraph 175 advises that the pupil should maintain contact with mainstream education where possible. Pupils can be dual registered at PRUs and schools or, alternatively, PRUs should provide the benefit of informal arrangements with local schools to facilitate the pupil's access to facilities which are not available at the PRU.

Paragraph 151 advises that LEAs and schools should ensure that excluded pupils are able to access core National Curriculum subjects. Specific needs should also be met, such as those of pupils with emotional and behavioural issues.

PRUs are also required to include personal, social and health education, information and communication technology (ICT) and citizenship in their curriculum.

5.6 REINTEGRATION

Paragraph 165 of Circular 0354/2004 provides guidance on reintegration panels for those LEAs that convene them to deal with exclusions and/or the provision of services for pupils out of school. It offers suggestions on the categories of individuals who should sit on these panels and emphasises the need for panels to meet promptly after each exclusion. LEAs are expected to decide for themselves how to run these panels and the extent of their remit, as the guidance envisages that some of the tasks required to ensure reintegration, can be undertaken either by the panel or by LEA staff members. These include assessing the pupil's needs and arranging actual provision.

The guidance acknowledges that not all LEAs convene panels, and those which do not have panels should have specific reintegration officers with responsibility for arranging reintegration, and monitoring ongoing support and progress of reintegrated pupils.

Paragraph 168 provides that an individual reintegration plan for each excluded child should be drawn up within one month of the governors' decision to uphold the exclusion. The plan should be attached to the pupil's individual education plan (IEP) and/or pastoral support programme and given to all relevant parties.

The reintegration plan should include details of the name of the school to which the child is to return, reintegration programme with the school and at least monthly dates for review of the plan by an LEA officer. It should include arrangements for interim and long-term provision.

Paragraph 177 provides that where the pupil is at Key Stage 4, a transition plan rather than reintegration plan should be prepared. More practical action should be considered, such as arranging placement at a further education college rather than a school.

Finding another mainstream school place

It is open to the parent to apply to alternative schools at any stage of the exclusion process. The LEA should offer assistance and involve the parent in discussions about alternative placement.

If an application is unsuccessful, the parent has a right of appeal to the admission authority's appeal panel under SSFA 1998, s.94(1) and (2) (see Chapter 3). This appeal right is restricted for a two-year period if the pupil has been permanently excluded twice; SSFA 1998, s.95 provides for special arrangements.

Section 96 of SSFE 1998 provides:

> The LEA may give a direction under this section if, in the case of any child in their area, either (or both) of the following conditions is satisfied in relation to each school which is a reasonable distance from his home and provides suitable education that is –
>
> (a) he has been refused admission to the school, or
> (b) he is permanently excluded from the school.

(2) A direction under this section shall specify a school –
   (a) which is a reasonable distance from the child's home, and
   (b) from which the child not permanently excluded.
   . . .
(4) A direction under this section to admit a child shall not specify a school if his admission would result in prejudice of the kind referred to in section 86(3)(a) by reason of measures required to be taken as mentioned in subsection (4) of that section
(5) Where a school is specified in a direction under this section, the governing body shall admit the child to the school . . .

This power of LEAs to direct does not appear to be commonly used. If acting for parents, advisers should make representations to LEAs to use this power where appropriate.

5.7 PUPILS WITH STATEMENTS OF SPECIAL EDUCATIONAL NEEDS

There may be a number of reasons why a pupil is not attending the school named in Part 4 of his/her statement. The LEA remains under a duty to arrange the provision detailed in the pupil's statement; if this is not feasible due to exclusion, steps should be taken urgently by the LEA to review the statement and enable the parent to express a preference for an alternative school. It is good practice to ensure that a meeting with an appropriate professional takes place as soon as possible after the exclusion; it may be prudent to arrange an early annual review.

Any maintained school which is expressed as a preference must be consulted by the LEA and given at least 15 days within which to respond before the LEA can contemplate naming it in an amended statement (see Chapter 7, p. 122). In theory, a pupil could be returned to school promptly if the parent expresses a preference immediately and the LEA, in turn, consults forthwith. In practice, however, it can take a significant period of time to identify a suitable alternative school, especially if the pupil has challenging behaviour; a prudent placement is vital to avoid further risk of exclusion.

Whilst steps are taken to identify a new school, the LEA is under a duty to make s.19 provision as detailed above. Paragraph 6.10 of Circular 11/99 advises that many pupils in PRUs have statements and many have emotional and behavioural difficulties; LEAs must consider carefully the provision to meet long-term need. It further advises that should a return to mainstream school prove unsuitable, the LEA should name a special school, as opposed to a PRU, on an amended statement.

Paragraph 179 of Circular 0354/2004 provides that placement in a PRU may be appropriate for the short term where pupils have statements, but their long-term needs generally require a school placement.

Paragraph 180 further emphasises that only in exceptional circumstances should a PRU or other alternative provision be the most appropriate placement for some pupils with statements who have emotional, behavioural and social problems.

Should the LEA fail to act expeditiously in seeking parental preference, consulting schools and making interim provision, the parent's likely remedy is that of judicial review based on breach of EA 1996, ss.324 and 19.

5.8 DAMAGES FOR PUPILS OUT OF SCHOOL

Article 2 of the First Protocol of the ECHR provides a negative right to education by providing that a pupil shall not be denied an education.

The Court of Appeal held in *A (Abdul Hakim)* v. *Head Teacher and Governors of the Lord Grey School* [2004] EWCA Civ 382 that the head teacher and governors were liable to pay damages under HRA 199, s.8 as they had the primary duty to educate and, on the facts of the case, had a primary duty not to exclude unlawfully.

At first instance, the Administrative Court held that a pupil's exclusion from a school might cause a breach of Article 2 of the First Protocol, but only where he/she had no access to alternative educational facilities. If an LEA had been responsible for the non-availability of provision, then it would be liable for damages.

Case law suggests that the High Court is not very keen on free-standing human rights damages claims, as demonstrated by *Anufrijeva* v. *London Borough of Southwark* [2004] 2 WLR 603, CA. In practice, damages claims are more likely to succeed if integral to a judicial review claim where the substantive matter is other than a damages claim. A claim founded, for example, on EA 1996, s.19 could, where appropriate, include a damages claim.

CHAPTER 6

Negligence

6.1 INTRODUCTION

This chapter considers the issues which may arise if a school or LEA has been considered to be negligent. This type of action will broadly fall into the following areas:

(a) claims involving personal injury or physical harm arising from, for example, inadequate supervision or defective premises;
(b) claims involving bullying;
(c) claims arising from the response to a child's SEN;
(d) claims arising from the delivery of the curriculum (for example failing to teach the correct public examination syllabus).

These potential claims affect both maintained and independent schools, with additional parental contractual rights in the case of independent schools.

The scope of this chapter does not encompass consideration of the detail of each type of claim. We have therefore focused on those claims which are particularly related to education and outside the usual range of general knowledge, even for a personal injury practitioner.

6.2 EDUCATIONAL NEGLIGENCE

Prior to 1995 it was generally understood that a common law claim in negligence was not available to a pupil or former pupil within the maintained school sector, in respect of the provision of education or SEN provision. The statutory framework, within which local authorities work in looking after children with SEN, is considered in Chapters 7 and 8. From the coming into force of the Education Act (EA) 1981, which first fully codified the statutory duties of LEAs in respect of pupils with SEN, it was clear that a mechanism for seeking redress when things arguably went wrong, would be sought by potential claimants.

The law was partially but not fully clarified in the House of Lords decision in *X* v. *Bedfordshire* [1995] 2 AC 633. In *X* v. *Bedfordshire* the House of Lords held that a claim might be brought against an LEA for vicarious responsibility for the acts or omissions of an educational psychologist in its employment and also recognised the responsibilities of teachers to pupils both with and without SEN. The important conclusions are set out and discussed in the speech of Lord Browne-Wilkinson at 756–759 and 766.

It was not until 1990 that a further decision of the House of Lords robustly confirmed the existence of a duty of care owed to pupils by 'education professionals' and further identified the existence of that duty as positively contributing to the maintenance of high professional standards.

The principles

A duty of care is owed by educational psychologists and other education professionals who assess, identify the needs of and advise on the remediation of pupils with SEN. The potential vicarious liability of an LEA for the negligence of an educational psychologist and/or other professional in its employment, was confirmed by the House of Lords in *Phelps* v. *Hillingdon London Borough Council* [2001] 2 AC 619 at 653H–654C, 665G–666A and 670D–675H. In recognising the impact that misdiagnosis or failure to advise properly may have, Lord Slynn pointed out at 651F:

> A failure to fulfil the duties by an authority either generally or in a particular case can have a serious effect on a child's education, his well-being and his future life.

The House of Lords also held at 664F–G:

> psychological damage and a failure to diagnose a congenital condition and to take appropriate action as a result of which a child's level of achievement is reduced (which leads to loss of employment and wages) may constitute damage for the purposes of a claim.

A similar duty of care is owed by teaching staff. In *X* v. *Bedfordshire* the House of Lords held that a claim might be brought against an LEA for vicarious responsibility for the acts or omissions of a head teacher or an advisory or specialist teacher in its employment. This was reinforced in *Phelps* by Lord Slynn at 658A–D and Lord Nicholls at 668D–H.

> If it comes to the attention of a headmaster that a pupil is underperforming, he does owe a duty to take such steps as a reasonable teacher would consider appropriate to try to deal with such under-performance.

The potential liability of an education officer was considered to have been left open for argument. Further judicial consideration of this issue in *Carty* v. *Croydon London Borough Council* [2005] 1 WLR 2312, CA confirmed the common law liability of education officers.

The damage caused is recognised as injury in the form of personal injury and may result in significant economic loss in later life (*Robinson* v. *St Helen's Metropolitan Borough Council* [2002] All ER (D) 388, CA).

However, simple lack of progress will not be sufficient to establish negligence. The actions of those for whom the LEA is vicariously liable must be judged against the test in *Bolam* v. *Friern Barnet Hospital Management Committee* [1957] 1 WLR 582, QBD, that is whether the conduct fell below the professionally recognised standards of the time.

6.3 WHO IS THE CLIENT?

The child, young person or adult concerned will be the client and potential claimant in any proposed litigation concerning maintained schools. The strong feelings which can be generated through many aspects of a pupil's education have already been identified. The potential claimant may have a burning sense of grievance at the perception of an inadequate response to his/her difficulties in school. Similarly the claimant's parent or carers may feel that they struggled against the school system, LEA and other professionals for virtually the whole of their child's education and have very high expectations as to what may be achieved on their child's and their own behalf.

The practitioner needs to recognise that many clients and their families have limited literacy and/or language skills and may struggle to understand the complex issues, which any claim of this sort raises and which can represent a significant challenge even for lawyers.

6.4 THE STATUTORY FRAMEWORK

Although this chapter considers common law claims, those claims arise within the context of a specific statutory framework within which the relevant duties of care arise. A claim may span several legislative changes. Therefore practitioners will need to be aware of some or all of the following:

- Education Acts 1981, 1993 and 1996;
- Special Education and Disability Act (SENDA) 2001;
- the relevant regulations;
- the Special Educational Needs Codes of Practice 1994 and 2001;
- earlier DoE guidance: Circular 1/83 and Circular 22/89 (in its original form and as amended in 1992);
- the Warnock Report (1979).

6.5 INITIAL INFORMATION NEEDED FROM THE CLIENT

The following points should be considered:

(a) whether the client is aged over or under 18: consider limitation and/or the need for a next friend;
(b) if the client is an adult there is still potentially an issue re capacity;
(c) the nature of client's difficulties, and whether these are confirmed or potentially open to dispute;
(d) the public funding/costs benefit analysis matrix;
(e) the time span of the potential claim: which, if any, legislation applies;
(f) the status of the client, i.e. whether he/she is recognised as having SEN and if so whether he/she has been statemented or not by the potential defendant(s);
(g) the client's qualifications, e.g. GCSEs or other qualifications, such as NVQs, ASDAN; A levels; further or higher education;
(h) the client's work status: earnings;
(i) the client's mental health status;
(j) identifying potential defendants: in particular, consider the reorganisation of local government (especially in 1997); status of any schools attended (maintained/non-maintained, independent, formerly grant-maintained, or foundation schools, voluntary aided, city technology colleges and city academies);
(k) whether there is any recent expert evidence: if so, does it confirm existing needs or diagnose new areas of difficulty? Are further assessments suggested?;
(l) what records does the client or parent/carer retain, e.g. school reports, statement documentation, old assessments, etc.?

6.6 WHAT DOES THE CLIENT NEED TO KNOW?

Many potential claimants will have become aware through the media that it is possible to 'sue' the LEA. They may be convinced they have a claim, without understanding the need for detailed expert evidence and analysis of the position. Equally, they may have an inflated idea of the sums likely to be recoverable even in a strong claim.

The client needs to understand:

(a) that there may be a lengthy period of investigative work, typically six to nine months, while school and LEA records are considered and expert evidence obtained. That will result in the preliminary merits of the claim being considered and may lead to a pre-action protocol letter being prepared and sent. If proceedings are initiated the likely timescale for the case to reach trial may be around two years, or more;

(b) that the damages recoverable are potentially not large and will focus on putting the claimant in the position in which he/she would have been had the negligence not occurred. In *Phelps* the successful claimant recovered approximately £45,000. A recent decision of the Court of Appeal, *DN* v. *Greenwich London Borough Council* [2004] EWCA Civ 1659, considered at 6.8 below, confirms the cautious approach which should be taken in relation to quantum;
(c) the implications of proportionality and the statutory charge;
(d) the emotional toll resulting from pursuing these types of proceedings, which can be considerable.

Once provided with the basis to consider the client's position, the following issues arise.

Limitation

Where the claim incorporates a personal injury element, the primary limitation period is three years from the date of the client's eighteenth birthday (Limitation Act 1980, s.11). It is possible to bring a claim after the client's twenty-first birthday, if the date of knowledge postdates his/her achieving majority, or by exercise of the court's discretionary power (Limitation Act 1980, s.33). However, the courts, in a series of recent cases considered since *Phelps*, have been extremely slow, even reluctant, to accept a post-21 limitation issue based on date of knowledge (*Robinson* v. *St Helens Metropolitan Borough Council*; but see, for example, the approach to limitation in *Smith* v. *Havering London Borough Council* [2004] ELR 629).

If a limitation period is pressing the claim should be issued and advantage taken of the four-month window which is allowed for service of the particulars of claim (CPR 7.5(2)).

6.7 DUTY OF CARE

It is essential to identify if at all possible the individuals in respect of whom the LEA is said to be vicariously liable. In many cases, this will be one or more educational psychologist, or advisory teacher. It is important to recognise that fleeting or passing contact with the pupil will not create the necessary relationship which establishes a duty of care.

Generally, the pupil will need to have been referred and/or assessed by the relevant professional in order to create the necessary nexus. It is not, however, a prerequisite for a report to have been prepared by the individual; indeed, failure to do so following assessment may constitute a specific particular of negligence.

The relationship between school staff at a school the pupil attended and the pupil should be sufficient to create the necessary nexus and establish a duty of care, even where a head teacher, for example, may have had little or nothing to do with the particular pupil, given the overarching responsibility implicit in the role.

Breach of duty

The *Bolam* test is flexible in its application to the differing professionals who may have been involved with a pupil. The test is essentially subjective and specific to the recognised and usual practice at the time. Therefore the standards and accepted good practice of 2005 cannot be used to judge and find wanting, for example, the approach of an individual in the early 1990s prior to the implementation of the first Special Educational Needs Code of Practice (1994). Hence the importance of considering old DfES and professional guidance from the time in question. Ofsted reports and HMI assessments may also be very relevant. However, a fairly standard approach was codified in the SEN Code of Practice of 1994, which has been developed and reinforced in a subsequently revised version of the Code (2001), which remains the relevant guidance.

Whilst the courts have recognised that departure from the statutory guidance is not necessarily indicative of incompetence, the more recent legislative framework provides a good context in which to consider the application of the *Bolam* test. The differing responsibilities of individual professionals, to whom a pupil may be referred and that of the schools he/she attends, need to be recognised. The role of schools is generally not to provide diagnostic or specialist advisory input for its pupils. However, if it clearly holds itself out as so doing that will be a relevant factor in considering the adequacy of the school's response to an individual pupil.

In *X* v. *Bedfordshire*, the court clearly envisaged appropriate recognition of a problem and referral for further assessment as potentially discharging the school's responsibilities to the pupil. However, a school cannot, in the authors' view, treat the act of referral in itself as the end of its role and where that referral leads to little or inadequate action, the school must have an ongoing responsibility to pursue appropriate intervention for its pupils.

6.8 DAMAGE

Damages will fall into the usual categories, broadly identified as special (specific) and general (non-specific). Typically there will be little difficulty in identifying the various areas of specific expenditure either already incurred, or prospectively arising, e.g. specialist tuition for dyslexia which aims to develop the claimant's literacy skills insofar as possible.

The position in relation to general damages is substantially more complex. Two possible categories of non-financial loss, not amounting to recognised psychiatric damage, may be identified. The first is what has been called psychological loss. This defies precise definition but appears to be something like loss of self-esteem and self-confidence arising from an unaddressed perception of lack of self-worth, which the tortfeasor failed to allay.

The second is what might be called educational deficit: the notion that the defendant's tort has prevented the claimant from acquiring the skills and knowledge necessary to lead a fulfilled life and to reach a level of attainment commensurate with the claimant's innate abilities. This is particularly difficult to characterise as 'loss' in any absolute sense. The claimant has suffered a loss in a relative sense, in that his/her educational gains have been slower in coming and less than they should have been, compared to the performance of others of the same ability, and judged against the level of expected performance deduced from the claimant's innate ability. But he/she has arguably not suffered loss in any absolute sense. In *Phelps* v. *Hillingdon London Borough Council* [1998] ELR 38 Garland J found that an educational psychologist had negligently failed to diagnose and recommend appropriate treatment for dyslexia. He asked himself the question:

> Can the plaintiff recover on the basis that on balance of probabilities, had her condition been diagnosed earlier, it would to some extent have been ameliorated, and by raising her level of literacy improved her quality of life and prospects of employment? Does the law of tort recognise a lost gain as well as an inflicted loss?

In *Phelps* it was held that it would be wrong to adopt an 'over-legalistic view' of what constitutes personal injury and it was also stated that the loss could be 'emotional'. In *Robinson* v. *St Helens Metropolitan Borough Council* Brooke LJ pointed out that the House of Lords has now recognised the existence of a duty of care 'where the foreseeable (and recoverable) damage resulting from a breach is not necessarily a physical or recognisable psychiatric injury' and indicated tentatively that in the latter type of claim such loss is 'the kind of damage the duty exists to prevent'.

How does that assist us in advising the client? A starting point is the judicial recognition that:

> The ability to read is a benefit that nobody would dream of undervaluing. It is not simply a benefit of economic value leading to enhanced employment prospects, although it certainly is that. It is a benefit that transforms the whole quality of life of the person who acquires it.
> (*Adams* v. *Bracknell Forest Borough Council* [2004] UKHL 29, [2004] 3 WLR 89, per Lord Scott at para. 67)

This approach is encouraging and allows for the broader impact of loss to be considered by the courts. However, difficult questions arise when considering the issue of loss where the claimant's potential is less certain, or where his/her difficulties would always have had a significant impact on functioning, for example those on the autistic spectrum.

An additional group is those whose educational difficulties, although not identified or addressed, have not prevented them, for example, obtaining a place at university, or having reasonable employment prospects. Given the inherent uncertainty in any educational outcome, the extent to which loss can be claimed for circumstances in which, for example, the individual becomes a nurse rather than a doctor, is debatable. There are further difficulties in defining loss where an individual may ultimately have had his/her difficulties recognised and addressed, but arguably at the 'too late to really make a difference stage' (see *Christmas* v. *Hampshire County Council* [1998] ELR 1, QBD).

In these claims, all roads can appear to lead back to the issue of causation. However, depending on individual circumstances, the claimant may seek to recover for the following, insofar as relevant to the claim:

- loss of earnings/loss of economic opportunity;
- recognised psychiatric injury;
- physical injury;
- care costs;
- 'psychological' harm of the type discussed above;
- expenditure incurred by the claimant or on his/her behalf, e.g. specialist tuition or school fees;
- prospective expenditure such as therapeutic provision, tuition, or computer equipment;
- counselling.

Quantum

The client needs to be aware that the case law and guidance on quantum is scant. In many cases the claimant's potential economic earning power may well have been limited, even in optimal educational circumstances.

Practitioners have been forced to look to the decision in *Phelps* for assistance; however, the facts of that case included the claimant's free-standing medical condition, which rendered her incapable of work and which depressed her potential claim for loss of earnings. The award was calculated as:

- loss of economic opportunity: £25,000;
- general damages: £12,500;
- various: approximately £8,000.

The approach of the judge, which might be described as instinctive rather than scientific, was endorsed by the House of Lords in the *Phelps* judgment. No other substantive awards have been achieved through trial, save *DN* v.

Greenwich London Borough Council [2004] EWCA Civ 1659, where the issue of quantum has been remitted to the trial judge for consideration. However, the Court of Appeal identified that, where expert evidence was uncertain on the issue of outcome for the claimant, the measure of damages would be small.

In settlements, it has been possible to agree awards of between £30,000 and £80,000 for individual claimants, generally where individuals of average intellectual ability who left school illiterate had not had their dyslexia recognised.

The authors' experience is that the straightforward and obvious claim will settle, with the more difficult claims proceeding to trial. However, the success rate at trial, as indicated above is not good.

6.9 CONTRIBUTORY NEGLIGENCE

This is an issue which potentially creates tension between the claim and the previous actions of the pupil's parents or carers. Some defendents will seek to argue vigorously that the pupil's own actions, or those of his/her family, have substantially contributed to their perceived loss.

Some examples include:

(a) a record of poor behaviour at school, exclusion or reluctance to accept support offered;
(b) failure to take up the available statutory remedies, when dissatisfied with the school or LEA's response. In particular, a failure to use the statutory appeal process now set out in EA 1996, may create future problems;
(c) withdrawal from school;
(d) truancy.

Where a client is still of compulsory school age, it is important to recognise that the family's energies may be better expended in seeking to improve the current position and achieve the best package of support within school, rather than pursuing a premature claim in negligence.

6.10 PROCEDURAL ISSUES

It is not the intention here to set out general information in respect of civil procedure. The following may be particularly relevant:

(a) pre-action discovery of records and information, to enable proper investigation of the potential claim;
(b) Data Protection Act 1998 searches;
(c) seeking the court's direction to bring a defendant into an alternative dispute resolution or mediation forum;

(d)   robust response to bullying Part 18 requests (CPR, 18.1);
(e)   limiting witnesses of fact to those who have a real contribution to make to relevant issues: well meaning family friends are rarely of assistance to the courts. School teachers who taught the pupil may be worthwhile witnesses;
(f)   focused witness statements: less is more, and additional statements can be filed if necessary to deal with further points;
(g)   joint expert reports or agreed memoranda of expert areas of agreement and disagreement;
(h)   a split trial may potentially benefit the claimant, particularly if facing potential LSC funding problems or difficulty in satisfying the LSC cost-benefit analysis matrix, as it may enable liability to be established more cost-effectively and maximise the chance of settlement.

Experts

It is important that the client realises that the expert's duty is to the court. The various judgments in educational negligence claims are littered with judicial criticism and comment on the expert evidence given in the trial. Any or all of the following experts may need to be considered:

- educational psychologist;
- expert in teaching practice and procedure;
- psychiatrist;
- speech and language therapist;
- occupational therapist;
- physiotherapist (less usual).

6.11   MEDIATION/ALTERNATIVE DISPUTE RESOLUTION

Educational negligence claims may be particularly suited to alternative forms of resolution, offering a real opportunity to address the client's concerns in a constructive and meaningful way. Defendants may, however, struggle to move beyond an entrenched view of their need to defend their position and to recognise that the 'alternative options', for example, an apology, may be more valuable to a claimant than the more limited remedies available to a court.

It is possible to address the needs of both parties through genuine dialogue, and mediation can be the least threatening option in seeking to bring parties to the negotiating table.

The following may be useful considerations:

(a)   the need to recognise and record that aspects of a pupil's education may not have been successful and that consequent difficulties have been experienced;

(b) whether the parties may agree that a formal apology should be offered to the claimant and his/her parents;
(c) the ongoing need for training and support and the role the LEA/school might play in supporting or facilitating that process, through provision of tuition, equipment (e.g. loaning or purchasing computer equipment) and financial support. Section 15 of EA 1996 specifically provides for LEA support to those beyond compulsory school age and can be a useful mechanism for 'arranging' such support;
(d) the role of other agencies in supporting the claimant, e.g. the local authority's social services department;
(e) a financial settlement or resolution of quantum issues.

6.12 INDEPENDENT SCHOOLS

The relationship between the independent school and pupil clearly creates a duty of care and the common law principles above will apply. The complicating factors may be the existence of a contractual relationship between the pupil's parents and the school (and potentially the pupil's third party rights) and the possible involvement of an LEA in supporting an independent school placement, through the terms of a statement of SEN, or otherwise. The latter point can bring into play public law remedies where normally none would exist (see, for example, *R. v. Cobham Hall School ex p. S* [1998] ELR 389; but also *R. v. Muntham House School ex p. R* [2000] ELR 287) due to the statutory framework within which the school is providing for a pupil.

The position of city technology colleges (now also applicable to city academies) was considered *R. v. Governors of Haberdashe's Aske Hatcham Community College Trust, ex p. T* [1995] ELR 350. These hybrid institutions are susceptible to both judicial review and the statutory framework for SEN. In addition, the common law principles set out in this chapter also apply in addressing any negligence issues.

6.13 OTHER CAUSES OF ACTION

Academic failure/negligent teaching

This type of claim arises where a school or LEA is vicariously liable for an individual staff member's failure to teach to a competent standard, most commonly in delivery of a specific public examination curriculum.

Bullying

Claims arising in respect of bullying may often co-exist with the type of claim considered above. The most detailed consideration of this type of relatively novel claim is in *Bradford-Smart* v. *West Sussex County Council* [2002] EWCA Civ 7, [2002] ELR 139, in which the Court of Appeal clearly identified the potential for negligence arising from a school's response to reports of bullying.

In *Faulkner* v. *Enfield London Borough Council* [2003] ELR 426, QBD the language of the House of Lords in *X (minors)* and *Phelps* was echoed in reflecting the reasonable expectations of society and parents, that schools should protect pupils and inform their parents of the problem and proposed action, so as to enable properly informed decisions to be made in respect of the child's safety.

6.14 PUBLIC FUNDING

Public funding currently remains available to investigate and pursue educational negligence claims, provided the claim can satisfy the LSC cost-benefit analysis matrix. However, this is the subject of current review by the LSC, which periodically seeks to bring these claims within the usual personal injury conditional fee agreement requirements. It is highly unlikely that any practitioner would be willing to run such a claim on a CFA basis. Research has established that no realistic insurance policy would be available for claimants, and in the absence of public funding, access to justice would in the authors' view be impaired for a vulnerable and disadvantaged group, which society should seek to protect.

6.15 CONCLUSIONS

The complex interrelationships of the public and private law rights and remedies require careful consideration. Whilst a small number of negligence claims will succeed, it is important to recognise that this remedy will be of little practical benefit to the majority of clients. Nevertheless, the sea change in judicial approach which has primarily taken place in the last 10 years is very much to be welcomed.

CHAPTER 7

Special educational needs: identification and assessment

7.1 INTRODUCTION

This is a complex area of law which is rooted in detailed legislation and guidance. This chapter outlines the process by which responsible bodies identify, assess and provide for pupils who have special educational needs (SEN). The following chapter deals with the appeal rights and procedures which arise in SEN law.

Due to the complex nature of SEN law, it is not uncommon to find that many parents are understandably at a loss when they first encounter its procedures. Because the process is convoluted and due to the voluminous documentation that is involved, it is particularly important to ensure that non-jargonistic language is used with parents and it may be necessary to explain the procedures and related time-frames more than once. Depending on the nature of the child's SEN, the parent may be coming to terms with a number of anxieties such as a possible long-term condition of their child, the ongoing stigma that others may attach to SEN and difficulty in seeing when the child's schooling is going to be finally resolved.

It is worth mentioning at an early stage that the current emphasis of SEN law is that children should be educated primarily within mainstream environments, particularly where this is the wish of the parent. This is due to the long-standing principle of inclusion which was given further statutory bite with the implementation of the Special Educational Needs and Disability Act 2001 and the related DfES Guidance on Inclusion.

7.2 THE STATUTORY FRAMEWORK

Historically, there have been several major revamps of SEN law. Suffice to state however that the enactment of EA 1996, Part IV and Scheds. 26 and 27 played a significant part in consolidating earlier legislation and introducing some coherence to this area of law.

Further developments took place on 1 January 2002 when provisions of the Special Educational Needs and Disability Act (SENDA) 2001 came into force along with the revised and comprehensive SEN Code of Practice (DfES 0581/2001, hereafter referred to as 'the Code'). Primary legislation provides that parties involved with SEN procedures must have regard to the Code.

There are a number of important statutory instruments. These are:

- Education (Special Educational Needs) (England) Consolidation Regulations 2001, SI 2001/3455 ('the Consolidation Regulations');
- Education (Special Educational Needs) (Provision of Information by Local Education Authorities) (England) Regulations 2001, SI 2001/2218;
- Education (Special Educational Needs) (Information) (England) Regulations 1999, SI 1999/2506 ('the SEN Information Regulations 1999').

The DfES has also issued guidance entitled 'Inclusive Schooling – Children with Special Educational Needs' (DfES Circular 0774/2001). There is also a Toolkit on the SEN Code of Practice (DfES 588/2001) which summarises the Code chapter by chapter.

7.3 DEFINITIONS

Definition of special educational needs

Section 312 of EA 1996 defines SEN as a 'learning difficulty which requires special educational provision'. 'Learning difficulty' is further defined as:

(a) a significantly greater difficulty in learning than the majority of children of the same age;
(b) a disability which prevents or impedes a child from making use of education facilities of a kind generally provided for children of the same age in schools within the area of the LEA;
(c) being under compulsory school age and falling within the definition of (a) or (b) above or would do so if special educational provision was not made for them.

Definition of special educational provision

'Special educational provision' is defined as:

(a) for children of two or over, educational provision which is additional to, or otherwise different from, the educational provision made generally for children of their age in schools maintained by the LEA, other than special schools in the area; or
(b) for children under two, educational provision of any kind.

Gifted pupils

Unsuccessful legal challenges have been brought which argue that the enhanced abilities of gifted children should fall within the definition of SEN. These arguments have been rejected so far by both the Special Educational Needs and Disability Tribunal (SENDIST) and the High Court.

7.4 RESPONSIBLE BODIES

The bodies responsible in law for identifying, assessing and meeting SEN are as follows:

- LEAs;
- governing bodies of maintained schools;
- (registered) early years' providers including childminders;
- statutory bodies involved with the statementing process, including health trusts and social services;
- SENDIST.

Local education authorities

These have a number of obligations which include the following:

(a) to maintain, publish and monitor a SEN policy pursuant to SI 2001/2218 (see above);
(b) to use best endeavours to ensure that the needs of children with SEN are identified and assessed as quickly as possible and matched with appropriate provision;
(c) to provide support to schools and early years settings;
(d) to monitor and evaluate their funding arrangements to schools;
(e) to make arrangements for Parent Partnership Schemes (PPSs) in their area (SENDA 2001, s.2 which incorporates a new EA 1996, s.322A);
(f) to provide an independent disagreement resolution service for parents in their area (SENDA 2001, s.3 incorporating a new EA 1996, s.332B).

Governing bodies of schools

Governing bodies' responsibilities include:

(a) to publish, monitor and report on the SEN policy of the school, pursuant to the SEN Information Regulations 1999 and the Code;
(b) to use their best endeavours to ensure that necessary provision is made for pupils with SEN, pursuant to EA 1996, s.317;
(c) to liaise appropriately with the LEA and other governing bodies;
(d) to inform parents when SEN provision is made for their child;

(e) to ensure that all relevant staff are informed that a child has SEN and recognise the importance of identifying and meeting those needs.

Early years settings

These include institutions in receipt of financial assistance from the LEA which are providers of relevant nursery education for the purposes of School Standards and Framework Act (SSFA) 1998, s.118 for four and five year-olds. Registered childminders are also included. The duties are akin to those of governing bodies.

Statutory bodies

These are typically health trusts and social services departments which work in conjunction with LEAs. They often play a role in identifying SEN through their professional involvement with families.

The Special Educational Needs and Disability Tribunal

When considering appeals, the tribunal must have regard to the Code.

7.5 MACHINERY FOR IDENTIFYING AND MEETING SPECIAL EDUCATIONAL NEEDS

The main components are:

- personnel;
- the Code;
- school-based support;
- the LEA.

Personnel

The special educational needs co-ordinator

In light of the responsibility on schools to identify and assess SEN, the Code requires schools to have a member of staff whose primary role is to address these important issues. Paragraphs 5.30 (primary sector) and 6.36 (secondary sector) of the Code provide that each school must have a SEN Coordinator (SENCO).

Paragraph 5.30 provides:

> The ... SENCO, in collaboration with the head teacher and governing body plays a key role in determining the strategic development of the SEN policy and provision in the school in order to raise the achievement of children with SEN. The SENCO takes day-to-day responsibility for the operation of the SEN policy and co-ordination of the provision made for individual children ...

Paragraphs 5.34 and 6.37 also provide that the SENCO should not usually also have other school-wide responsibilities. This is in recognition of the important and demanding functions of the SENCO. In practice, many schools allocate the role of SENCO to a senior member of staff.

LEA officers

Most LEAs have an SEN section within the education department which divides up among its personnel the many tasks and functions exercised by the LEA in order to comply with its statutory duties towards children with SEN. The officers with such responsibilities include statementing officers who conduct the assessment process. There is also a Named Person for each statement of SEN to enable the parent to identify a specific officer who has knowledge of the particular statement and who is a point of contact within the LEA.

Parent partnership officer

In consequence of the LEA's duty to arrange a PPS, each LEA appoints a parent partnership officer (PPO) to administer the scheme.

Some LEAs fund the PPS in such a way that it is physically separate from the LEA, for example, in the form of a parents' centre. Some LEAs contract the function out to voluntary sector organisations. Some PPOs are based within the LEA. This sometimes leads parents to feel that they are less likely to obtain impartial information and support within the statementing process.

One of the roles of the PPO is to recruit and train volunteers who support and assist parents through the assessment and statementing process. These volunteers are known formally as independent parental supporters (IPS). Many parents find their assistance invaluable in situations such as attending meetings with the LEA to discuss the contents of draft statements and making representations. The IPS is also able to provide information which may not otherwise be easily available to the parent on issues such as school placement and the funding policy of the LEA.

The Special Educational Needs Code of Practice

The current Code came into effect in November 2001. It differs from its predecessor in a number of respects. There is a greater emphasis on a multi-agency approach to SEN and on interested parties working in partnership.

The Code is an extremely detailed and comprehensive document which consists of 10 chapters and a number of annexes. The preceding Code was based on a five-stage model of identifying and providing for SEN. In contrast, the current Code places emphasis upon a 'graduated approach' to meeting SEN and viewing the child's education as a continuum which is monitored closely by teaching staff. The current model consists of three stages: School Action; School Action Plus; and ultimately, statemented provision.

The underlying philosophy of the Code is that most children with SEN can have those needs met within a school's resources and without the necessity of the LEA issuing a statement of SEN.

Structure of the Code

The Code consists of the following chapters:

1. Principles and policies
2. Working in partnership with parents
3. Pupil participation
4. Identification, assessment and provision in early education settings
5. Identification, assessment and provision in the primary phase
6. Identification, assessment and provision in the secondary phase
7. Statutory assessment of SEN
8. Statements of SEN
9. Annual review
10. Working in partnership with other agencies

The annex to the Code consists of relevant SEN regulations.

There is also a Toolkit which consists of a summary booklet which streamlines and summarises the detailed information contained in each chapter. It is useful for quick reference purposes and readers are advised to obtain it from the DfES. It is also important to read the relevant sections of the actual Code when seeking clarification on issues. There is such an abundance of guidance in each chapter that it is difficult to retain it all. Direct quoting from the relevant paragraphs places one in good stead when negotiating or making representations.

SPECIAL EDUCATIONAL NEEDS: IDENTIFICATION AND ASSESSMENT

Identifying special educational needs

Chapter 4 of the Code deals with nurseries and other relevant early years settings. Chapters 5 and 6 deal with primary and secondary schools respectively. Similar provision apply for each sector, but readers are strongly advised to read the pertinent sections of the Code as necessary. There is too much detail to summarise fully for the purposes of this chapter, although an overview is provided.

School-based support

The graduated approach to identifying need is referred to above. In practice, one envisages that where a child has SEN, this will come to the attention of the parent, staff working with the child or some other professional. Usually this occurs because the child is not making 'adequate progress' as defined in para. 5.42 of the Code, which provides that progress is adequate which:

(a) closes the attainment gap between the child and his/her peers;
(b) prevents the attainment gap growing wider;
(c) is similar to that of peers starting from the same attainment baseline but less than that of the majority of peers;
(d) matches or betters the child's previous rate of progress;
(e) ensures access to the full curriculum;
(f) demonstrates an improvement in self-help, social or personal skills;
(g) demonstrates improvements in the child's behaviour.

Referral should be made to the SENCO. Discussion should also take place regarding the nature of the child's difficulty which is prohibiting adequate progress and the provision which appears most appropriate to meet the need, halt the decline or delay and enable the child to comply with para. 5.42.

Individual education plan

Paragraphs 5.50 and 6.58 outline the role of the IEP, which is to record the strategies employed to facilitate the child's progress. The IEP should be a concise document which records the provision or strategies which are additional to or different from the provision which is in place for all children. The Code advises that it should focus on three or four individual targets which match the child's needs.

The plan should set short-term targets, identify the strategies and provision to be implemented, record the review date and identify success or exit criteria.

In many cases, an IEP will be drafted and discussed with the parent. Steps should be taken, where necessary, to differentiate the curriculum for the child. This often takes the form of additional or different input to assist the child.

The IEP identifies the areas of difficulty, sets targets to mark the child's progress, confirms the action which is to be taken to enable the child to meet the targets and records the date when the child's performance should be reviewed.

Sufficient time should be given for the additional or alternative provision to take effect, after which the child should be monitored to ascertain whether adequate progress has been made or not. This should all take place with parental involvement and understanding.

If the child fails to make adequate progress, staff should make a decision on whether the child requires increased provision.

In early years settings, the increased provision is called Early Action or Early Action Plus. In primary and secondary settings, the increased provision is called School Action or School Action Plus. For the purposes of this chapter, reference will be made to the latter, which operate in the same manner as Early Action and Early Action Plus.

School Action

This mode of support should be considered when the child has failed to make adequate progress despite receiving differentiated provision over a reasonable period of time.

Paragraphs 5.44 and 6.51 of the Code set out the likely circumstances which should prompt a decision to place a pupil on School Action support. These are where the child:

(a) makes little or no progress even when teaching approaches are targeted particularly in the identified areas of weakness;
(b) shows signs of difficulty in developing literacy or mathematics skills which result in poor attainment in some curriculum areas;
(c) presents persistent emotional or behavioural difficulties which are not ameliorated by the behaviour management techniques usually employed in the school;
(d) has sensory or physical problems and continues to make little or no progress despite the provision of specialised equipment;
(e) has communication and/or interaction difficulties and continues to make little or no progress despite the provision of a differentiated curriculum.

The nature of the provision required at School Action is determined by the SENCO in conjunction with the class teacher(s), taking into the account the child's difficulties, the school's resources, and facilities which may be available within the LEA, such as behaviour management services. The Code acknowledges that provision of one-to-one tuition for the pupil is not necessarily the most effective input and refers to other approaches, such as provision of different learning materials, special equipment, or introduction to group or individual support.

At this stage, the additional support is usually drawn from within the school's own resources, although it is open to the school to seek external advice, support and provision. Nothing is written in stone. Each child's needs are very individual and should be treated as such, thus there is no set formula. Schools generally operate within the SEN policy issued by the governing body which influences the actual practice and delivery.

School Action Plus

Where the child still fails to make adequate progress despite the provision of additional support at School Action, a decision has to be made on whether the child should proceed to School Action Plus. The likely triggers for moving on to School Action Plus are outlined in paras. 5.56 and 6.64 of the Code as where, despite the child's receipt of school action support or an individualised programme, the child:

(a) continues to make little or no progress in specific areas over a long period;
(b) continues working at National Curriculum levels substantially below those expected of children of a similar age;
(c) continues to have difficulty in developing literacy and mathematical skills;
(d) has emotional or behavioural difficulties which substantially and regularly interfere with the child's own learning or that of the class group, despite having an individualised behaviour management programme;
(e) has sensory or physical needs and requires additional specialist equipment or regular advice or visits by a specialist service;
(f) has ongoing communication or interaction difficulties that impede the development of social relationships and cause substantial barriers to learning.

This level of support invariably entails obtaining external support and advice. The school may, for example, make a referral to the LEA's psychology service for the child to be assessed by an Educational Psychologist. Other provision may be obtained, for example specialist teaching or the child's attendance at support services within the LEA.

The IEP should be amended to reflect the transition to School Action Plus, new targets and the provision made. A review meeting with the parent should also take place as a matter of good practice.

The local education authority

Statutory assessment

Under EA 1996, s.323 a request can be made to the LEA to initiate a statutory assessment of a pupil's SEN. Requests can be made by the child's school or other educational setting, the parent or through referral by another agency such as the health authority or social services.

Request by the school

Section 329A of EA 1996 provides that

> Schools and relevant nursery education providers have a statutory right to ask the LEA to conduct a statutory assessment or reassessment of a child's educational needs.

Schools are defined as maintained schools, maintained nursery schools, pupil referral units (PRUs), independent schools including city technology colleges, city academies, city colleges for technology or the arts, and funded early education settings.

If, following a period of School Action Plus, the school determines that the pupil is still failing to make adequate progress, the school can make a formal request to the LEA to initiate a statutory assessment of the pupil's SEN under EA 1996, s.323. This is usually, but not always, preceded by advice from the LEA's psychology service in those terms.

The school should provide reasons for the request and make documentation available to the LEA which includes the parent's views, IEPs, evidence of the child's progress, evidence of professionals' advice and the steps taken by the school to follow it.

The purpose of requesting a statutory assessment is to obtain the benefit of a detailed multi-disciplinary professional assessment of the child's needs, with a view to the LEA taking a decision on whether or not the child requires a statement of SEN in order to have his/her needs met appropriately.

Section 8 of SENDA 2001 provides that where a request is made by the child's school, should the LEA refuse to make a decision to assess, the parent is entitled to appeal against the said decision to SENDIST.

Request by the parent

The parent can also make a request to the LEA for a statutory assessment provided no assessment has taken place in the preceding six months.

The request must be made in writing to the LEA and can be by way of a letter which should include the child's full name, date of birth and school attended.

It is, however, advisable for the parent to provide detailed information about why the request has been made, including the support given to date, the nature of the child's difficulties and why the parent believes that the child requires input which is over and above that possible within School Action Plus.

7.6 PROCEDURE FOR REQUESTING A STATUTORY ASSESSMENT

The statementing procedure is set out in the Consolidation Regulations 2001, regs. 6–13.

The regulations draw distinctions between the different scenarios in which a request is made. These are: where the LEA, of its own volition, makes the decision to assess; where a responsible body makes a request; and where a parent makes a request.

Where the LEA makes a decision of its own volition, reg. 6(1) specifies that it is required to send notices to the social services department, the health authority, the child's head teacher, if applicable, or the head of SEN in relevant early years provision.

Regulation 6(3) specifies that if the parent makes the request and at least six months has passed since a previous assessment, the LEA is required to notify the afore-mentioned agencies of the request and the likely information which the LEA may require. This also applies where the request is made by a responsible body.

On receiving the request for an assessment, the LEA is required to make a decision on whether or not to initiate a full statutory assessment, within six weeks of the request.

Before making the decision, the LEA should seek the advice of the LEA's psychology service and other relevant experts. It should also consider the pupil's school records and steps already taken within the school to meet the child's SEN.

The LEA usually refers to its 'Criteria for Initiating Statutory Assessments' or similar document. This sets out the criteria by which the LEA determines whether it is appropriate, within its SEN policy, to assess. The full assessment process is costly and time-consuming. Most LEAs also anticipate that the majority of pupils with SEN do not require statements, on the basis that resources within schools can meet most needs. This is partly due to funding arrangements between LEAs and schools, whereby the former delegate sums of money to schools to meet the needs of pupils with SEN who do not have statements.

LEAs prepare their criteria individually and not in accordance with any particular model. The criteria will usually indicate the level and nature of need and educational delay that is required to meet the LEA's threshold for a statutory assessment. It is these criteria which are used to measure each individual request and to form the basis of the final decision.

The criteria are not, however, binding on SENDIST, which has the role of considering the individual child's circumstances, should the parent pursue an appeal against a decision of the LEA refusing the request to assess. It must have regard to the Code when determining the appeal. Although the LEA's criteria will be a relevant consideration, this is by no means a determining factor.

The request is usually considered by the assessment team or its equivalent within the LEA. In order to make a decision on the request, the LEA will often liaise with its psychology service and obtain information from the school. The information is passed to the SEN panel of the LEA, or an equivalent body, for a decision.

The LEA must formally notify the parent of the decision by way of a letter. If the request was made by a responsible body, the LEA must also notify it of the decision. If the LEA decides to initiate an assessment, the letter should advise the parent of the procedure which will follow.

If the LEA refuses the request to assess, the decision letter must inform the parent of the right of appeal to SENDIST within two months of receiving the decision letter, and give the address of SENDIST. The letter should also inform the parent of the availability of the PPS and the authority's disputes resolution scheme and should make clear that resort to either facility does not affect the statutory right of appeal to SENDIST. Parents must, however, be aware that the two-month time limit is strict.

Delay

If the LEA fails to make a decision within six weeks of the request, the parent must ensure that the LEA gives prompt reasons for the delay.

Regulation 12(5) of the Consolidation Regulations contains statutory exceptions for complying with the six-week deadline. These include where the LEA has sought advice from a school one week before the school closes for at least four weeks and the response is due one week before the school reopens, where there are exceptional personal circumstances affecting the child or parent during the six-week period or where the parent and child are absent from the LEA's area for at least four weeks.

If the LEA fails to make a decision within 6 weeks in circumstances which do not fall within the above regulation and no reasonable timescale is given by which the decision will be made, the parent's potential remedy is judicial review. Proceedings could be considered on the grounds that the LEA is in breach of statutory duty through its failure to comply with the statutory time limit of 6 weeks.

7.7 DECISION TO ASSESS

Timescale

Paragraph 12(6) of the Consolidation Regulations requires the LEA to complete the assessment within 10 weeks of making the decision to assess. There are however some statutory exceptions to this time-frame permitted by reg. 12(7) of the Consolidation Regulations. These include where:

(a) the LEA, in exceptional circumstances, considers it necessary to seek further advice after receiving the prescribed advice;
(b) the parent informs the LEA that he/she wishes to provide advice more than six weeks after the LEA requested the information and where the LEA has agreed to consider the late advice;
(c) exceptional personal circumstances affect the child or parent during the 10-week period;
(d) the child or parent are absent for at least a continuous four-week period from the LEA's area;
(e) the child fails to keep an appointment for an examination or test within the 10-week period;
(f) the LEA has sought professional advice from the health trust or social services and those agencies have failed to provide the reports within the six weeks;
(g) the LEA has sought reports from a school or head of SEN during a period which begins within one week of the school closing for vacation for at least four weeks and ends one week before the establishment re-opens.

Regulation 12(8) specifies that social services and the health authority should provide requested information to the LEA within six weeks of the LEA request.

Regulation 12(9) sets out exceptions which include where exceptional circumstances affect the child or parent, where the child fails to keep an appointment or attend a test and where the child or parent are absent from the area of the authority for at least a continuous four-week period.

The remedy available to the parent where the agencies in question fail to provide reports within a reasonable period of time is not outlined in the Consolidation Regulations. In practice, the parent should consider pursing a complaint within the agency's internal complaints procedure.

Procedure

When the LEA decides to initiate a statutory assessment, a letter is sent to the parent advising him/her of the professionals who will assess the child and prepare a report.

The parent is also given an opportunity to make representations within the assessment by way of completing Form SA2. This is a detailed form which enables the parent to provide background information about the child, to outline the nature of any difficulties and to express his/her views generally about the child's educational needs.

The parent is entitled to submit additional advice such as his/her own professional reports. Sometimes, independent experts are instructed by parents and the resulting reports as submitted as parental representations.

The decision to issue a statement

The LEA is required, subject to the above-mentioned statutory exceptions, to conclude the assessment within 10 weeks of making the decision to assess. Regulation 17(1) of the Consolidation Regulations specifies that it then has to make a decision within two weeks on whether or not it will issue a proposed or draft statement of SEN, in the case of a child who does not have a statement. Where a child already has a statement, reg. 17(2) specifies that it has to decide whether it will issue a proposed amended statement.

Where the LEA decides that it will not issue a draft or proposed amended statement, it must inform the parent in writing of the refusal. The letter must advise the parent of the right of appeal to SENDIST within two months of receipt of the refusal. The letter should also advise the parent of the availability of the LEA's alternative disputes resolution services but make clear that using the service does not affect the parent's right of appeal to SENDIST. Again, the two-month time limit is strict.

The LEA can alternatively make a decision not to issue a statement but to issue instead a note in lieu of a statement. This decision is usually made when the LEA concludes that the child's needs are not sufficiently significant to warrant a statement but that the child still requires additional advice or input. The note can set out additional provision or strategies to meet the child's needs. Parents must be aware that it is not binding on the child's school or nursery setting and must not make the mistake of believing that there is no need to appeal to SENDIST if they believe that a statement is required.

7.8 THE PROPOSED (AMENDED) STATEMENT

Regulation 17(1)(a) and (2)(a) of the Consolidation Regulations requires the LEA to serve the proposed statement and an accompanying notice on the parent within two weeks of completing the assessment.

The notice must contain prescribed information which is appended to the Consolidation Regulations at Parts A and B of Sched. 1 and which is partly prescribed by EA 1996, Sched. 27, para. 4.

In summary, the notice must: advise the parent that the proposed statement is enclosed with the attached professional advice; explain the structure of the statement; explain that Part 4 (placement) is blank so that the parent can advise the LEA of his/her preferences; outline the circumstances when the LEA does not have to comply with parental preference; advise the parent of the entitlement to suggest a non-maintained special school or independent school; outline the right to make representations, and how and when to do so; set out the procedure for the LEA finalising the statement; and outline the right of appeal to SENDIST. The notice must also refer the parent to enclosed information about schools, access to the PPS and the authority's disputes resolution service.

The format of the proposed statement is prescribed. Schedule 2 of the Consolidation Regulations appends a draft statement and highlights the information or provision which should be in each part of the document.

Part 1 is an introduction and records details of the parent(s) and child. It also lists the reports obtained by the LEA during the assessment process.

Part 2 sets out the child's SEN and any medical diagnoses which impact on the child's learning difficulties. On average, Part 2 is at least one page long, as it should contain a current description of the child's needs in summary form. Ideally, Part 2 should conclude with a list of the child's areas of difficulties, as this gives focus to the statement.

Part 3 sets out the objectives which the special educational provision should aim to meet. The list of objectives should therefore correspond with the list of difficulties highlighted in Part 2.

Part 3 then goes on to set out the actual educational provision which is required to meet the child's needs and the objectives set out at the beginning of Part 3. It will usually describe the type of educational environment that the child requires in order to have his/her learning difficulties met. This may be either a mainstream or a specialist environment. The latter may be described in such terms or it may be more specific. If the child requires residential accommodation, this should be detailed in Part 3. The description of the type of school required for the child is important as this will impact upon the decision made by the LEA with regard to Part 4 of the statement.

Part 3 should contain details of any required facilities, equipment, curriculum, staffing and the nature of the curriculum which should be made available in light of the child's SEN.

Part 3 also sets out the arrangements for monitoring the implementation of the statement. It will usually provide that a review meeting should take place within six to eight weeks of the date on which the statement is issued.

Part 4 sets out the arrangements for the child's placement. It may either outline the type of school the child should attend, name a specific school or confirm arrangements which have been made by the parent.

Part 5 sets out the non-educational needs of the child which require provision in order to assist the child to benefit from the special educational provision.

Part 6 sets out non-educational provision which is to be made available for the child either by another agency such as social services or the health authority.

Specificity

The child's learning difficulties may be such that he/she requires direct or specified provision. Examples include learning support assistant (LSA) provision, specialist teaching, speech and language therapy, occupational therapy, and physiotherapy.

Paragraph 8.36 of the Code provides:

> A statement should specify clearly the provision necessary to meet the needs of the child. It should detail appropriate provision to meet each identified needs . . .

Paragraph 8.37 further provides:

> LEAs must make decisions about which actions and provision are appropriate for which pupils on an individual basis. This can only be done by a careful assessment of the pupils' difficulties and consideration of the educational setting in which they may be educated. Provision should normally be quantified (e.g. in terms of hours of provision, staffing arrangements) although there will be cases where some flexibility should be retained in order to meet the changing SEN of the child concerned. It will always be necessary for LEAs to monitor, with the school or other setting, the child's progress toward identified outcomes, however provision is described. LEAs must not, in any circumstances, have blanket polices not to quantify provision.

See also the Court of Appeal decision in *R. (on the application of IPSEA Ltd) v. Secretary of State for Education and Skills* [2003] ELR 393.

Decisions on quantification of provision should be based on professional advice. Quantified provision is significant because it must be provided to the child. It therefore carries funding obligations for the LEA.

Section 324 of EA 1996 requires an LEA to maintain any statement which it issues. Ultimately, therefore, if provision is quantified in Part 3, the parent is entitled to ensure that it is made available to the child. If necessary, judicial review proceedings on the grounds of breach of statutory duty can be pursued by the parent acting as litigation friend for the child.

Therapies

Disputes can arise on whether particular therapies are an educational requirement or not. LEAs may argue that some are required primarily to meet the child's medical or social needs and should not therefore be named in Part 3 as educational provision which is funded by the LEA.

Whether or not a therapy is called for on educational grounds will depend upon the particular needs of the child. Case law establishes that speech and language therapy can be educational or non-educational (*R. v. Lancashire County Council ex p. M* [1989] 2 FLR 279). It has clarified, however, that as communication is crucial to the learning process, speech and language will usually be regarded as educational, in the absence of exceptional reasons.

Many LEAs have a practice of making general provision in Part 3 in the format of 'speech and language programmes' and provision for monitoring the implementation of such programmes. This is often on the basis that the child will, where necessary, receive input from the health authority.

This approach is not always appropriate for the individual child. Advisers of concerned parents should consider commissioning an assessment by an independent speech and language therapist. This can be done either during the assessment process, for the purpose of making submissions on the proposed statement, or it may become necessary if the parent pursues an appeal to SENDIST so that a report can be used as parental evidence.

Other therapies such as occupational therapy and physiotherapy are not necessarily assumed to be educational needs. Again, this will depend on the degree of the child's need for such input and whether lack of input will significantly prohibit the child from accessing the curriculum. Where differences in opinion arise between the parent and LEA, consideration should be given to obtaining an independent assessment.

Part 4 and parental preference

Paragraph 3(1) of Sched. 27 to EA 1996 provides:

> Every LEA shall make arrangements for enabling a parent on whom a copy of a proposed statement has been served ... to express a preference for a maintained, foundation or foundation special school that he/she wishes the child to attend, and to give reasons.

Paragraph 3(3) provides that the LEA shall name the school expressed as a preference by the parent in the child's statement unless:

(a) the school is unsuitable to the child's age, ability or aptitude or to his SEN, or
(b) the attendance of the child at the school would be incompatible with the provision of efficient education for the children with whom he would be educated or the efficient use of resources.

On receiving the proposed statement and information on prospective schools from the LEA, the parent should make investigations with a view to expressing a preference. Paragraph 4 of Sched. 27 entitles the parent to make representations on the proposed statement either by way of written representations within 15 days of the date on which the notice was served, or by requesting a meeting with an LEA officer within 15 days of service. The parent can make written representations within 15 days after meeting an LEA officer. The parent should make representations on school preference during this process.

After the parent makes representations to the LEA, the latter must then consult relevant schools pursuant to para. 3(4) of Sched. 27. Where the parent wishes the LEA to consult a maintained school within the authority, the LEA should consult the governing body of the said school. This entails sending the child's proposed statement with the appendices to the governing body which has 15 days within which to respond. If the school is maintained by another authority, the LEA must also consult the maintaining authority.

If the maintained school fails to respond within 15 days, the LEA can proceed to name it in Part 4. If the school responds by raising concerns and indicating that it cannot meet the child's needs, the LEA is still empowered to name that maintained school, provided it consulted properly and complied with the required timescale for a response. In practice, many LEAs seek to address any concerns raised by schools or may seek to consult further to clarify issues.

Non-maintained schools

An LEA is under a duty to consult maintained schools which are expressed by the parent as the parent's preference in light of the provision in para. 3(3) of Sched. 27. Subject to the statutory exceptions, the LEA must comply with parental preference for a maintained school and name it in the statement.

However, a parent may make representations for a non-maintained school. The LEA should ascertain whether the school can meet the child's SEN, although the LEA is only required to have regard to the parent's wishes so far as that is compatible with the efficient education of the child and so far as it avoids unreasonable public expenditure. Section 9 of EA 1996 therefore applies.

If the LEA does not agree with the representations for a non-maintained school it should advise the parent accordingly, and the parent should then have an opportunity to express a preference for a maintained school before the LEA proceeds with naming a school in Part 4.

In practice, many LEAs, on issuing the draft statement, provide the parent with a list of maintained and non-maintained special schools to enable the parent to make full enquiries before stating a preference.

There are two categories of non-maintained special schools: those that are registered with the DfES, and those that are not. The distinction is relevant if the parent subsequently appeals to SENDIST, seeking a placement at a non-maintained school. Where a school is not registered with the DfES, the parent is required to make an application to the DfES for Enabling Consent to have the school named by SENDIST. Further details are provided in Chapter 8.

Before an LEA or SENDIST can determine whether the school is suitable, evidence is required from the school that it can meet the pupil's needs. This is usually established through the school's assessment process. Some schools will only assess a child if the maintaining LEA formally consults by sending the pupil's draft statement and related paperwork. If the LEA refuses to send the documentation, this prohibits the parent's ability to have the school named unless a Direction is obtained from SENDIST.

In contrast, some schools' assessment procedures enable the parent to make a direct application. Following assessment, the school will then confirm to the parent whether or not it can meet the pupil's needs and whether it can offer a place. The LEA will then determine whether placement at the school is compatible with the efficient use of resources.

7.9 INCLUSIVE SCHOOLING

The entitlement of most pupils with SEN to receive their education in mainstream schools is given statutory bite in SENDA 2001, s.1, which amends EA 1996, s.316 to provide:

(1) This section applies to a child with special educational needs who should be educated in a school.
(2) If no statement is maintained under section 324 for the child he must be educated in a mainstream school.
(3) If a statement is maintained under section 324 for the child he must be educated in a mainstream school unless that is incompatible with –
   (a) the wishes of his parent, or
   (b) the provision of efficient education for other children.

Before an LEA can rely upon the exception to the mandatory duty to educate a child within mainstream education on the latter ground, it has to establish that there are no reasonable steps which can be taken to prevent incompatibility with the provision of efficient education. Reference must be made to current statutory guidance 'Inclusive Schooling – Children with Special Educational Needs' (DfES Circular 0774/2001). This provides guidance on the statutory framework for inclusion. It gives specific advice on different types of SEN including autism and emotional and behavioural difficulties. It highlights common traits of these conditions and the types of difficulties displayed by pupils. It also gives guidance on the types of measures that should be considered by schools and LEAs to address the manifestations of these conditions which may assist the pupil to cope in a mainstream environment. Specific measures are suggested which, if successful, can enable the school to meet the pupil's needs without causing adverse impact on other pupils. The guidance also acknowledges that, in some circumstances, it may not be possible to include pupils in mainstream schools.

R. (MH) v. *Special Educational Needs and Disability Tribunal and Hounslow LBC* [2004] EWCA Civ 770 clarified the relationship between Sched. 27 and s.316 when an LEA is faced with a parent who is requesting a mainstream school. In summary, the Sched. 27, para. 3 procedure has to be exhausted by the LEA before s.316 comes into play. If, after applying para. 3, the LEA is not minded to name the parent's stated preference, it must then apply s.316 to determine whether the particular school or another mainstream school should be named. A special school should only be named if the LEA determines that the naming of a mainstream school would be incompatible with the provision of efficient education for other children.

7.10 THE FINAL STATEMENT

Regulation 17(3) of the Consolidation Regulations requires the LEA to finalise the draft statement within eight weeks; however, statutory exemptions are provided in reg. 17(4) which include:

(a) exceptional personal circumstances affecting the child or parent during the eight-week period;
(b) absence of the child or parent for at least four weeks;
(c) parental representations made later than the 15-day period;
(d) the parent requesting a further meeting with the LEA;
(e) the LEA seeking the Secretary of State's consent which is still outstanding after six weeks.

On finalising the statement, the LEA should name a school in Part 4. It is permitted however, to not name a school if the parent has made arrangements for the child's schooling. Part 4 can therefore contain wording which confirms the private arrangements made by the parent for the child's placement.

The LEA is required to date and issue the final statement with a decision letter enclosing the statement. The letter must inform the parent of his/her right of appeal to SENDIST within two months of receipt of the statement and provide the address. The letter will also inform the parent of the authority's alternative disputes resolution scheme and should explain that resort to the scheme does not affect the right of appeal to SENDIST. The two-month time limit is strict.

7.11 TRANSPORT

Each LEA should have a transport policy with criteria for deciding when free transport should be provided for a child. The general rule of thumb, however, is that if an LEA names a school in Part 4 and the child is unable to travel independently to the school, or the parent has not made suitable arrangements, the LEA should provide transport (*R. v. Havering London Borough Council ex p. K* [1998] ELR 402, QBD; *R. v. Islington London Borough Council ex p. GA* [2000] EWHC 390).

Section 324 of EA 1996 empowers the LEA to provide transport for pupils with statements. Guidance is provided in 'Home to School Transport for Children with SEN' (DfES Circular 68/2001). The guidance highlights that the decision should be based on the pupil's needs. If the child's needs do not automatically necessitate the provision of free transport, the LEA should apply the standard distance criteria; free transport is usually provided for children under the age of eight if the walking distance to school is over two miles, and for children over that age if the walking distance is over three miles.

Where an LEA provides transport, case law establishes in *R. v. Hereford and Worcester County Council, ex p. P* [1992] 2 FLR 207, QBD, that the journey must be 'non-stressful'.

If SENDIST names a school, the LEA has to provide transport unless the parent chooses to make transport arrangements.

Provision for transport is very rarely detailed in a statement, and SENDIST does not have jurisdiction to determine disputes about transport.

7.12 MAINTENANCE OF STATEMENTS

Chapter 9 of the Code sets out the detailed requirements on the LEA to ensure that statements are maintained. This takes place primarily through reviews. Part 3 of a well-drafted statement usually makes provision for the monitoring and review of statements. Provision is often made for the first review meeting to take place within six to eight weeks of the date on which the statement is issued.

Paragraph 9.1 of the Code provides that statements must be reviewed annually, with the exception of statements for children under the age of two. It remains open and indeed is good practice, for LEAs and schools to hold review meetings at more frequent intervals. This may be particularly appropriate for very young children whose needs and development can change rapidly.

The purpose of the annual review is to consider the effectiveness of the provision in the statement and to assess the child's progress against targets set at the last annual review and/or the IEP. Participation from all relevant professionals and the parents is crucial. It is an opportunity for parents and professionals alike to raise concerns or to confirm that the provision and placement are suitable. Essentially, the review needs to ascertain whether the pupil is making adequate progress; whether the provision or statement need amendment, and whether the placement remains suitable.

It is technically the responsibility of the LEA to arrange the annual review. Regulation 18(1) of the Consolidation Regulations provides that the LEA must serve a notice on head teachers at least two weeks before the beginning of each term which lists the pupils in attendance at the school who have statements maintained by the authority and whose annual reviews are due before the second term after the notice is given.

In practice, it is the school which makes the practical arrangements for the annual review. This involves arranging for teaching staff and therapists to prepare detailed reports on the pupil's work and progress, arranging the date of the meeting and sending invitations to relevant parties including the LEA.

The school compiles a report in advance of the annual review meeting which consists of all the advice prepared by relevant professionals. Reports by teaching staff play a central role.

The actual meeting provides an opportunity for positive discussion to take place on the pupil's attainments. Regulation 20(8) of the Consolidation Regulations sets out the specific matters which must be considered at the annual review. These include:

(a) the child's progress towards meeting the objectives detailed in the statement;
(b) the progress of the child with the provisions of the National Curriculum;
(c) progress made with any provision substituted for the provision of the National Curriculum;
(d) any significant changes in the child's circumstances since the date of the statement or the last review.

It is important that parents feel able to express their views fully and to raise any issues of concern. The report following the meeting will specifically record the views of the parent.

The meeting concludes with a consideration of any changes that are considered necessary to the statement. It will then consider recommendations that should be made to the LEA. Regulation 20(9) sets out the matters on which the meeting can make recommendations. These are:

(a) any identified steps, including whether the statement should be amended or ceased;
(b) the setting of targets to further the objectives set in the statement.

SPECIAL EDUCATIONAL NEEDS: IDENTIFICATION AND ASSESSMENT

Within 10 working days of the meeting, the head teacher must prepare a report summarising the discussions, issues and recommendations. Recommendations may be agreed by all parties, but in some cases they are not.

Regulation 20(10) provides that where differing recommendations are made, these shall be made where it appears necessary to do so by the participants.

The annual review report must be sent to the LEA which is required, under reg. 20(13) to consider the report and specifically the recommendations. It must then make a decision on whether or not it will make amendments to the statement or cease to maintain it. No time limit is specified; however, the LEA is arguably required to make a decision within a reasonable period of time.

Regulation 20(14) requires the LEA to send copies of its decision or recommendations to the parent, head teacher and any other appropriate person within one week of completing its review of the statement.

7.13 TRANSFER BETWEEN DIFFERENT PHASES

Regulation 19 of the Consolidation Regulations provides that where a child is within 12 calendar months of a phase transfer, the LEA must issue an amended final statement by 15 February in the calendar year of the child's transfer. This does not, however, apply when a child transfers from nursery to primary school.

The purpose of the provision is to allow sufficient time for the parent to appeal to SENDIST to resolve any dispute before the transfer takes place. It also overcomes the previous anomaly of schools allocating all or most of their places to pupils without statements before considering those with statements.

7.14 ANNUAL REVIEWS FROM YEAR 9

These reviews are of particular significance as their functions extend to planning the pupil's longer-term provision and the eventual transition from the secondary phase. Paragraph 9.45 of the Code deals specifically with these important reviews and advises that the review has to not only review the pupil's statement but also draw up the pupil's transition plan.

The school must invite the Connexions service and all other agencies which are involved in the pupil's life to the annual review. The meeting's objective is to establish the pupil's aims and to ensure that professional advice is made available to assist the young person to start making decisions on post-16 provision, whether that be continued attendance at school, further education, sixth form, vocational courses or employment. The aim of the transition plan is to assist the young person to prepare for adult life, and the plan should be prepared in conjunction with the Connexions service.

The transition plan is reviewed in Year 10 and Year 11. The young person must be fully involved. The Connexions service plays a role in assisting the pupil and parent to determine post-16 provision, offering support and counselling.

7.15 CEASING TO MAINTAIN A STATEMENT

If the pupil remains in school beyond the age of 16, the LEA can remain responsible for maintaining the statement until he/she attains the age of 19.

If post-16 provision is pursued at a further education institution, the young person becomes the responsibility of the Learning and Skills Council, and the statement automatically lapses.

By Year 11, in view of the transitional annual review in Year 9 and consideration of the transition plan in Year 10, the pupil and parent are likely to have a view on post-16 provision. If the pupil wishes to remain at a school maintained by the LEA, the latter has to make a decision on whether to maintain the statement or whether to cease to maintain it. Decisions to cease to maintain can be made at any time of a pupil's schooling, usually following an annual review.

If the issue arises in Year 11, the LEA should make a decision by 15 February so that there is sufficient time for the parent to appeal the decision to SENDIST and obtain a hearing date within the academic year. When the LEA makes a decision to cease to maintain, it has to maintain the statement pending the outcome of any appeal to SENDIST.

7.16 TRANSFER OF STATEMENTS

When a parent moves from one LEA to another, the statement automatically transfers to the new authority. Regulation 23 of the Consolidation Regulations sets out the requirement on the new authority to serve a notice on the parent within six weeks of the transfer confirming:

(a) that the statement has been transferred;
(b) whether it proposes to make an assessment;
(c) when it proposes to review the statement.

The regulation details the latest date by which the review should take place.

CHAPTER 8

Special educational needs: appeals

8.1 THE STATUTORY FRAMEWORK

Parents have a statutory right of appeal against prescribed decisions of an LEA on SEN. The appeal is made to and determined by the Special Educational Needs and Disability Tribunal (SENDIST) which is an independent body constituted by the Department for Constitutional Affairs and the DfES.

Sections 325 and 326 of EA 1996, as amended by the Special Educational Need and Disability Act (SENDA) 2001 provide rights of appeal to the tribunal. The tribunal's procedure and powers are regulated in the Special Educational Needs Tribunal Regulations 2001, SI 2001/600 ('the Tribunal Regulations') which came into force on 1 September 2001. These regulations apply to both England and Wales.

Appeals on disability discrimination grounds are also made to SENDIST and are regulated by the Special Educational Needs and Disability Tribunal (General Provisions) (Disability Claims Procedure) Regulations 2002 (SI 2002/85). The procedure outlined below is also applicable to disability discrimination claims brought to the tribunal.

By virtue of EA 2002, s.195 and Sched. 18, Wales has its own separate tribunal. Paragraph 5 of Sched. 18 provides an amendment to EA 1996, s.336 by the insertion of s.336ZA which provides that there shall be an SEN tribunal for Wales. Sections 333 to 336 of EA 1996 apply to the Welsh tribunal as they apply to SENDIST. The Secretary of State is substituted by the National Assembly for Wales, whose powers are only exercisable with the agreement of the Secretary of State.

Paragraph 7 of Sched. 18 also amends the Disability Discrimination Act (DDA) 1995 to give the SEN tribunal for Wales jurisdiction to hear disability discrimination claims.

8.2 WHOSE RIGHT OF APPEAL?

It is the parent who has the right of appeal and not the pupil. Eligibility for Legal Help or public funding for appeals from SENDIST decisions is therefore determined on the parent's means.

8.3 AGAINST WHICH DECISIONS CAN A PARENT APPEAL?

Appeals to SENDIST can be made against the following decisions:

(a) refusal of an LEA to initiate a parent's request for a statutory assessment or reassessment (EA 1996, s.329);
(b) refusal to initiate a statutory assessment following a request by a school (EA 1996, s.329A);
(c) refusal of an LEA to issue a statement of SEN after conducting a statutory assessment;
(d) refusal to make amendments to an existing statement following a re-assessment (EA 1996, s.326);
(e) refusal to carry out a reassessment following a parental request (EA 1996, s.328);
(f) refusal to carry out a reassessment following a request from a school (EA 1996, s.329A);
(g) challenging the contents of a statement of SEN (EA 1996, s.326);
(h) challenging the refusal of an LEA to amend Part 4 of the statement where the parent has asked it to substitute the named school for another maintained school and where the statement was issued at least one year before the parent made the request (EA 1996, Sched. 27);
(i) challenging the decision of an LEA to cease to maintain a statement (EA 1996, Sched. 27).

8.4 TIMESCALES AND PROCEDURE FOR APPEAL

The appeal must be lodged at the tribunal within two months of the date on which the parent receives the decision in question. If the two-month period expires during the month of August, the appeal must be lodged by the first working day in September of the same year. The notice of appeal must be signed by the parent.

The appeal must be made on a prescribed notice of appeal which is contained in a booklet produced by the DfES, 'Special Educational Needs: How to Appeal' (DfES TRI 022). The booklet must be made available to the parent by the LEA. In practice, many LEAs do not automatically send the booklet to the parent with the decision letter, which must inform the parent of the right of appeal to the tribunal, the two-month time limit and that further information about appealing can be obtained from the LEA. In such circumstances, the parent can ask the LEA for the booklet. Parents who seek legal advice often obtain the booklet from their adviser.

The booklet is an informative document, written in non-technical language, which provides useful general information about the right of appeal. Importantly, it explains that the tribunal is unable to deal with a range of problems and issues which commonly arise between parents, LEAs and schools.

The appeal form must be fully completed with details of the parent, child, LEA and the decision which is the subject of the appeal. The parent is required to provide sufficient reasons for appeal to enable the LEA to respond to the substance of the appeal. These should be detailed under the section entitled 'Grounds of appeal' or on an attached appendix to the appeal if there is insufficient space on the form.

Regulation 8 of the Tribunal Regulations sets out the requirement on the parent to provide reasons. It specifies that where the President of SENDIST decides that insufficient reasons have been provided by the parent to enable the LEA to respond, a direction shall be given to the parent requiring him/her to send particulars of the reasons to the tribunal within 10 working days. Those particulars are then treated as forming part of the notice of appeal. If the parent fails to provide the requested details within the time limit the tribunal can dismiss the appeal.

Where the President considers that insufficient reasons have been given, SENDIST usually declines to register the appeal formally until satisfactory particulars have been provided. In these circumstances, the appeal is retained by the pre-registration section of the tribunal. It is important to bear this in mind when drafting appeal grounds because of the delay which is caused to the appeal process if a direction is issued.

The notice of appeal specifies the address at which the appeal must be lodged. In London, parents are directed to the tribunal in Darlington. This can present problems if time is short. In practice, many appeals are lodged at the central tribunal in London which then forwards the appeal to Darlington. Where the time limit is imminent, serious thought should be given to lodging the appeal in person. It is not the general practice of SENDIST to allow late appeals.

Transfer of local education authority

Regulation 43 of the Tribunal Regulations provides that where a parent moves to a new LEA after appealing a decision of the original authority, the new authority is substituted for the first authority within the appeal. Before the President of SENDIST makes an Order, the old LEA, new LEA and parent have an opportunity to be heard.

The new LEA is treated as if it made the original decision which is the subject of the appeal and the appeal process restarts with a new case statement period.

What must be lodged with the notice of appeal?

The required documentation depends upon the nature of the decision under appeal. The decision letter of the LEA must always be lodged with the notice of appeal. Where the appeal is against the refusal of the LEA to assess, reassess, issue a statement, or cease to maintain a statement, the appeal can be registered with minimum documentation, comprising the notice of appeal and decision letter. It is, of course, open to the parent to lodge any other documentation which is considered material to the appeal.

Where the appeal is against the contents of a statement, the parent must lodge a copy of the statement with the appendices. The parent must indicate on the notice of appeal whether the appeal is against Parts II, III or IV. It is open to the parent to appeal against all or some of these parts of the statement. Unless the parent is absolutely certain that no amendments, however minor, are necessary to any of these parts, it is advisable to keep their options open by appealing against all three parts if this is possible, and if there are sufficient reasons which can be provided for appealing against each part.

Sometimes the parent may not be in possession of all appendices to the statement. There is the option of requesting the documents from the LEA at the earliest opportunity. Alternatively, if time is short, the appeal can be lodged with a covering letter explaining why the full appendices are not included and asking SENDIST to issue a direction to the LEA requiring it to provide the missing documents. This is a prudent step to take as SENDIST may otherwise decline to register the appeal and write to the parent requesting a copy of the missing documents. This will have the effect of delaying the appeal and effectively wasting time unnecessarily if the parent does not have the documentation.

Appeals against Part IV

Where the parent is challenging the named school either through an appeal against the contents of the statement or through a limited appeal against the refusal of the LEA to change the named school, SENDIST requires information about the preferred school.

The notice of appeal requires the parent to provide details of the preferred school or to give an indication of the type of school which is sought. In the latter case, the parent can give a general description such as 'a specialist school for pupils with emotional and behavioural difficulties'.

Where the parent indicates that he/she wishes to have a specific school named in Part IV, SENDIST requires evidence, before registering the appeal, that the school has been notified of the parent's wishes. In practice, this can be satisfied if the parent writes to the school before lodging the appeal, notifying it of the appeal and the parent's wish to have the school named in Part IV. The parent should attach a copy of that letter to the notice of appeal.

In many cases, the parent may be considering more than one school. A letter should be written to each, and a copy of each letter should be attached to the notice of appeal.

Optional documents to be included with the notice of appeal

The parent has a choice of either lodging a very full appeal with detailed documentation, or alternatively, lodging the essentials and waiting until later in the proceedings to lodge additional documentation which is material to the appeal. It may be helpful to the grounds of appeal and from a tactical stance to lodge supportive documents if they illustrate and significantly corroborate the parent's arguments. This may be instrumental in prompting the LEA to negotiate or review its decision with a view to settling the appeal, thus avoiding the expense and time delay of preparing for a hearing and awaiting the outcome.

Documents that may be lodged with the appeal include old statements of SEN, professional reports which are not included in the appendices to the current statement, Individual Education Plans, annual review documentation, school brochures, examples of the child's school work and school reports.

8.5 REGISTRATION OF THE APPEAL

Once the appeal is received at the tribunal, it aims to register the appeal within 10 working days if the documentation is in order and if sufficient reasons for the appeal have been provided by the parent.

The tribunal then writes to the parent or the parent's representative and also to the LEA. On the notice of appeal, the parent has to indicate whether the tribunal should communicate with the parent or a representative.

A registration letter is sent to the parties which confirms that the appeal has been registered, provides the appeal number and outlines the proposed time-table for the appeal.

On registering each appeal, SENDIST also sends a video of a precedent hearing to the parents. This is a useful video and it is advisable that parents view it.

8.6 POST-REGISTRATION REQUIREMENTS FOR PART IV APPEALS

If the parent has indicated in the notice of appeal that an alternative maintained school is sought, the tribunal writes to the school in question seeking its views on a proposed placement.

If the school is non-maintained and is not registered with the DfES, the tribunal sends an application form to the parent for enabling consent. This is a form which must be signed by the parent and submitted to the DfES with a copy of the child's statement and appendices. The application should be made only if the school in question has already assessed the child and decided that it can meet the child's needs. The school must also complete a provision of place form.

On receiving the application, the DfES considers the child's documentation and the nature of the provision at the school. It then decides whether the school appears suitable for the child's needs. If it believes the school is suitable, it issues an enabling consent letter. This then permits the tribunal to name the school if it believes that would be an appropriate order. The enabling consent letter does not guarantee that the tribunal will name the school; it purely enables it to name the placement.

If the parent wishes the child to attend a non-maintained school that is approved by the DfES, the tribunal only sends the parent a provision of place form with the registration letter. The form has to be signed by the head teacher of the school and submitted to the tribunal before or at the hearing. The head teacher has to confirm that there is an available place at the school either at the date of the hearing or at the start of the term following the hearing. If, at the date of the hearing, the date on the form has passed, the tribunal will be unable to name the school. The parent must therefore ensure that an additional letter or a further form with more current dates is provided by the school.

The tribunal has to satisfy itself that the child's needs match those which the school can cater for and for which it obtained registration from the DfES.

8.7 HEARING DATE

The letter informs the parties of the period within which the appeal is likely to be listed for a hearing. Usually the tribunal gives a proposed fortnight some months in advance. It notifies parties that dates to avoid within that period must be communicated to the tribunal, usually within a fortnight of the registration letter, otherwise the tribunal will fix a hearing date and there will be no automatic right to obtain a subsequent adjournment.

8.8 CASE STATEMENT

This is the second stage of the appeal process. The parties have a period of 30 working days within which to prepare the appeal further. The registration letter highlights the expiry date of the case statement period, which is the date by which parties must submit documentation upon which they intend to rely and which is guaranteed by the tribunal to be included in the subsequent tribunal bundle and therefore admitted as written evidence before the tribunal. The case statement is the next stage of formal pleading within the appeal as the parties can lodge a written statement addressing the issues in the appeal.

From the parent's perspective, the case statement is an opportunity to elaborate upon the appeal grounds. The parent can lodge a further statement in support of the appeal but it is not compulsory to do so. It is usually important if the grounds of appeal were minimal or if there have been significant developments since the appeal was lodged and the parent wishes to draw those to the attention of the tribunal.

If the parent lodged the appeal with minimal documentation, the case statement is an essential opportunity to lodge further important documents. Often, the parent will have taken steps to obtain assessments of the child by independent experts since lodging the appeal. The resulting reports may contain crucial evidence not previously available.

The LEA's first voice within the proceedings is through its case statement which is effectively similar to a defence. If it opposes the parent's appeal, it will confirm this and give reasons why it does not agree with the appeal. The LEA can attach to its case statement any documents which it considers relevant to its defence. Sometimes the LEA may concede some aspects of the parent's appeal. It will often confirm those concessions within its case statement. This is useful for negotiation purposes. It is open to parties to have meetings to discuss the appeal with a view to negotiating or mediating. Similarly, negotiations can take place through correspondence. These steps are advisable so that the parties can clarify exactly what they can agree upon and therefore identify the precise areas of dispute which call for determination by the tribunal.

If the LEA fails to lodge a case statement, reg. 15 empowers the tribunal to:

(a) determine the appeal on the basis of the notice of appeal without a hearing; or
(b) without notifying the authority hold a hearing at which the authority is not represented.

8.9 AFTER THE CASE STATEMENT PERIOD

The tribunal compiles the consolidated tribunal bundle and sends it to the parties advising them to keep it safe as no further documents will be sent out.

On receiving the bundle, the parent becomes appraised of the LEA's defence to the proceedings through its case statement. This is the first time that the LEA's position is officially notified to the parent despite the parent having prepared his/her case in full through the notice of appeal and case statement.

Negotiations at this stage can be helpful as each side is now aware of the other side's case and the extent, if any, of concessions or common ground. Some LEAs routinely offer to meet with the parent to discuss the appeal. If the parent is represented, the adviser may attend the meeting. If the adviser cannot attend, it is advisable that the parent should refrain from making any significant decisions at the meeting before having an opportunity to liaise with the adviser.

In appeals against the contents of a statement, if the LEA is agreeable to making some of the requested amendments, it is often helpful for one of the parties to prepare a draft amended statement which incorporates the agreed amendments and which can be used as a working document within the appeal. This document can be presented to SENDIST as late evidence or on the day of the hearing, thereby assisting the tribunal and saving valuable court time.

Where there is a dispute about Part 4, the parent sometimes first becomes aware of the LEA's proposals for an alternative school after the case statement period. This may require the parent to seek further expert advice on the suitability of the proposed school with a view to submitting it as late written evidence.

8.10 LATE EVIDENCE

The significance of the case statement period is that any documentation submitted before its expiry is certain to be admitted by SENDIST as evidence within the proceedings.

Any documentation which is submitted at a later stage must be submitted as late evidence and must meet specific criteria before it is admitted by the tribunal.

Regulation 33 of the Tribunal Regulations provides for two modes of submitting late evidence. The first arises when a party serves the late evidence on the tribunal and the other side at least five working days before the hearing. An application has to be made by the serving party at the outset of the hearing before the tribunal for admission of the evidence. The tribunal will listen to any representations from the other side. Unless those are given overriding weight, it will admit the evidence provided:

(a) it was not and could not reasonably have been available before the end of the case statement period;
(b) a copy of the evidence was served on the tribunal and other side at least 5 working days before the hearing; and
(c) the nature of the evidence is such that it is not likely to impede the efficient conduct of the hearing.

The second mode of seeking to submit late evidence applies when the party has not served the evidence five working days before the hearing. An application has to be made at the outset of the hearing and the tribunal listens to representations from the other side. The criteria are more onerous as the evidence will only be admitted if:

(a) the case is wholly exceptional; and
(b) unless the evidence is admitted, there is a serious risk of prejudice to the interests of the child.

8.11 WITNESSES

Regulation 20 empowers the tribunal to ask the parties to confirm who will attend the hearing on their behalf.

When the tribunal sends the registration letter to parties, it encloses an attendance form which should be returned to the tribunal by the expiry of the case statement period. The form has to be completed with details of the parent's representative, if any, witnesses who will attend the hearing and any other person who the parent wishes to attend in the capacity of a friend or supporter. The form also asks parents to indicate if they have any special requirements due to physical impairment or if they require an interpreter and will need to have the tribunal determination translated. The parent is advised that unless the form is returned, there is no guarantee that the tribunal will allow the parent to be accompanied at the hearing by representative, witnesses or supporters. Witnesses and representatives can be disbarred if the tribunal is not notified. If the attendance form is mislaid, the tribunal usually accepts the information by letter.

Parties are entitled to have two witnesses attend the hearing. If they require more than two, an application can be made to the President of SENDIST who has discretion to refuse or allow the request.

It is sometimes necessary to consider summonsing a witness to the hearing. This is commonly the case when teaching staff or other professionals in the employment of the LEA or school are not in a position to attend voluntarily. Regulation 26 of the Tribunal Regulations deals with the summonsing of witnesses. A party is required to apply to the tribunal for the summons at least eight working days before the hearing but can apply later if the prospective witness consents to the application in writing. A witness is required to attend the hearing if he/she has been given at least five working days' notice, unless the witness informs the tribunal that he/she will accept a shorter period of notice. A witness is not required to attend the hearing unless his/her expenses are paid or offered.

Information is given to the parent about the limited expenses that can be claimed by witnesses in general guidance notes provided by the tribunal.

8.12 DIRECTIONS

It is open to either party to apply to the tribunal at any stage of the proceedings for a direction against the other side. Regulation 21 of the Tribunal Regulations provides that the President, either of his/her own accord or on the application of a party, may give directions to enable parties to prepare for the hearing or to assist the tribunal to consider the issues. Common applications relate to requests for further particulars of an appeal, supplementary statements and service of documentation.

Practitioners should use this regulation proactively. There may be other situations when requests to the other side have been unsuccessful and potentially hamper the availability of evidence to the tribunal. An example is where a parent may have unsuccessfully asked an LEA to consult a preferred school so that the school can assess the child and determine whether it can meet his/her needs. If the parent is seeking an order from the tribunal to name the preferred school, an application can be made to the tribunal for a direction on the grounds that assessment by the school is material to the appeal and important for the tribunal's deliberations.

8.13 REPRESENTATION

Parents can feel disadvantaged at the hearing if they cannot afford to pay for representation or meet the full cost of their expert witnesses. Whilst the Legal Help Scheme covers the cost of an adviser preparing the appeal, it does not cover the costs of representation by advocates or witnesses. LEAs, on the other hand, are better resourced and often have a number of professional expert witnesses in addition to an experienced advocate.

Parents should be aware that the Independent Panel for Special Educational Advice (IPSEA) does have some resources for providing advocates free of charge in a limited number of cases. If representation is required, IPSEA should be contacted at the earliest opportunity. Some law centres are also able to offer free representation.

Regulation 12(6) states that the parent shall be represented by one person; however, permission can be sought to be represented by more than one person. There is a corresponding provision for the LEA in reg. 16.

If the LEA does not attend the hearing, it is permitted by reg. 16(3) to submit further written representations at least five working days before the hearing.

8.14 VIEWS OF THE CHILD

The appeal procedure requires the LEA to ensure that the views of the child, where possible, are represented within the appeal ('The SEN Disability Tribunal: A child's right to be heard' [2003] Fam Law 745). In practice, many LEAs ascertain the child's views, depending on age and understanding, through their educational psychology service. Where the child lacks capacity to express any views, the LEA can simply state this in its case statement.

It is also open to the parent to present the child's views. This can be achieved by permitting the child to attend the hearing. Regulation 30(2)(a) of the Tribunal Regulations specifies that the child is entitled to attend the hearing. The tribunal has the power, however, under reg. 30(4)(b) to exclude the child if his/her presence would make it 'difficult for any person to adduce the evidence or to make the representation necessary for the proper conduct of the appeal'.

In practice, if the child is old enough and has capacity to express a view at the hearing, the parent can inform the tribunal that the child will attend. It is usually undesirable for the child to attend the entire hearing, and therefore the tribunal usually writes to the parent requesting that the parent bring an adult who can sit with the child in a waiting area once the child has made his/her contribution to the hearing.

8.15 THE HEARING

It is commonly the case that frantic discussions and negotiations take place at the tribunal shortly before the hearing. The early arrival of all parties is beneficial, as this is often the first opportunity for advocates and experts to thrash out the issues. Many appeals settle in part or completely at this vital hour, and draft amended statements are often produced or finally agreed upon.

Where there are still areas of dispute, or where the LEA maintains an original refusal, SENDIST has to determine the appeal. The tribunal consists of a three-member panel. The legally qualified chair is appointed by the Department for Constitutional Affairs. The two lay members are appointed by the DfES and are required to have some experience of SEN. Some lay members are experts, such as educational psychologists.

The tribunal aims to officiate the appeal as informally as possible. Often, the parent is not represented. At the outset of the hearing, the chair may seek an update on the outcome of any negotiations and then clarifies to the parties the panel's understanding of the issues which remain in dispute. Those issues are then addressed by the parties one by one so that the proceedings do not become confused and disjointed.

Applications for admission of late evidence are made at the outset of the hearing and the tribunal listens to representations from the other side. It then makes a decision on whether or not the evidence is to be admitted.

If the child is in attendance, the tribunal will determine when the child will give evidence and ensure that he/she does not remain in the hearing longer than necessary.

When considering the specific issues in dispute, the tribunal often asks the LEA to give evidence first. The parent is then given an opportunity to ask questions of the LEA before then presenting his/her evidence on the issue. Tribunal hearings are less formal than those of other courts, thus the conduct of proceedings is determined by the chair. The hearing is usually more akin to a round table discussion than an adversarial hearing regulated by strict rules of evidence. There is often a history of disagreement between the parties and relationships are sometimes fraught. The tribunal is trained to deal with these difficulties. The role of the tribunal is to ensure that all the issues are addressed in full and everybody at the hearing has the opportunity to ask questions and make representations.

The panel members often have specific questions to ask the parties and their witnesses. Once all the issues have been discussed and all the evidence given, the chair invites the LEA to sum up its case followed by the parent. Where the parent is represented, most panels ensure that the parent is given an opportunity to state his/her views in person in addition to the advocate. Of overriding importance is the necessity for the chair to ensure that all parties have an opportunity to state fully their position and views and to feel satisfied that they have done so.

Where parties have discussed and agreed a draft amended statement, it can be presented to SENDIST, which will subsequently decide whether or not to incorporate it into an order with or without amendments.

8.16 ADJOURNMENTS

Regulation 35 empowers the tribunal to adjourn hearings. In so doing the tribunal can also give directions and announce a provisional conclusion which is not the equivalent to an actual decision.

Adjournments may be ordered when the tribunal concludes that further steps need to be taken by the parties before a decision can be reached. A common example is where parties are in dispute about Part 4, and none of the schools put forward to the tribunal appears satisfactory. The tribunal can adjourn and give directions that parties attempt to identify and agree an alternative school. Sometimes adjournments are ordered to enable parties to attempt negotiation of Parts 2 or 3 on the understanding that they return to the tribunal if agreement is not reached.

8.17 THE DETERMINATION

It is not the usual practice of the tribunal to make a decision immediately after hearing oral evidence as it has to consider carefully the written and oral evidence of the parties. Sometimes, however, the tribunal will give an indication of the likely decision. The more likely course is that the tribunal reserves its decision, and the determination is sent to parties within approximately 10 working days of the hearing. The tribunal is required to produce a determination that gives sufficient reasons and should make findings of fact (*S* v. *Swansea City Council* [2000] ELR 315 and *Crean* v. *Somerset County Council* [2002] ELR 152, QBD).

The tribunal has to make up its own mind, based on the evidence submitted within the appeal. It is allowed to draw on its own expertise and should draw to the parties' attention that it is using its own expertise in place of expert evidence submitted by the parties. Parents should be aware that it open to a tribunal to accept neither the expert evidence of the parent nor that of the LEA. It should, however, make clear on the face of its determination why it takes such a view.

The tribunal is not bound by earlier SENDIST decisions; however, good practice requires each tribunal to have regard to earlier decisions.

8.18 COSTS

Regulation 40 empowers the tribunal to make an order in respect of costs and expenses. The prescribed circumstances include where a party has acted frivolously or vexatiously, or has failed to attend or be represented at a hearing. An order can also be made against an LEA where it has failed to file a case statement or where the tribunal concludes that the LEA's disputed decision was wholly unreasonable.

Costs orders are rarely made.

8.19 ENFORCEMENT OF TRIBUNAL DETERMINATIONS

Where there is no challenge to the decision, the LEA is required to implement the tribunal decision within statutory time-scales provided in reg. 25(2) of the Consolidation Regulations.

The following timescales apply and run from the day after the issue of the tribunal order:

(a) to start an assessment or reassessment: 4 weeks
(b) to make a statement: 5 weeks
(c) to amend a statement: 5 weeks
    (issue a proposed statement)
(d) to change the school named in Part 4: 2 weeks
(e) to cease to maintain a statement: immediately or on date proposed by the LEA, whichever is the later

Regulation 25(4) of the Consolidation Regulations provides exemptions which permit the LEA not to comply with the time limits if it is impractical to do so. These include exceptional circumstances affecting the parent or child within the relevant period; absence of the child or parent from the LEA's area for a continuous period of at least two weeks; and where the parent makes representations on a draft statement after the expiry of the statutory 15 days.

8.20 REVIEW OF THE DETERMINATION

Regulation 39 of the Tribunal Regulations provides that a parent can request a review within 10 working days of notification of the decision if he/she believes that:

(a) the decision was wrongly made as a result of an error on the part of tribunal staff;
(b) there was an obvious error in the tribunal decision;
(c) the interests of justice so require;

On considering the application, the President can set aside or vary the decision. The President can also, on his/her own accord, review a decision of the tribunal. Where this occurs, the parties are notified by the President within 10 working days after notification of the determination and are given an opportunity to attend a hearing. Where a decision is set aside or varied, the records are amended accordingly and the parties are notified.

8.21 STATUTORY APPEAL

A party can appeal on a point of law only by way of a statutory appeal to the Administrative Court of the High Court under CPR Rule 52. Judicial review is not a remedy. Examples of points of law include: grounds based on the tribunal's misunderstanding of material evidence; the tribunal's failure to make findings of fact to support its conclusions; irrationality and perversity; unexplained conclusions which fly in the face of expert evidence; a misdirection in law.

Only the parent or the LEA may appeal. Public funding is therefore based on the parent's eligibility. The appeal has to be lodged within 28 days of the date of the determination and the sealed notice of appeal must be served on the respondent LEA and tribunal. Service on the latter is effected by serving the Treasury Solicitor. Appeals must be lodged within the 28 days unless there are acceptable reasons for delay and must usually be accompanied by a skeleton argument; the procedural rules provide for some exceptions to this. It may also be appropriate to serve a witness statement with the appeal.

The procedural rules require the appellant to file a skeleton argument and trial bundle at least 21 days before the hearing date; the Respondent is required to file a skeleton argument 14 days before the hearing.

The most likely remedy, if the appeal is successful, is an order quashing the tribunal's decision and remitting the appeal to the tribunal for a *de novo* hearing.

8.22 CONCESSIONS OF APPEAL BY THE LOCAL EDUCATION AUTHORITY

Where the LEA concedes appeals against:

(a) refusal to initiate an assessment;
(b) refusal to initiate a re-assessment;
(c) refusal to change the named school for another maintained school.

SENDIST treats those appeals as having been determined in the parent's favour and the LEA has to implement the decision within the timescale referred to above under implementation of tribunal orders (see 8.19).

8.23 LEGAL HELP/PUBLIC FUNDING

Legal Help covers full preparation of appeals and disbursements for experts. This is invaluable for obtaining essential evidence such as reports by educational psychologists and speech and language therapists. The scheme does not cover the cost of representation at the tribunal.

Public funding is available only if the parent pursues a statutory appeal to the High Court. Eligibility for both forms of funding is based upon the parent's means.

CHAPTER 9

Disability discrimination

9.1 INTRODUCTION

The Special Educational Needs and Disability Act (SENDA) 2001 amended the Disability Discrimination Act (DDA) 1995 by the introduction of Part IV which extended the scope of DDA 1995 to education. The main provisions of DDA 1995, Part IV came into effect in September 2002, with the provisions on auxiliary aids and services coming into effect in September 2003, and those on accessibility in September 2005. The aim of Part IV was to cover all aspects of education. Some areas of education are not, however, covered by Part IV, most notably general examination boards (e.g. Edexcel), but the prominent aspects of education, including exclusions, admissions, school curriculum, children out of school, etc. are all within its scope. This chapter deals with under-16 provision in schools.

9.2 WHO IS THE CLIENT?

Under DDA 1995 as it applies to education, only the parent can bring a claim for unlawful discrimination. There is no provision enabling the child to bring his/her own claim.

The DDA 1995 introduces a special form of discrimination, namely 'victimisation'. This protects a person with a disability; parents; siblings; classmates, etc. who either make a complaint of discrimination or give evidence in relation to a complaint. An example could be a fellow student giving evidence in support of a complaint of discrimination who finds that his/her homework has not been marked. This could amount to 'less favourable treatment' and would amount to discrimination for the purposes of DDA 1995, Part IV.

9.3 THE STATUTORY FRAMEWORK

Relationship between special educational needs and disability discrimination

It would be wrong to assume that every child with SEN is a person with a disability for the purposes of DDA 1995, Part IV. That would usually be the case, but a consideration of the definitions under the relevant legislation illustrates that there are specific differences.

The more familiar concepts of SEN provision are set out in particular in EA 1996, s.312 and the SEN Code of Practice (November 2001) which sets out:

> A child has 'special educational needs' for the purposes of this Act if he/she has a learning difficulty which calls for special educational provision to be made for him/her.

The emphasis is on 'learning difficulties' and 'educational provision'.

By contrast DDA 1995, s.1 defines a person with a disability for the purposes of Part IV as follows:

> a person has a disability for the purposes of this Act if he has a physical or mental impairment which has a substantial and long-term adverse effect on his ability to carry out normal day-to-day activities.

The definition under DDA 1995 is broader insofar as it is not restricted to learning difficulties or to educational provision. A pupil with severe asthma may qualify for protection under DDA 1995 but will not necessarily have a learning difficulty. Conversely, a pupil with educational behavioural difficulties related to home or school may have 'learning difficulties', but may not be disabled for the purposes of DDA 1995 as he/she may not come within the definition under DDA 1995 of 'mental impairment'. Representatives of parents of children with ADHD, Asperger's Syndrome or even dyspraxia or dyslexia should bear in mind that they cannot automatically assume that the child will be disabled within the meaning of DDA 1995, s.1. It is natural for parents to assume that their child who has a special educational need will also be disabled but this may not be the case. Meeting the definition under DDA 1995, s.1 will depend on individual facts and the extent the impairment affects their access to education.

Codes of Practice and Regulations

Section 53A of DDA 1995 provides for the Disability Rights Commission (DRC) to draw up Codes of Practice in relation to under-16 and post-16 educational provision (henceforth referred to as 'the Code of Practice for Schools' and 'the Post-16 Code of Practice'). Under s.53A, if the contents of

PRACTICAL EDUCATION LAW

the code of practice appear to the court, tribunal or other body hearing proceedings to be relevant, the code must be taken in account. Failure to follow the provisions of the code of practice does not in itself make any person liable to proceedings (s.53A(8)).

Regulations may be made by the Secretary of State to clarify provisions of DDA 1995, for example, the Disability Discrimination (Meaning of Disability) Regulations 1996, SI 1996/1455, which clarify the definition under s.1.

9.4 DEFINITION OF DISABILITY

Section 1 of DDA 1995 provides the definition of disability, which has four main features:

1. Is there a physical or mental impairment? (Impairment is given its ordinary meaning: *McNicol* v. *Balfour Beatty Rail Maintenance Limited* [2002] EWCA Civ 1074.)
2. Does the impairment have a substantial adverse effect?
3. Does the impairment have a long-term effect?
4. Does the impairment affect normal day-to-day activities?

Meeting the definition under DDA 1995, s.1 can be complex and SENDIST may order a preliminary hearing to determine if the definition is met.

Physical/mental impairment

All physical impairments are covered, including impairments of sight and hearing or mobility, and medical conditions such as diabetes, epilepsy, etc. Schedule 1 to DDA 1995 and the Code of Practice for Schools provide examples of physical and mental impairment.

Mental impairment is intended to cover a wide range of impairments including learning difficulties. However, it does not include any impairment resulting from or consisting of mental illness, unless that illness is a clinically well-recognised illness. A clinically well-recognised illness is one that is recognised by a respected body of medical opinion. There is no similar requirement for physical impairment (*College of Ripon and York St John* v. *Hobbs* [2002] IRLR 185).

People who have a severe disfigurement are covered by DDA 1995. The severe disfigurement is taken as having an adverse effect on a person's ability to carry out normal day-to-day activities, and it is not necessary to prove the disfigurement has that effect.

The Disability Discrimination Act 2005, s.18 extended the definition of disability to people with HIV/Aids, multiple sclerosis and some forms of cancer. At the time of writing, there was no fixed date for implementation.

Substantial adverse effect

A substantial adverse effect is something which is more than a minor or trivial effect and goes beyond the normal differences between people (*Goodwin* v. *Patent Office* [1999] ICR 302, EAT, a decision which gives useful general guidance in the approach to be taken when dealing with cases of disability discrimination).

In the case of *R. (on the application of H)* v. *R School and Special Educational Needs Tribunal* [2004] EWHC Admin 981, the court considered a decision of SENDIST made in response to an application by the school to strike out (Special Education Needs (General Provision and Disability Claims Procedure) Regulations 2002, SI 2002/1985, reg. 44) the claim of disability through discrimination made by *H*, on the basis that *H* was not disabled within the meaning of DDA, s.1. SENDIST reached the conclusion that H was not disabled and struck out the claim. On considering the decision of SENDIST, the court took the view that the tribunal had fallen into the trap of concentrating on what the claimant could do rather than looking at what the claimant could not do or could only do with difficulty. It concluded that if SENDIST focuses on what the individual can do then it may fall into the trap of deciding that the adverse effect clearly cannot be substantial, whereas it clearly would be so regarded if the tribunal focused on what the individual cannot do (*Leonard* v. *Southern Derbyshire Chamber of Commerce* [2001] INLR 19).

Long-term effect

A long-term effect of an impairment is defined in DDA 1995, Sched. 1, para. 2 as an effect:

(a) which has lasted at least 12 months; or
(b) where the total period for which it lasts is likely to be at least 12 months; or
(c) which is likely to last for the rest of the life of the person affected.

Effects which are not long term are not covered. A pupil with a broken limb or an infection, which is likely to heal or be cured in a 12–month period would not be covered.

Conditions which come and go over a period of time will come under Part IV if:

(a) the condition has a substantial adverse effect on day-to-day activities;
(b) there is likely to be at least one recurrence of the substantial effect 12 months or more after the initial occurrence;
(c) the impairment remains.

Likelihood will be determined by the condition as it currently was or would seem to have been when the discrimination took place and 'likely' should be given the meaning 'more probably than not' (*Latchman* v. *Reed Business Information Limited* [2002] ILR 1453, EAT).

For example, in the case of a person with rheumatoid arthritis whose impairment has a substantial adverse effect which then goes into remission and ceases to be substantial, the effects are to be treated as if they are continuing and likely to continue beyond 12 months if the tests above are met.

Paragraph 8 of Sched. 1 to DDA 1995 deals with progressive conditions which have changed and developed over time. Conditions which have had or continue to have an effect on the ability to carry out day-to-day activities, but which are not or were not having a substantial adverse effect are likely to be deemed to have that effect if the condition is likely to result in such an impairment. An impairment which results from the treatment of a progressive condition is likely to satisfy the requirements of para. 8(1)(b) (*Kirton* v. *Tetrosyl* [2003] EWCA Civ 619; [2003] ILR 353, CA).

Pupils receiving treatment which alleviates or removes the effects but not the impairment will be covered under DDA 1995, Sched. 1, para. 6. The treatment will be ignored and the impairment is taken to have the effect it would have without the treatment. An illustration would be that a person with epilepsy is disabled and the effect that the medication has in controlling seizures would be discounted. If the substantial adverse effect is not likely to recur even if the treatment stopped, the person in question is no longer to be treated as having a disability (Post-16 Code of Practice, para. A.10).

Certain conditions are specifically excluded from cover under DDA 1995. These include hay fever, addiction to alcohol or nicotine, etc. (see Appendix 1 of the Code of Practice for Schools for a list of conditions specifically excluded and Disability Discrimination (Meaning of Disability) Regulations 1996, SI 1996/1455, regs. 3 and 4). The exclusions from the definition of impairment as set out in the Regulations only cover conditions which are free-standing and not those which are a direct consequence of a physical or mental impairment covered by DDA 1995, s.1.

People who wear glasses or contact lenses are not covered by the Act. The effect of the glasses or contact lenses on the impairment is taken into account.

Normal day-to-day activities

This refers to activities that are carried out by most people on a regular and frequent basis.

The test of whether an impairment affects normal day-to-day activities is whether it affects one of the broad categories of capacity set out in DDA 1995, Sched. 1, para. 4. The categories of capacity are:

- mobility;
- manual dexterity;

- physical co-ordination;
- continence;
- ability to lift, carry or otherwise move everyday objects;
- speech, hearing or eyesight;
- memory or ability to concentrate, learn or understand;
- perception of risk or danger.

Reference is made to para. A1.9 of the Post-16 Code of Practice which sets out that normal day-to-day activities are those carried out by most people on a fairly regular basis. It goes further and clarifies that they do not include activities which are normal only for a particular person or group of people, for example, playing a musical instrument or sport to a professional standard, or performing a skilled or specialist task related to a particular academic discipline, education or training course. Someone who is affected in this way but is also affected in normal day-to-day activities is covered by the definition.

Employment case law provides guidance on what activities fall within the meaning of normal day-to-day activities. For instance, they must be determined by reference to gender (*Ekpe* v. *Metropolitan Police Commissioner* [2001] IRLR 605, EAT); the circumstances of the relevant claimant (*Abadeh* v. *British Telecommunications plc* [2001] IRLR 23, EAT); and where the condition may fluctuate, then the ability to perform tasks in an educational setting and outside should be considered (*Cruickshank* v. *Vaw Motorcast Ltd* [2002] ICR 729, EAT).

9.5 WHAT EDUCATION SETTINGS DOES PART IV COVER?

Part IV of DDA 1995 covers the following institutions:

Schools

Independent, non-maintained and LEA-maintained schools and PRUs are covered at primary and secondary level.

Nurseries

All LEA-maintained nursery schools, nursery classes, and nursery school provision both independent and grant aided, is covered.

Private, voluntary and statutory providers of pre-school provision which is not constituted as a school are covered by DDA 1995, Part III as service providers. This is dealt with later in this chapter.

Post-16 provision

Sixth form provision not at school is covered under further and higher education.

Who is the 'responsible body'?

The DDA 1995 introduces the concept of the 'responsible body' which is defined for schools by DDA 1995, Sched. 4A as inserted by SENDA 2001, Sched. 2. It mirrors the provisions in relation to sex and race discrimination. The responsible body will depend on the type of school (see Table 9.1).

Table 9.1 Responsible body for schools

Type of school	Responsible body
Maintained school	Governing body but not for admissions as LEA retains responsibility for admissions to community schools
Pupil referral unit	LEA
Maintained nursery school	LEA
Independent school	Proprietor
Special school not maintained by LEA	Proprietor

In the independent/private and voluntary sector when trying to determine who is the responsible body it should be considered who is responsible for the management of the school. This may vary but is likely to include the board of trustees, the governing body, a private owner or a management group.

Examination boards

Examination boards are not covered by either Part IV or Part III of DDA 1995 (*Palmer* v. *(1) RSA; (2) AQA* (unreported, 26 March 2004, Central London County Court)). External examination boards are not schools or providers of higher education and are not covered by Part IV of the Act. They are not direct providers of services to the general public. They merely act as service providers to educational institutions and therefore are not covered by Part III (DDA 1995, ss.19–20). Section 19 requires a direct relation between service provider and the person complaining. This is not the case with examination boards, where any application for disapplication or alteration of usual arrangements for an examination is made by the school or college which is acting as an examination centre. The examination board will give a decision, and the examination centre conducts the examination in accordance with the decision.

Since October 2004 it has been unlawful to discriminate on grounds of disability in the provision of 'professional or trade qualifications', the reason being that Article 13 of the Treaty of Rome provides that there should not be discrimination in the manner in which examinations are provided for those who are training to enter into a trade or profession. There may be an argument that these provisions should apply to GCSEs or A level examinations if they are a necessary prerequisite to being able to obtain a professional qualification or to entering a trade.

9.6 WHAT ACTIVITIES ARE COVERED BY PART IV?

The aim of Part IV is to cover every part of school life. This includes:

- admissions;
- education and associated services; and
- exclusions.

Admissions

Part IV (under s.28A(1)) places a duty on responsible bodies not to discriminate in arrangements made for determining admissions of pupils to school.

Section 28A of DDA 1995 places a duty on a responsible body not to discriminate against a disabled person. The duty is similar to those duties imposed by the Sex Discrimination Act 1975, s.22 and Race Relations Act 1976, s.17. The duty imposed by DDA 1995 is wider than the duties under those Acts as it includes the arrangements which the responsible body makes for determining admission to school as a pupil. The duty begins at an earlier stage and applies to the time before any particular pupil applies to the school.

As it applies to 'prospective pupils' this will cover the criteria which have been determined for deciding who will be admitted to oversubscribed schools and how the criteria are operated. It will cover the terms of any offer of admission and a refusal or deliberate omission by failure to accept an application for admission from someone who is disabled.

The DDA 1995 does allow 'a permitted form of selection'. This enables schools to continue to operate selection criteria as set out in the Admissions Code of Practice 1999.

Education and associated services

The aim of s.28A(2) is to cover all aspects of school life both for pupils and prospective pupils. This would include preparation for entry to school, school clubs and activities, the serving of school meals, school trips, etc. (see the Code of Practice for Schools for a full list). It does not cover adult education provided by the school, or services to parents which are covered under DDA 1995, Part III. For instance, when a parent teacher association holds a car boot sale, this is covered under Part III, and the same applies to services provided by other bodies such as providers of health services which may take place in school.

Out-of-school clubs run with the knowledge and authority of the school will be covered by DDA 1995. The Act makes responsible bodies liable for anything done by their agents if it is done with their authority.

Section 28A(3) provides that the Secretary of State may make regulations to prescribe what services count as education and related services.

Exclusions

It is unlawful for a responsible body to exclude a pupil for a reason related to his/her disability. This applies to both fixed-term and permanent exclusions.

A recent decision (*Governing Body of PPC* v. *DS* [2005] All ER (D) 64, QBD confirmed that the duty to make reasonable adjustments does apply to exclusions. In contrast to s.28A, exclusion is not expressly referred to under s.28C.

9.7 THE DISCRIMINATION TEST

What is discrimination?

For the purposes of s.28A the test of discrimination is defined by DDA 1995, s. 28B(1) and (2). There are two types of discrimination as follows:

- s.28B(1) sets out the less favourable treatment test;
- s.28B(2) requires that it must be shown that there has been a failure to comply for the purposes of s.28A without justification and to the detriment to the disabled pupil.

Less favourable treatment

The less favourable treatment test under s.28B(1) raises three questions:

1. Is the treatment less favourable for the reasons related to the pupil's disability?
2. Is the treatment less favourable than the treatment received by another actual or (hypothetical) pupil to whom the reason does not apply?
3. Can less favourable treatment be justified?

The Act places an anticipatory duty on the responsible body, and the pupil only has to show that the other pupils would have been treated better, not that they actually were treated better.

The comparator test in determining 'less favourable treatment' is not a pupil with similar problems but someone who is not disabled and has no associated difficulties (*McAuley Catholic High School* v. *C and Others* [2003] EWHC Admin 3045; see also Code of Practice for Schools, para. 5.10).

Can the treatment be justified?

If there has been a failure to comply for the purposes of s.28A then school must show that the treatment is justified on the following grounds:

(a) under a permitted form of selection – this covers the cases of selective schools who select on academic ability, and specialist schools which can give priority to a proportion of pupils who show a particular aptitude for the subject in which the school specialises;
(b) where there is a clear connection between the reason the responsible body gives and the circumstances of the particular case, and that reason is substantial, i.e. more than minor or trivial (DDA 1995, s.28B(6) and (7)).

The justification would have to be valid even after a 'reasonable adjustment' has been made (DDA 1995, s.28B(8)).

It is not clear from s.28B(7) and (8) who bears the burden of proof on the issue of justification. It is likely that the burden of proof would be on the responsible body, and some guidance is given in the Code of Practice for Schools at para. 5.17C where an example is given of the operation of this section and it assumed that it will be for the responsible body to prove that it can justify its actions.

Reasonable adjustment duty

Section 28C imposes a duty on the responsible body to take such steps as it is reasonable to ensure that disabled pupils and prospective pupils are not placed at a substantial disadvantage in comparison with those pupils who are not disabled. The responsible body discriminates if it fails to the detriment of the pupil and without justification to take those steps (DDA 1995, s.28B(2)).

The requirement of reasonable adjustment relates to:

(a) admission to school; and
(b) education and associated services.

The nature of the duty

The test again is a comparative test. The position of the disabled pupil should be compared with that of pupils who are not disabled.

Is the disabled person at a 'substantial disadvantage'? The Code of Practice for Schools sets out some examples to take into account when determining 'substantial disadvantage', for example:

(a) time and effort which may need to be expended by the disabled child;
(b) inconvenience, indignity or discomfort a disabled child may suffer;
(c) diminished progress in comparison with non-disabled peers;
(d) loss of opportunity.

The duty is anticipatory and a school should not wait until a disabled pupil is admitted before complying. A school should review its policies and procedures regularly to anticipate what should be done and make reasonable adjustments accordingly.

This is an evolving duty with the aim of raising the 'baseline' for reasonable adjustments and to ensure provision is continually improving.

A duty is also owed to disabled parents under DDA 1995, Part III, e.g. to provide sign language interpreters at parent evenings.

What is reasonable?

The DDA 1995 does not define 'reasonable adjustment'. It requires a weighting exercise – substantial disadvantage to the disabled pupil against relevant factors, which may prevent participation of the pupil in school life. The Code of Practice for Schools lists relevant factors, and the responsible body is required to have regard to these relevant factors when making its decision (DDA 1995, s.28C(4)):

(a) the need to maintain academic, musical, sporting and other standards (schools can still choose their best pupils in these categories to enter inter-school competitions, but must ensure the standards do not bar a disabled pupil from participating in an activity);
(b) the extent to which it is practical to take the step;
(c) the interests of other pupils in school or who may be admitted;
(d) health and safety requirements;
(e) the cost of taking a step;
(f) the financial resources of the school;
(g) the extent to which aids and services are to be provided to a disabled pupil under SEN provision.

Case examples

The following example is taken from the DRC Report of 5 March 2003.

A six-year-old pupil was told that he must wear the regulation school uniform trouser even though the flannel material inflamed the eczema on his legs. Medical evidence from his GP and hospital supported the fact that the boy needed to wear 100% cotton to stop his eczema flaring up to the extent that he could barely walk. The school disregarded the medical evidence and insisted that the boy had another medical examination. His mother refused as she felt that more than enough medical evidence had been provided and that the school was being unreasonable. She withdrew her son from school.

The school could reasonably have been expected to adjust its policy on school uniform to allow the disabled pupil to wear trousers of a different material.

The case of *Governing Body of PPC* v. *DS* [2005] All ER (D) 64, QBD considered the relationship of the duty to make reasonable adjustment and the defence of justification to alleged less favourable treatment. The case concerned the exclusion of N, a pupil with Asperger's syndrome. N's parents had appealed to SENDIST against the decision of the governing body of an independent mainstream school to permanently exclude N. The governing body appealed the decision of SENDIST that reasonable steps could have been taken as an alternative to exclusion and that the exclusion amounted to unjustified less favourable treatment on grounds of N's disability. The court was asked to consider whether the failure to make reasonable adjustment could be considered by the tribunal when it was raised in the context of a justification defence to less favourable treatment but not as a distinct complaint. The court found that there was no need to separate the failure to carry out reasonable adjustments as a cause of action in its own right from the anticipatory reply to a justification defence in relation to a cause of action for less favourable treatment.

In the above case the court found it was clear that the parents were challenging both less favourable treatment and adjustment in the Tribunal and advisers must be sure that they consider and if necessary claim under both heads.

Exceptions to the reasonable adjustment duty

The DDA 1995 does not place a duty on a responsible body to provide auxiliary aids and services which should come under a statement of SEN, e.g. radio aids for deaf pupils, specialist computer equipment, etc. There is not necessarily any correlation between the full range of a pupil's needs and the provision in a statement of special needs. A child may not have a statement of SEN and/or the need may not be an educational need, e.g. a need for nursing care. As a pupil may have a disability but not have SEN assessing these services can prove problematic.

Pastoral support may be covered and a school can be required to provide support during unstructured times, e.g. through a mentor, planned managed disruptive behaviour, etc. This would not necessarily amount to auxiliary aids and services to be provided under a statement of SEN (*McAuley Catholic High School* v. *C and Others* [2003] EWHC Admin 3045).

Independent schools can charge parents for specialist tuition. Discrimination may occur if the charges levied were so high that they deterred disabled pupils from applying to the school.

Alteration/removal of physical features

The DDA 1995 does not place a duty on a school to make physical adjustments to accommodate disabled pupils. These should be dealt with either under the planning duties or the duties on the school and LEA to produce accessibility plans (ss.28D and 28E).

Maintained schools must publish their accessibility plans in their annual report to parents.

The duties on schools and LEAs to draw up plans and publish them are general and really offer no protection to an individual disabled pupil. Breach of the duties under ss. 28D and 28E will not enable a disabled pupil to bring a claim to SENDIST that he/she has been unlawfully discriminated against. There may be an entitlement to bring a judicial review claim for breach of statutory duty, but as the duties are so non-specific it is difficult to see what practical relief the court could award.

Adjustments which fall short of physical alterations could be required, e.g. moving the school library to the ground floor to ensure accessibility.

Defences to less favourable treatment and reasonable adjustment duties

There are two defences, which may be available:

(a) lack of knowledge;
(b) confidentiality.

Lack of knowledge

Did the responsible body know or could it have reasonably been expected to know that the pupil was disabled and was the failure to take the step attributable to that lack of knowledge? A responsible body cannot rely on not having direct knowledge of the disability if it could have taken reasonable steps to have found out about the pupil's disability. This places a burden of proof on the responsible body in three ways:

(a) that it did not, in fact, know that the person concerned was disabled;
(c) that it could not have reasonably have been expected to know that the person was disabled;
(c) that its failure to take the step in question could be attributed to that lack of knowledge.

Generally, pupils will fall under the SEN framework, and the disability will be known to the school. If this is not the case then it should be checked with the parents if discussion of disability was facilitated at key points in the child's school life i.e. admission, transition between schools, school trips, etc.

Underachievement and difficult behaviour may be indicators that the pupil is experiencing problems related to a disability. If a parent has expressed concern and nothing has been done then the school may be precluded from relying on lack of knowledge. Similarly, if the disability has been disclosed to a member of staff, e.g. the school secretary, who has not passed this on, then the lack of knowledge defence will not be arguable.

Confidentiality

Confidentiality is discussed in DDA 1995, s.28C. A request for confidentiality by a parent or pupil, if he/she has the capacity and can understand the effect of the request, may limit what a responsible body can do. The effects of the request should be explained by the school to the parent or pupil and discussion to allay fears or possible disadvantage to the pupil should be facilitated. If a claim is made, advisers should consider what the school did in answer to the request: was it reasonable, could they have explained more, were policies and procedures properly discussed?

There is nothing in DDA 1995, which overrides the Data Protection Act 1998, and information about a disabled pupil should not be disclosed without the parent or pupil's consent as it is classified as 'sensitive personal data'.

9.8 PRE-SCHOOL PROVISION

Much early years provision is not in maintained nursery school classes. Often it is in playgroups or pre-school centres run by the private and voluntary sector (see Table 9.2). The social care of young children has been covered under DDA 1995, Part III and since September 2002, educational provision has also been included under Part III (see the DRC Code of Practice under Part III – Right of Access to Goods, Facilities, Services and Premises).

9.9 SCHOOL ACCESSIBILITY STRATEGIES

The LEA has to prepare an accessibility strategy for the schools for which it is responsible. Under DDA 1995, s.28D accessibility strategies must be in writing, and are defined by s.28D(2) as strategies for:

(a) increasing the extent to which disabled persons can participate in the school's curriculum;

Table 9.2 Early years education providers

Duties under Part III	Schools' duties under Part IV	LEA's residual duties under Part IV
LEA Day Nurseries (not on school premises), Family Centres, etc.	LEA maintained schools	Home teaching services for young people, i.e. portage.
	LEA maintained nursery schools	
Private and voluntary playgroups and pre-schools	Independent schools	
Accredited childminders	Non-maintained special schools	

(b) improving the physical environment of the school to increase the extent to which disabled pupils are able to participate in education and associated services; and
(c) improving the service delivery to disabled pupils, within a reasonable time and in ways which are decided after taking account of their disabilities and any preferences expressed by the pupils or their parents.

The LEA must keep its accessibility strategy under review during the time to which it relates and must, if necessary, revise it. The LEA is under a duty to implement its strategy, and its performance of these duties can be subject to an inspection under EA 1997, s.38.

Similar responsibilities to those imposed on the LEA are imposed on responsible bodies in relation to maintained schools, independent schools and schools which are not maintained but which are approved by the Secretary of State, or in Wales, the National Assembly. Again, performance of these duties can be the subject of an inspection under the School Inspection Act 1996.

9.10 THE LOCAL EDUCATION AUTHORITY'S RESIDUAL DUTIES

Under DDA 1995, ss.28F and 28G, an LEA will be under a duty to comply with Part IV when it is acting as a responsible body for a school, e.g. as an admission authority for community schools.

It also has 'residual duties' outside schools which are covered by the provisions of Part IV. These residual duties include:

- LEA policies such as those in relation to SEN, capital building programmes, transport, early years provision, arrangements for home and hospital tuition;
- LEA policies on school admissions and exclusions;
- deployment of the LEA's non-delegated budget;
- services to pupils, e.g. weekend or after-school leisure and sporting activities, school trips, etc.

Advice on 'residual duties' is likely to arise in the areas of both home tuition and transport. For example, if an LEA has a policy that all transport for disabled primary school pupils collects these pupils at 3.30 pm, this may result in some disabled pupils not being able to stay for after-school clubs. The LEA should review its transport policy and consider whether a reasonable adjustment needs to made to allow later departures from school.

9.11 APPEALS TO THE SPECIAL EDUCATIONAL NEEDS AND DISABILITY TRIBUNAL

Since September 2002, the remit of the Special Educational Needs Tribunal (now SENDIST) was extended to hear claims of unlawful discrimination in the following areas:

- fixed-term exclusions from all schools;
- permanent exclusions from all schools except maintained schools and city academies;
- admissions to all schools except maintained schools and city academies;
- the provision of education and associated services.

Provision was made for the procedure for SENDIST claims to be dealt with by regulations made under DDA 1995, s.28J.

The procedure for appeal to SENDIST is dealt with in detail in Chapter 8. It will not be repeated here, except insofar as there are certain aspects of the procedure which differ in respect of disability discrimination claims.

Time limits

An appeal to SENDIST must be lodged within six months of the alleged discrimination. The time limit is extended to eight months if the DRC conciliation procedure is used (see 9.13). The tribunal has a discretion to extend time where it considers it is just and equitable to do so (SENDIST Regulations 2002, Sched. 3, para. 10).

A disability claim and an SEN claim can be run together but the time limits differ. The SEN time limit of two months will prevail in a mixed SEN/DDA 1995 claim.

Expedition

SENDIST usually aims to list a matter for hearing two to three months after registration of the appeal. If a parent needs an earlier remedy, i.e. to allow a pupil to attend a school trip, it is necessary to obtain the agreement of the responsible body to expedition and a proposed date. A responsible body may decide to delay and therefore frustrate an effective remedy.

Preparing a case for appeal

What evidence is needed to show a pupil is disabled?

Definitions of disability under DDA 1995, s.1 of can be contentious, particularly if the pupil's disability comes under 'mental impairment'. The tribunal will need good medical evidence, and specific evidence should be gathered which demonstrates the way in which the physical and/or mental impairment has a substantial adverse effect on normal day-to-day activities.

'Impartial expert evidence' will be necessary for the tribunal to decide whether the actions of the pupil are relevant to his/her disability, particularly in relation to disruptive behaviour where the expert evidence would assist in linking the behaviour to the disability. In *McAuley Catholic High School*, the school relied on the evidence of the head teacher who had previously been the head teacher of a school with an autistic unit. The court held that the head teacher could not be sufficiently independent to be regarded as an 'expert' in the dispute.

A recent SENDIST decision (DRC/03/8674) illustrates the difficulties which may be encountered when deciding on the applicability of DDA 1995, s.1. The case concerned a pupil with ADHD, which the tribunal accepted was a clinically well recognised mental impairment. However, the tribunal went on to decide that, as the diagnosis of ADHD postdated the alleged discrimination, the child was not disabled at the time of the alleged discrimination and therefore not protected by DDA 1995. An appeal against this decision was lodged in the High Court and was conceded by the tribunal. The claim was referred back to SENDIST for reconsideration.

Employment case law

Many of the provisions of DDA 1995 about discrimination in education are set out in identical terms to those relating to discrimination in employment. The decision in *McAuley Catholic High School* case makes it clear that employment case law should apply to education. Attention should be paid to employment case law decisions particularly in the areas of:

- the comparator test for less favourable treatment;

- the definition of disability, set out under DDA 1995, s.1, which is identical for all claims;
- the meaning in general of less favourable treatment;
- the reasonable adjustment duty;
- justification of less favourable treatment or failure to make reasonable adjustments;
- the issue as to whether or not the tribunal considers justification standing in the shoes of the school or merely reviews the decision of the school to see if it was within the reasonable range of responses available to the school at the time (*James* v. *Post Office* [2001] EWCA Civ 558, CA).

Factors for consideration in preparing a DDA 1995 claim

Is there justification for the discrimination?

1. Does the less favourable treatment relate to admission? First consider whether there is a 'permitted form of selection'.
2. If it does not relate to admission or a permitted form of selection, carry out a balancing exercise of the effect of the discrimination on the pupil as against relevant factors such as costs implications for other pupils, etc.
3. Are there health and safety issues? Consider whether a 'risk assessment' has been undertaken by the responsible body to comply with the health and safety legislation.

Is there a reasonable adjustment that could have been made?

1. Consider again the effect that the alleged discrimination is having on the pupil. What evidence needs to be produced to show the pupil is not progressing appropriately compared with other non-disabled pupils, whether actual or hypothetical? This is a comparative test, and evidence will need to be presented of the level of performance of non-disabled pupils.
2. Can evidence be produced of the added time and effort the disabled pupil is expending?
3. Does the reasonable adjustment require auxiliary aids and services? Are these auxiliary aids and services which could be dealt with under SEN provision?

Strike out

Under SENDIST Regulations 2002, reg. 44, the secretary of the tribunal can at any stage of proceedings, on the application of a responsible body or if the President so directs, serve a notice on the parent stating that it appears that

PRACTICAL EDUCATION LAW

Step 1
Does the disbled child meet the definition of disability under DDA 1995 s.1 → No. Unlikely to be discrimination on grounds of disability.

↓ Yes

Step 2
Is the child a pupil or potential pupil? → No. Unlikely to be discrimination under DDA 1995, Part IV.

↓ Yes

Step 3
Is the institution covered by DDA 1995, Part IV?
Who is the responsible body?
Is the education service covered by Part IV? → No. Unlikely to be discrimination under DDA 1995, Part IV.

↓ Yes

Step 4
Has the disabled child received less favourable treatment for a reason related to his/her disability?
Has the responsible body failed to take all reasonable steps to ensure that the disabled child is not placed at a substantial disadvantage (reasonable adjustment duty)? → No to all of these. Unlikely to be unlawful discrimination.

↓ Yes to any of these

Step 5
Was it reasonable for the responsible body not to know the child was disabled?
AND
Was the failure to make reasonable adjustment related to the lack of knowledge?
Can the responsible body justify the less favourable treatment?
Is the failure to make a reasonable adjustment Justified? → Yes to all of these. Unlikely to be unlawful discrimination.

↓ No to any or all. May be unlawful discrimination.

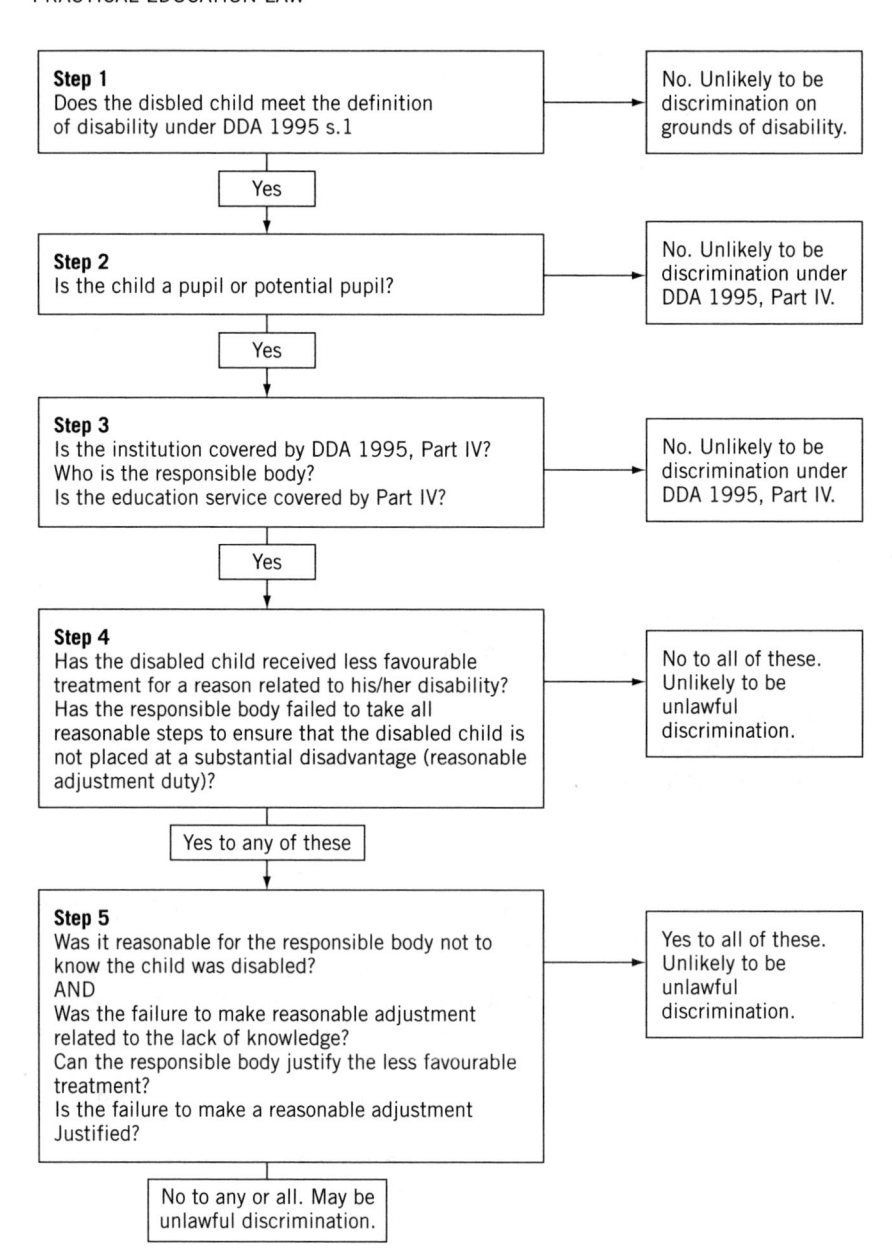

Figure 9.1 Five steps in a disability claim

the claim should be struck out on one or both of the grounds specified in reg.44(2) or for want of prosecution.

The grounds referred to in reg. 44(2) are:

(a) the claim is not, or is no longer, within the jurisdiction of the tribunal; and
(b) the notice of claim is, or the claim is or has become, scandalous, frivolous or vexatious.

The procedure as set out under reg. 44 does not give SENDIST the power to hold a preliminary issue hearing to determine discrete issue relating to the appeal. This is a mechanism which exists in employment tribunals. In the case of *R. (on the application of H)* v. *R School and Special Educational Needs Tribunal* [2004] EWHC Admin 981, the judge reached the conclusion that 'strike out' was not the correct forum for determining the complicated issue of whether or not a person has a disability under DDA 1995. In a case where there is substantial medical evidence which appears to demonstrate that the child concerned does or could have an impairment. The DRC complained at the time when the SENDIST Regulations 2002 came into force that by the admission to give SENDIST the power to hold a preliminary issue hearing limited the tribunal's effectiveness in determining complex issues such as whether a pupil was disabled within the meaning of DDA 1995, s.1.

Orders that the tribunal can make

If SENDIST finds there has been unlawful discrimination, it can make a declaration that a pupil has been unlawfully discriminated against and can make other orders, for example that an institution must implement or review policies and procedures, provide training for staff, make an apology, etc. (see DRC Code of Practice for Schools for a full list). SENDIST is limited in the effectiveness of its remedies as it cannot make an order for monetary compensation. It can impose time limits for compliance with its orders.

Case examples

A six-year-old boy with learning difficulties was left out of his school play; he was not allowed to take part in other Christmas activities. It emerged that the school had not employed the full-time LSA as required under his statement of SEN and the pupil had not been able to partake fully in class activities. He was excluded from class for photographs and when the class were taken to a local museum. His mother brought a claim of disability discrimination.

The tribunal found that the boy had been discriminated against and his treatment had been 'less favourable' because of his disability. The tribunal ordered:

(a) a written apology to the pupil and his mother;
(b) that the school revise all its policies for disabled pupils and for recruiting and retaining staff;
(c) that the governing body and all staff attend disability equality training (SENDIST 03-50019 (DIS)).

Another case (SENDIST 04-50116, 18 April 2004) concerned a claim against a responsible body for unlawful discrimination against a visually impaired child (A). The responsible body selected A to attend a school ski trip which was self-funding. Four months before the trip, the responsible body advised A's mother that she would have to pay an extra £1,000 to cover the extra supervision and tuition that A would require. The responsible body had not undertaken a risk assessment. Due to the lateness of the request A's mother was not able to raise the extra money and A did not go on the trip. SENDIST found that the responsible body had discriminated against A and ordered the responsible body to apologise, review and implement new policies, and train staff. SENDIST had no power to order compensation and could not have ordered the responsible body to pay the additional monies. As the responsible body refused to agree to expedition the school trip had already taken place by the time of the SENDIST hearing.

Direction by Secretary of State

SENDIST can set deadlines for the compliance of orders. If a responsible body fails to comply with the deadlines set by SENDIST, or it has acted or is proposing to act unreasonably in complying with SENDIST orders, the Secretary of State can make a direction requiring compliance. This is enforceable through the courts if necessary.

Complaints procedures

Prior to making any SENDIST claim, an adviser should consider whether the complaint could be resolved through the responsible body's complaints procedure. When advising a client on pursuing the complaints procedure:

(a) bear in mind the time limits for claims to SENDIST and independent appeal panels – the time limit for SENDIST will not be extended to facilitate complaints procedures, *only* for conciliation by the DRC;
(b) include with any initial letter to a responsible body a request for abridgement of complaint procedure time limits;
(c) a complaint can be made at the same time as or during a SENDIST claim.

9.12 EXCLUSION AND ADMISSION APPEAL PANELS

It should be remembered that not all complaints of discrimination in admissions and exclusions will be heard by SENDIST. The appropriate remedies are shown in Table 9.3.

Time limits and procedure for admission and exclusions appeals are dealt with in Chapters 3 and 4 and are not repeated here. Bear in mind that different time limits will apply to different appeal procedures for different categories of schools.

9.13 ROLE OF THE DISABILITY RIGHTS COMMISSION

Part IV of DDA 1995 emphasises the role of the DRC in drawing up Codes of Practice and in running a conciliation service.

The DRC runs a helpline for parents and a casework service to try to resolve disputes prior to conciliation and any claim.

Reference to the DRC conciliation service extends the time limit for claims to SENDIST by two months. Both parties must agree to conciliation. The

Table 9.3 Remedies

Category	Type of school	Remedies
Admissions	Maintained schools/ city academies	LEA appeal procedure
	Independent/private schools and voluntary or non-maintained special schools	SENDIST
Exclusions		
(a) Fixed term	Maintained schools, independent/private and voluntary or non-maintained special schools	SENDIST
(b) Permanent	Maintained schools	LEA appeal procedure
	Independent/private schools and voluntary or non-maintained special schools	SENDIST
Education and associated services	All	SENDIST

DRC does not have the power to impose a settlement, and conciliation does not prevent a parent pursuing a tribunal claim or other action. No information disclosed in conciliation can be used in a tribunal or other claim without the consent of both parties.

Conciliation is available for admission and exclusion disputes but, given the short time limits for appeal panels, it is an impractical remedy.

9.14 PUBLIC FUNDING

Appeals to SENDIST under DDA 1995 will need to be prepared under the LSC's Legal Help Scheme. The reason for this is that public funding is not available for tribunal representation or for admission or exclusion appeals.

The Legal Help Scheme will cover preparation, obtaining expert reports and preparing for the hearing, but not representation at the hearing. At the time of writing, the cost limit under the Legal Help Scheme was £500, but obviously, given the likely need for expert reports, an application would need to be made to the LSC to increase the limit.

As at the time of writing, the LSC was bringing in a fixed fee scheme as from April 2005 which will limit fees paid under contract for categories of work to a figure allocated by the LSC. It is likely that the cost of conducting a DDA 1995 claim to SENDIST or an appeal panel would exceed the fixed fee level. This has obvious implications for advisers in the future.

Public funding certificates may be granted to cover appeals from SENDIST to the High Court, or claims to the county court. On appeals from SENDIST, certificates will be in the name of the parents and based on the parents' means.

Claims to the county court or possible judicial review claims for breach of the DDA 1995 will be issued in the child's name with the parent shown as litigation friend.

CHAPTER 10

School transport

10.1 INTRODUCTION

The responsibilities of LEAs in respect of the provision of school transport affect:

- children with SEN;
- children of compulsory school age and beyond;
- pre-school children attending nurseries;
- students attending institutes of further education;
- institutions providing further or higher education either maintained or assisted by the LEA (as defined in EA 1996, s.579(6)–(7)).

This chapter primarily considers school age pupils.

10.2 THE STATUTORY FRAMEWORK

The LEA's statutory responsibilities in respect of school transport are set out in EA 1996, s.509(1), which requires the LEA to:

> Make such arrangements for the provision of transport and otherwise as they consider necessary, or as the Secretary of State may direct, for the purpose of facilitating the attendance of persons receiving education.

The LEA's responsibility is general and wide ranging, requiring it to facilitate physical access to educational institutions from nursery through to university for pupils and students attending. It has duties and powers to provide free school transport and/or to charge in certain circumstances.

However, the duty is framed in terms that require the LEA to make subjective value judgements as to what is 'necessary', defined by the House of Lords in *R. v. Devon County Council ex p. George* [1989] AC 573, as really needed. The obligation to comply with the 'duty' imposed by s.509, is not triggered until there has been a determination that some form of transport arrangement has been considered necessary. Whilst the precise nature of the duty imposed on LEAs by the section may be the subject of an interesting debate, the practical implications of any failure to provide school transport can be extremely significant for individual families.

In considering whether it is necessary to provide school transport, there are a number of statutory factors which the LEA must take into account (s.509(4)), including:

- the age of the individual;
- the nature of the route or alternative routes as the individual could reasonably be expected to take;
- any expressed parental preference for a child to be educated at a school offering a particular religious ethos;
- other factors, which might include health or other social factors and/or other issues affecting parental preference, for example an expressed preference for a single-sex or mixed-gender school.

The LEA has a discretionary power to provide transport even where it is not considered 'necessary', through the operation of s.509(3).

Pre-school pupils may be provided with assistance with travel arrangements to and from a nursery (s.509A). The LEA may provide transport, or make arrangements, including the payment of travel expenses, provided it is satisfied that without LEA assistance the child would be unable to attend the nursery. However, an LEA may charge for the provision of any arrangements made under this section.

In seeking to challenge an LEA's failure to exercise its discretionary powers, the logical starting point may be a complaint to the LEA, as judicial review will generally require an 'unreasonableness' argument to be run.

10.3 TYPES OF ASSISTANCE/ARRANGEMENTS

The types of assistance which might be provided include:

- LEA run and operated vehicles;
- transport run by private contractors, e.g. coaches, mini buses, taxis;
- provision of travel passes or permits;
- a mileage allowance to carers or a designated driver for a particular school route;
- payment to individual schools which arrange transport for their pupils;
- escorts or carers.

10.4 WHO IS THE CLIENT?

The majority of school transport challenges have been made in the name of the pupil. In the authors' view, the pupil both has standing and is most closely concerned with the duties which may be at issue, particularly within any judicial review proceedings.

However, within certain proceedings, the parent may be the more appropriate client, principally when seeking to defend any prosecution brought pursuant to EA 1996, s.444 in respect of which the failure of the LEA to provide school transport will provide a parent with an effective defence, provided the child lives beyond walking distance of the nearest school. Walking distance is defined by statute as two miles in respect of children under the age of eight years and three miles in respect of children over the age of 8 years, with the distance being measured by reference to the nearest available route (EA 1996, s.444(5)). (A contrary view is set out in R. McManus, *Education and the Courts*, second edition (Jordans, 2004).)

In cases involving further and higher education, the client will be almost always be the student.

10.5 POTENTIAL ISSUES

Prosecution of a parent

Where a parent is being prosecuted under s.444, he/she will have a defence provided that:

(a) the school at which the child is registered is not within walking distance of the child's home; and
(b) no suitable arrangements have been made by the LEA or the funding authority for any of the following:

  (i) for transport to the school at which the pupil is registered; or
  (ii) for boarding accommodation for the pupil at or near the school; or
  (iii) enabling the pupil to become registered at a school nearer to his/her home.

The parent will have a good defence if all of the circumstances outlined above are absent (*R.* v. *Devon County Council ex p. George* [1989] AC 573 at 604B; see also *R. (on the Application of Jones)* v. *Ceredigon County Council* [2004] EWHC Admin 1376; [2004] ELR 506). However, the LEA will have discharged its duties by making any of the suitable arrangements defined in the section.

Nearest available route

The judgements involved in considering whether a child lives outside the statutory definition of walking distance can create considerable debate. As set out above, the LEA must have regard to the child's age and the route he/she can take in deciding whether it is necessary to provide transport or not.

Consideration by the House of Lords has created no clear criteria against which issues such as a child's safety in walking and the need for either an accompanying adult or a degree of supervision can be considered. In *George*, was held that an LEA may not be obliged to provide free transport simply because the nearest available route was too hazardous for an unaccompanied child to use. The fact that it was not possible for the child to be accompanied may be insufficient to create necessity.

However if, as is acknowledged, transport arrangements to and from school must be non-stressful, in the authors' view, walking arrangements must be so also (see *R. v. Hereford and Worcester County Council ex p. P* [1992] 2 FLR 207 particularly, but not exclusively in relation to SEN).

Parental preference

As we have already seen in considering admissions, the right to express a parental preference is often misunderstood as providing an entitlement for the pupil to attend a school of the parent's choice. However, in circumstances where a child is admitted to the school in respect of which his/her parents have expressed a preference, that does not mean that the LEA is obliged to provide school transport. Analysis of the case law suggests that, in general, the LEA will not be obliged to provide transport to a school which falls outside the statutory definition of walking distance if the child's attendance at that school is solely as a result of parental preference.

Clearly if a child is attending a school further away from the family home, because of a lack of local places or other factors outside the family's control, the circumstances are likely to satisfy the 'necessary' test of s.509(1) (*R. v. East Sussex County Council ex p. D* (1991) COD 374; *R. v. Essex County Council ex p. C* [1994] ELR 54, see 65G, and [1994] ELR 273, CA).

The Court of Appeal has concluded that parental preference was one of the factors which the LEA was obliged to take into account, but that it would not be determinative in the subjective consideration of whether the provision of transport was 'necessary' or not. On that basis, it would appear difficult to mount any form of meaningful challenge to an LEA's refusal to provide transport, where the requirement for transport arises through the attendance of the child at a particular school where a place in a school closer to home is available.

However, as set out above, the statute requires the LEA specifically to consider those parents who express a particular preference, based on their wish for their child to attend at a school which provides a particular religious education, or which has a particular religious ethos. The logical interpretation of this part of the legal framework would appear to require LEAs to give greater weight to a parental preference based on a particular religious adherence than to parental preference based on other grounds, which may be of equal importance to the family. However, we have already seen in the operation of the HRA 1998 and ECHR, First Protocol, Article 2 in relation to admissions, an acknowledgement of the weight which must be given to a parent's desire for the education of his/her child in a particular religious environment (*R. (on the application of K)* v. *Newham London Borough Council* [2002] ELR 390, paras. 29, 38). An LEA will therefore need to consider very carefully these particular factors, amongst others, when reaching their decision.

Special educational needs

Where a particular school, either independent or maintained, is named in Part 4 of a child's statement of SEN, the LEA must provide assistance with transport if asked to do so. The transport costs associated with pupils with SEN can be as high, or sometimes higher, than the cost of the school placement itself. However, even when expensive transport arrangements may potentially be put in place, the LEA (and ultimately the court or tribunal) must be satisfied that the transport provided is not stressful (*R.* v. *Hereford and Worcester County Council ex p. P* [1992] 2 FLR 207).

It is not uncommon for parents to reach agreement with LEAs resulting in a child with SEN being placed within a school which the parents prefer, subject to the parents agreeing to meet the transport costs. The difficulties inherent with this type of situation, were considered in *R.* v. *Havering London Borough Council ex p. K* [1998] ELR 402. In that decision, Sedley J made clear that the matter would have to be fully reconsidered. However, the court did not take the view that, in the absence of the parents' ability to continue to provide transport, even where the cause was genuine and outside parental control, the LEA became automatically responsible in meeting the additional costs arising from those circumstances. The matter would therefore need to be reconsidered, taking into account the child's circumstances at the time.

Policy changes

The courts have recognised that where LEA transport policies change the parents have a legitimate expectation to be consulted over the new transport proposals (*R.* v. *Rochdale Metropolitan Borough Council ex p. Schemet* [1994] ELR 89). However, although LEAs are obliged to consult over proposed substantive changes, the ultimate arbitrator of strategic policy will remain the LEA.

10.6 REMEDIES

The particular circumstances of the case will determine the most appropriate remedy. Remedies include:

(a) judicial review, which will be the most useful remedy in the majority of cases. The issues which arise for determination are likely to fall within a public law remit, as they are likely to concern the lawfulness of the LEA's decision-making process and exercise or fettering of discretion, and to have a significant degree of urgency. Within judicial review proceedings, particularly where publicly funded, consideration must always be given to mediation (see *R. (on the application of Cowl) v. Plymouth County Council* [2002] 1 WLR 803). The principles in respect of judicial review set out in other chapters apply. However, the need to act promptly (i.e. within days or weeks *not* months) cannot be overemphasised;

(b) complaint to the Secretary of State for Education which, whilst an option, may be extremely slow and unsuited to both the issues under consideration and the timescales within which a decision is needed (a recent complaint had not been determined within nine months);

(c) complaint to the local authority and/or local authority monitoring officer;

(d) applying for exercise of the local authority's discretionary power under s.509(3).

10.7 PUBLIC FUNDING

Public funding is available to pursue a claim for judicial review, subject to the appropriate means test. The issue of standing may be relevant as a defendant may seek to argue that a claim brought and publicly funded in the name of the child seeks to abuse the system by circumnavigating the likelihood of the parents not qualifying for public funding.

For the reasons considered above, the authors' view is that the child will be the proper claimant in the majority of cases, and therefore public funding, supported by counsel's opinion if necessary, should be sought. The benefit provided by school transport to an individual pupil or student would make any necessary application proportionate.

Investigative help in relation to other remedies may be available.

APPENDIX A

Particulars of claim

IN THE HIGH COURT OF JUSTICE   Claim No.
QUEEN'S BENCH DIVISION
BETWEEN:

                                                 Claimant

and

                                                Defendants

PARTICULARS OF CLAIM

1. The Claimant was born on [*date*]. At all material times the Claimant was a child with special educational needs within the meaning of the Education Acts 1981, 1993 and 1996.
2. The First Defendant was at all material times the local education authority responsible for the Claimant's education, within London Borough of [*name*], by reason of its statutory duties under the Education Acts 1944, 1981, 1993 and 1996, for, *inter alia*, identifying any child with special educational needs, determining the special educational provision which should be made for him/her, maintaining, where necessary, a statement of his/her needs and arranging that the special educational provision specified in any statement was made. The First Defendant was also under a duty when making an assessment of special educational needs to seek written advice from, *inter alia*, the child's parents, teachers, medical practitioners and psychologists.
3. Throughout the period of operation of its statutory duties in respect of the Claimant, the First Defendant owed to the Claimant a duty of care in the conduct of its employees or agents, who offered specialist and/or professional help, in the form of advice and assistance to the Claimant and the Claimant's parents. In particular, in fulfilling the requirements of its duty of care, the First Defendant owed the Claimant a duty in assessing and diagnosing his special educational needs, in determining the appropriate response to the Claimant's special educational needs and in arranging special educational provision for the Claimant. The employees or agents of the First Defendant, who were employed

APPENDIX A

by the First Defendant to provide those services, owed the Claimant a duty of care when carrying out their duties in accordance with their employment. The First Defendant was and is vicariously liable for the negligence of its employees or agents, acting in the course of their employment by the First Defendant.

4. In particular, the First Defendant was vicariously liable for the negligence of its employees and/or agents acting in the course of their employment as educational psychologists, within the First Defendant's educational psychology service for the London Borough of [*name*], whose specific duties involved assessing and determining the Claimant's special educational needs. The First Defendant is and was at all material times vicariously liable for the negligence of its employees and/or agents, acting in the course of their employment as Education Officers for the Defendant.

5. Further, both Defendants were vicariously liable for the negligence of their employees and/or agents who were employed by the Defendants as school teachers and/or head teachers. Further, both Defendants, through their employees or agents, including school teachers and/or head teachers, owed a duty to the Claimant to take reasonable steps to achieve progress in respect of any identified and/or potential special educational needs which the Claimant experienced, and to advise the Claimant's parents on the nature of the Claimant's difficulties and/or any appropriate referral and/or other actions necessary in respect of the Claimant.

6. Throughout the Claimant's education until the events pleaded below, the Claimant's parents relied upon the advice and information offered by the said schools in respect of the Claimant. At all material times the Claimant's parents relied upon the professional care and skill of the Defendants' employees and/or agents in determining what, if any, provision was necessary to develop the Claimant's basic educational skills and/or ameliorate any special educational needs experienced by the Claimant, until they realised the said advice was wrong and negligent.

7. Between 1986 and 1996 the Claimant attended the following schools:
[*list schools*]
Thereafter, the Claimant was not offered a school place and received no educational input at all, until he commenced part-time attendance at the Tuition Centre, maintained by the First Defendant, where he completed his education, until [ ]. The Claimant was made the subject of a statement of special educational needs, dated [*date*], which provided for him to be educated within a mainstream school environment, with the support of a learning support teacher for six hours each week.

8. During his primary education it became apparent that the Claimant was exhibiting difficulties in acquiring academic skills and displaying difficulties with behaviour, concentration, and attention. The Claimant's mother drew the Claimant's difficulties with acquiring basic literacy and numeracy skills to the attention of his primary and secondary schools on a number of occasions, during parents evenings and meetings. During his primary education the Claimant was not referred, by his schools, to an educational psychologist and/or any other external specialist teaching service, whether maintained by the First Defendant or otherwise.

9. The Claimant was referred for an assessment of his basic skills by an education social worker in the first half of 1994, while attending [*name*] School. As a result, the Claimant was assessed by an educational psychologist employed by the Defendant, at a chronological age of approximately 11 years 6 months. However, the educational psychologist did not produce a report or communicate any recommendations in respect of the Claimant to his parents or school. The Claimant was referred to and attended the Project, where he was assessed by

PARTICULARS OF CLAIM

[name], a teacher who concluded that the Claimant had specific learning difficulties/dyslexia. At approximately 12 years 3 months of age, the Claimant was assessed as reading at a 6 year 9 month level.
10. In December [year] the Claimant transferred to [name] School, a mainstream secondary school, maintained by the First Defendant. A statutory assessment of the Claimant was initiated in December [year] and the Claimant was assessed by [name], an educational psychologist employed by the First Defendant, in [month] and [month], who produced a report dated [date].
11. On assessment the Claimant demonstrated retardations of between 7 years 5 months and 6 years 4 months behind his chronological age of 13 years 6 months in literacy. His numeracy does not appear to have been the subject of assessment.
12. The Claimant was permanently excluded from [name] School on 2 February 1996.
13. The Claimant did not receive any education until [date], when he was offered and accepted a part-time place at a pupil referral unit, the Tuition Centre. No further or better details can be given pending discovery.
14. The Claimant has undertaken and continues to undertake further education courses. He has had and continues to experience problems with all aspects of his further education due to his lack of literacy and numeracy skills and poor language skills.
15. Throughout the period 1986–1999 the Claimant was a pupil of average intellectual ability, whose primary special educational needs were his severe specific learning difficulties, speech and language difficulties, and consequent need for an appropriately modified curriculum and differentiated educational opportunities to enable him to develop basic literacy and numeracy skills, language skills and to address his consequential emotional and/or behavioural problems.
16. Had his class teachers, head teachers and/or other teachers/professionals identified the Claimant as a pupil whose marked and increasing under-achievement warranted the need for further referral and/or investigation of the nature of his difficulties, and/or diagnosed his specific learning difficulties and/or disabilities, and/or acted upon the possibility that the Claimant experienced language skills difficulties, and/or recommended appropriate education and/or treatment to ameliorate those difficulties, the Claimant could and should have been provided with specialist structured tuition and therapy and support, which would have addressed his specific learning difficulties, language difficulties and any consequent emotional and/or associated problems. Had this course been adopted the Claimant would have overcome his specific learning difficulties and language difficulties either entirely, or to a much greater extent than has been the case to date, and would have done so sooner and would not have developed the level of consequential emotional and/or behavioural difficulty he experienced.

PARTICULARS OF NEGLIGENCE

17. The Defendant and its servants or agents were negligent in that they:
    (a) failed between [date] and [date] to correctly diagnose the Claimant's specific learning difficulties/dyslexia and/or the full cause of his underperformance at school. Following diagnosis in [month and year] by [name], there was failure on the part of [name] School and [name] School to take appropriate action to address the Claimant's difficulties, by way of further referral and/or provision within school;
    (b) failed to recommend that the Claimant be the subject of referral and/or further investigation and/or assessment and/or receive specific specialist

APPENDIX A

provision. In particular, by the Claimant's primary school head teachers and teachers, in failing to refer the Claimant for assessment by the Defendant's educational psychology service and/or another specialist referral service as the Claimant was underperforming at all, and by his secondary schools, in failing to refer him for assessment by an educational psychologist/for statutory assessment until [*date*];

(c) failed through the assessment processes between [*date*] and [*date*] to prescribe appropriate remediation in respect of the Claimant's specific learning difficulties/dyslexia;

(d) failed to conduct an assessment of the Claimant by an educational psychologist between the periods September [*year*] and December [*year*]. In particular, by the Claimant's teachers in failing to act upon the parental concerns expressed during that period;

(e) failed through the assessment of educational psychologist in [*month and year*], to provide a report or information in respect of the assessment and/or to act on the outcome of the assessment;

(f) failed through the assessment of [*name*] to conduct a full and competent assessment of the Claimant's difficulties, and/or failed to make appropriate recommendations as to how to address the Claimant's difficulties, and/or negligently failed to produce a report until 13 months after the completion of the assessment;

(g) failed to produce a statement of special educational needs within a reasonable time-scale and further failed to produce an adequate or appropriate statement of special educational needs which properly defined the Claimant's needs and the necessary provision to meet his needs;

(h) failed to arrange for the Claimant to attend a mainstream school on a full-time basis between [*date*] and [*date*];

(i) failed to arrange for any, or any adequate, programmes to ameliorate the Claimant's specific learning difficulties and/or language problems to be devised, instituted, implemented and monitored for the Claimant between [*date*] and [*date*], or thereafter through the Tuition Centre;

(j) failed to assess properly, or at all, the Claimant's difficulties and/or to appreciate the nature and extent of the Claimant's difficulties, in particular, failing to identify the need for referral to a speech and language therapist for assessment and diagnosis of the nature of the Claimant's difficulties;

(k) failed to monitor and review adequately the Claimant's learning difficulties properly or at all and/or failed to appreciate the significance of the relatively worsening retardations exhibited by the Claimant over time during his attendance as a pupil at both primary and secondary school and at the Tuition Centre;

(l) failed to make any, or any adequate, level of specialist and/or other learning support available to the Claimant, throughout his educational career between [*date*] and [*date*].

By reason of the particulars of negligence, the Claimant has suffered injury, loss and damage.

PARTICULARS OF INJURY, LOSS AND DAMAGE

18. The Claimant has and continues to suffer from severe specific learning difficulties and speech and language difficulties, together with emotional vulnerability

and social difficulties. The Claimant has little self-confidence or sense of self-esteem. The Claimant has suffered severe retardation in all basic learning skills as a result of the failure to address his special educational needs. If his condition had been correctly diagnosed and/or if recommendations for further assessment had been made, appropriate remedial treatment could have been instituted and his educational handicap, together with the consequential emotional problems and low self-esteem, would have been substantially ameliorated. In particular, the relatively worsening retardations, which occurred between [*date*] and [*date*] would have been avoided, and the Claimant's problems would have been addressed within his primary and secondary school environments. The Claimant would not have lost the educational opportunities during his period out of education from [*date*] and thereafter. The Claimant would not have experienced the widening gap between his skills age and chronological age, together with his reduced prospect of successfully undertaking public examination courses and/or of undertaking further and higher educational courses within his range of overall cognitive ability, and/or adequately and sufficiently ameliorating his difficulties, due to the failure to diagnose and treat the Claimant's difficulties at a sufficiently early stage.
19. The Claimant will rely upon the report served herein in compliance with CPR Practice Direction 15, para. 4.3.

PARTICULARS OF DAMAGE

20. The Claimant's losses are set out in the attached schedule of expenses and losses attached to the particulars of claim in compliance with CPR Practice Direction 15, para. 4.2.
21. The Claimant claims and is entitled to interest pursuant to Supreme Court Act 1981, s.35A:
    (a) on general damages at such rate and for such period as the court shall deem just;
    (b) on special damages at the full rate in the special circumstances that earnings have been lost and expenses incurred on the Claimant's behalf, which will be irrecoverable from the Defendant until the trial of this matter.

AND THE CLAIMANT CLAIMS:

(i) Damages.
(ii) Interest as pleaded in para. 29 above.

This claim concerns personal injury and other damage sustained by the Claimant and has a value in excess of £50,000.

STATEMENT OF TRUTH

The Claimant believes that the facts stated in these oarticulars of claim are true. I am duly authorised by the Claimant to sign this Statement.

Signed ....

Dated ....
Claimant's Solicitors

APPENDIX B

Special educational needs: reasons for appeal

IN THE SPECIAL EDUCATIONAL NEEDS AND DISABILITY TRIBUNAL

APPEAL NUMBER

[*Child's name*] (DOB: [*date*])

APPEAL AGAINST FINAL STATEMENT OF SPECIAL EDUCATIONAL NEEDS ISSUED BY COUNTY COUNCIL DATED [*date*] AND RECEIVED [*date*]

REASONS FOR APPEAL

1. Mr and Mrs [*name*] appeal against Parts 2, 3 and 4 of [*child*]'s statement of special educational needs issued by [*name*] Council on [*date*].
2. There has been a period of considerable delay on the part of the LEA in this case. A statutory reassessment of [*child*]'s educational needs was commenced on [*date*]; a proposed amended statement of special educational needs was issued by the LEA on [*date*]. On [*date*], Mrs [*name*] responded to that statement yet it was not until we wrote to [*name*] Council on [*date*] that the LEA issued a final statement.
3. The LEA received a letter from the head teacher of [*name*] School dated [*date*], which stated 'I would strongly argue that [*name*] School would not be an appropriate placement for [*child*] as we are unable to ensure that she is able to maintain her skills and to support her in developing to her potential as she grows older'. Faced with this evidence, the LEA effectively did nothing for a further five months.
4. Due to the severity and complexity of [*child*]'s needs, the local authority's social services department currently funds 85 nights respite care per annum for [*child*] within [*name*], which is a specialist respite centre at a cost of £370 per night.
5. In relation to Part 2 'Special educational needs', this will need to be changed to reflect:
    - the fact that she has congenital abnormalities which have caused delayed development;

SPECIAL EDUCATIONAL NEEDS: REASONS FOR APPEAL

- the fact that she finds it extremely difficult to initiate any functional motor movement and all areas of daily function are affected;
- the fact that she is too large to be lifted by one person;
- the fact that her posture is deteriorating and scoliosis has developed;
- the fact that she is unable to dress herself and has no self-help skills at all;
- the fact that she is totally dependent on others for all aspects of physical living, learning and comfort.

A summary of her specific educational needs at the end of Part 2 will be required. In relation to Part 3 'Special educational provision objectives': these will be need to be amended to reflect the changed description of [*child*]'s needs in Part 2 of her statement.

6. In relation to Part 3 – 'Educational provision to meet needs and objectives':

    (a) This section should be deleted completely. It does not comply with paragraph 8:37 of the SEN Code of Practice. No specific levels of provision are specified (see *L* v. *Clarke and Somerset County Council* [1998] ELR 129, QBD).

    (b) Although a draft statement of special educational needs will be produced in advance of the hearing and circulated to the LEA and tribunal for use as a working document at the hearing, which will contain details of all amendments sought to the statement in terms of Parts 2, 3 and 4, this section of [*child*]'s statement should include the following:

    – provision for [*child*] to be placed in a residential school specialising in the education of children with complex special needs which is able to offer a holistic and seamless approach to her difficulties and to allow her educational needs to be dealt with as a whole so as to ensure that she can make educational progress;
    – the specification of an environment which has a high staff to pupil ratio and very small classes, and which is able to provide a structured and protective environment;
    – the need for a risk assessment of her needs to be carried out, particularly having regard to her lack of movement and need for additional adult support when bathing, going to the toilet, etc.;
    – provision for social interaction opportunities, including group cooperative work with adult support;
    – the use of non-verbal signals used by an adult to encourage and sustain concentration;
    – the provision of on-site speech and language therapy delivered by a speech and language therapist on a one-to-one and group basis. Further evidence as to the precise amount of input required will be provided in advance of the hearing;
    – for [*child*] to receive access to the National Curriculum appropriately modified to take account of her individual needs;
    – the provision of special programmes of study to provide the most appropriate method of communication including a specific augmentative communication system (further evidence as to this will be given at the hearing) and other alternative methods of augmentative communication;
    – on-site occupational therapy and physiotherapy delivered by an appropriately qualified paediatric occupational therapist and physiotherapist to address [*child*]'s fine and gross motor difficulties. Details of the precise levels of therapy being sought will be made available in due course. [*child*] will also require hydrotherapy on at least a weekly basis;

APPENDIX B

- a class group chosen on the basis of age, ability and personality in order to ensure a cohesive and compatible group;
- for all teachers to be empathetic and experienced in dealing with children who have complex motor and communication difficulties;
- for the provision of a programme to develop toileting, eating, dressing and other aspects of personal independence;
- for the provision of a programme to develop her ability to control her attention and to respond to the direction of an adult;
- for a learning activity programme to be provided to improve [*child*]'s concentration time;
- for the school to be able to provide an on-site rehabilitation and engineering unit able to tailor, make, adapt and modify postural equipment and to ensure that [*child*]'s postural management needs are met throughout the day in terms of sitting, lying, and standing;
- for [*child*] to be provided with a powered wheelchair together with access to on-site maintenance, as well as being taught how to drive this, thereby increasing her independent mobility and ability to explore her environment;
- for the school to be able to provide a tracking system extending around the school in order to assist pupils in modified powered wheelchairs to develop early driving and switch skills, spatial awareness and independence of movement;
- for the school to be able to provide a multi-sensory room;
- for [*child*] to be able to use an on-site riding centre to improve independence skills;
- for [*child*] to be provided with music therapy;
- for [*child*] to be provided with monitoring and advice from an expert in visual impairment or qualified teacher of the visually impaired who will also provide on-going advice to teaching staff;
- access to on-site or nearby medical expertise which is able to ensure care of her gastrostomy and which can provide assistance with gastrostomy feeding, where there can be ongoing monitoring of her spinal curvature (scoliosis), access to orthopaedic advice and access to further medical advice for management of other complications arising from her physical difficulties, e.g. the recent inflammation of her knees.

7. In relation to Part 4 – Placement:
   (a) The LEA states that [*child*]'s needs can be met in 'a day special school able to meet the needs of pupils with physical difficulties and severe learning difficulties'.
   (b) A day placement is no longer appropriate for [*child*] but, in any event, there is no school locally or within day travel from distance of home which is able to provide the considerable levels of provision which [*child*] needs.
   (c) For all these reasons therefore, Mr and Mrs [*name*] propose that [*name*] School be named in Part 4 of [*child*]'s statement of special educational needs on the basis that it can meet all her needs as identified in this provision.

APPENDIX C

Special educational needs: parental statement to SENDIST

IN THE SPECIAL EDUCATIONAL NEEDS AND DISABILITY TRIBUNAL

APPEAL NO

IN THE MATTER OF THE EDUCATION OF
[*child*]

PARENTAL CASE STATEMENT

1. Attached to this case statement are the following additional documents, which supplement the information already lodged with our reasons for appeal:

    (a) interim report of [*name*], educational psychologist, dated [*date*];
    (b) report of [*name*], speech and language therapist, dated [*date*];
    (c) prospectus in relation to [*name*] School;
    (d) the most recent Ofsted inspection report in relation to [*name*] School;
    (e) national care standards inspection report in relation to [*name*] School;
    (f) completed provision of place form in respect of [*name*] School.

2. The report of [*name*]; educational psychologist, confirms the views of [*name*], LEA educational psychologist, concerning both the extent and severity of [*child*]'s difficulties and his resistance to testing.

3. However, notwithstanding those concerns, on a day-to-day basis, even within the specialist environment of [*name*] School, [*child*] presents as a boy with severe and entrenched dyslexia (see para 2.2.2 of the report). In the view of [*name*]:

    > [*child*] has made good progress in all areas during his time ... but it is slow and laboured; however, the intense revision and structure would seem to be essential for [*child*] to continue to progress.
    >
    > Mrs [*name*] notes that [*child*] needs a lot of support and attention. Consolidation tasks can now be carried out independently by [*child*] but one-to-one support or small group support is often needed for most other tasks. [*child*] needs sessions on a weekly, and daily if possible, basis with the school's motor development specialists and these sessions really do seem to help him concentrate. He will often return to lessons more focused and ready to work.

4. The speech and language therapist's report identifies [*child*]'s language difficulties and their impact on his general functioning, as well as his acquisition of literacy skills.

APPENDIX C

5. [*child*]'s emotional response to testing is identified by the educational psychologist throughout her report (see, e.g., paras. 3.2 and 3.11).
6. The educational psychologist concluded that the complexity and severity of [*child*]'s needs could not be properly analysed within her initial assessment and is scheduled to revisit [*child*] in [*month*] 2005. In addition, appointments were made for [*child*] to see an occupational therapist and a speech and language therapist, and those reports will be submitted to SENDIST and served on the LEA, as soon as they are available pursuant to reg. 33 of the Special Educational Needs Tribunal Regulations 2001, SI 2001/600.
7. Based on the current available evidence, [*child*] has thrived within the small specialist and supportive environment that [*name*] School offers and it is difficult to envisage, on analysing all the available information, how his needs could be met with any lesser level of provision.
8. We will attempt to liaise with the LEA and ensure that insofar as possible, issues arising in respect of Parts 2, 3 and 4 of [*child*]'s statement are resolved in advance of the scheduled hearing in this matter. In order to expedite that process, we will ensure that any additional information is served on the LEA directly, as well as filed with SENDIST.

APPENDIX D

Exclusion: grounds of appeal to the independent appeal panel

BETWEEN:

N

Appellant

v

BOARD OF GOVERNORS OF S SCHOOL

Opponent

GROUNDS OF APPEAL AGAINST PERMANENT EXCLUSION OF M FROM S SCHOOL

1. The Appellant challenges the validity of the head teacher's letter dated 6 February 2004 which communicates the decision to exclude permanently.
2. M was excluded from the school originally on 15 January 2004 for a fixed-term period of 35 days. Attached to these Grounds of Appeal is a copy of the decision letter dated 15 January 2004. The exclusion was imposed in response to an incident which occurred on 12 January 2004 and which is detailed in an incident report. The exclusion letter dated 15 January 2004 made no reference to the head teacher conducting any further investigations and gave no indication that the 35-day fixed-term exclusion was anything other than the finite sanction for the incident. Having made a decision to punish M with a 35-day fixed-term exclusion, it was not then open to the head teacher to impose a permanent exclusion for the same incident; this was effectively an attempt to punish M twice.
3. Paragraph 12(a) of the DfES Guidance, 'Improving Behaviour and Attendance: Guidance on Exclusion from Schools and Pupil Referral Units' requires the head teacher to conduct a thorough investigation before making a decision to exclude. It is submitted that the subsequent decision to exclude permanently would only have been valid if the initial decision to exclude for a fixed-term period was imposed on the condition that there were further investigations with a view to a final decision being made on the ultimate sanction.
4. M accepts that his behaviour was below standard; however, he believes that there are strong mitigating circumstances, details of which will be provided to the independent appeal panel in submissions.

APPENDIX D

5. The incident arose in response to an attack upon M's younger brother E, on 12 January 2004. There were therefore circumstances of provocation. It is also the Appellant's contention that the school could have taken more proactive preventative steps to avoid a confrontation between M and the victim.
6. Prior to 15 January 2004, M had never been excluded from school either on a fixed-term basis or permanently. The Appellant submits that his behaviour was out of character and due to the extreme circumstances of the day in question. For this reason, he believes that a 35-day exclusion was adequate and that a permanent exclusion is disproportionate.
7. M is deeply remorseful for his actions and made this clear during the hearing before the governing body. In light of his remorse and the issues outlined above, the Appellant believes that it would be just and equitable for the independent appeal panel to overturn the permanent exclusion.
8. Further grounds to follow.

APPENDIX E

Exclusion: judicial review – claim form

Judicial Review
Claim Form

In the High Court of Justice
Administrative Court

Notes for guidance are available which explain how to complete the judicial review claim form. Please read them carefully before you complete the form.

For Court use only	
Administrative Court Reference No.	
Date filed	

Seal

SECTION 1 Details of the claimant(s) and defendant(s)

Claimant(s) name and address(es)
- name: M (by his litigation friend and father N)
- address: 20 Fet Road, Barley, N22 3HP
- Telephone no.:
- Fax no.:
- E-mail address:

Claimant's or claimant's solicitors' address to which documents should be sent.
- name: Roach Solicitors
- address: 40 Fet Road, Barley, N22 3HW
- Telephone no.: 29050 39229
- Fax no.: 29050 38511
- E-mail address: roachsolicitors@oar.co.uk

Claimant's Counsel's details
- name: Sarah Huges
- address: Mark Chambers, Temple Court, Barley, N22 9PD
- Telephone no.: 29050 333333
- Fax no.: 29050 232323
- E-mail address: sarahhuges@plt.co.uk

1st Defendant
- name: Independent appeal panel of X County Council

Defendant's or (where known) Defendant's solicitors' address to which documents should be sent.
- name: Havey Solicitors
- address: 20 Darland Road, Harley, P2 2RF
- Telephone no.: 09529 20202020
- Fax no.: 09529 2393956
- E-mail address:

2nd Defendant
- name: X County Council

Defendant's or (where known) Defendant's solicitors' address to which documents should be sent.
- name: Harvey Solicitors
- address: 20 Darland Road, Harley, P2 2RF
- Telephone no.: 09529 202020
- Fax no.: 09529 2393966
- E-mail address:

N461 Judicial review claim form (03.02)

The Court Service Publications Branch

APPENDIX E

SECTION 2 Details of other interested parties

Include name and address and, if appropriate, details of DX, telephone or fax numbers and e-mail

name

address

Telephone no.   Fax no.

E-mail address

name

address

Telephone no.   Fax no.

E-mail address

SECTION 3 Details of the decision to be judicially reviewed

Decision:
1. Decision of IAP to uphld a permanent exclusion
2. Breach of s.19 Education Act 1996

Date of decision:
1. 21 June 2004
2. Continuing breach.

Name and address of the court, tribunal, person or body who made the decision to be reviewed.

name

address

SECTION 4 Permission to proceed with a claim for judicial review

I am seeking permission to proceed with my claim for Judicial Review.

Are you making any other applications? If Yes, complete Section 7.	☐ Yes	☑ No
Is the claimant in receipt of a Community Legal Service Fund (CLSF) certificate?	☑ Yes	☐ No
Are you claiming exceptional urgency, or do you need this application determined within a certain time scale? If Yes, complete Form N463 and file this with your application.	☑ Yes	☐ No
Have you complied with the pre-action protocol? If No, give reasons for non-compliance in the space below.	☑ Yes	☐ No

Does the claim include any issues arising from the Human Rights Act 1998? If Yes, state the articles which you contend have been breached in the space below.   ☑ Yes   ☐ No

Article 2 of the first protocol

190

EXCLUSION: JUDICIAL REVIEW – CLAIM FORM

SECTION 5 Detailed statement of grounds

☐ set out below ☑ attached

SECTION 6 Details of remedy (including any interim remedy) being sought

See attached

SECTION 7 Other applications

I wish to make an application for:-

APPENDIX E

IN THE HIGH COURT OF JUSTICE
QUEEN'S BENCH DIVISION
ADMINISTRATIVE COURT

BETWEEN:

M

(A minor, suing by his father and litigation friend N)

Claimant

and

(1) INDEPENDENT APPEAL PANE OF X COUNTY COUNCIL
(2) X COUNTY COUNCIL

Defendants

Draft Order

Upon reading the Claim Form, the grounds of review, the application for urgent consideration

AND Upon reading the witness statement of N

IT IS ORDERED THAT:

(1) The Claimant be given permission to move for judicial review
   (a) On the breach of s19 provision and/or
   (b) On the permanent exclusion from school
(2) The Claimant be provided with full time education suitable to his age, aptitude and special educational needs from the commencement of the school term in September 2004 by the Defendant.
(3) The Defendant do be given 14 day to file and serve its acknowledgement of service from today.
(4) Both parties to file and serve any evidence by 31st August 2004.
(5) The matter is listed for a substantive hearing on or before 15 September 2004 with a time estimate of one day.
(6) This matter is certified fit for vacation business.
(7) This case be subject to a Reporting restriction under section 39 of the CYPA 1969 and CPR 39.2 apply in relation to the Claimant and his litigation friend, who are hereafter to be referred to "M" and "N".
(8) Costs reserved.
(9) Detailed assessment of the Claimant's legal costs subject to paragraph 4 of the CLS Funding Order 2000.

EXCLUSION: JUDICIAL REVIEW – CLAIM FORM

SECTION 8 Statement of facts relied on

Statement of Truth

I believe (The claimant believes) that the facts stated in this claim form are true.

Full name _Charlotte Mary Brown_

Name of claimant's solicitor's firm _Roach Solicitors_

Signed _C.Brown_ Position or office held _Solicitor_
   Claimant ('s solicitor)   (if signing on behalf of firm or company)

APPENDIX E

SECTION 9 Supporting documents

If you do not have a document that you intend to use to support your claim, identify it, give the date when you expect it to be available and give reasons why it is not currently available in the box below.

Please tick the papers you are filing with this claim form and any you will be filing later.

☐ Statement of grounds	☐ included	☑ attached
☐ Statement of the facts relied on	☐ included	☑ attached
☐ Application to extended the time limit for filing the claim form	☐ included	☐ attached
☐ Application for directions	☐ included	☐ attached

☑ Any written evidence in support of the claim or application to extend time

☐ Where the claim for judicial review relates to a decision of a court or tribunal, an approved copy of the reasons for reaching that decision

☑ Copies of any documents on which the claimant proposes to rely

☑ A copy of the legal aid or CSLF certificate *(if legally represented)*

☑ Copies of any relevant statutory material

☑ A list of essential documents for advance reading by the court *(with page references to the passages relied upon)*

Reasons why you have not supplied a document and date when you expect it to be available:-

The CLSLF Certificate will be lodged once received from the Legal Services Commission

Signed __C. Brown__ Claimant ('s Solicitor)_____

APPENDIX F

Exclusion: judicial review – application for urgent consideration

Judicial Review
Application for urgent consideration

This form must be completed by the Claimant or the Claimant's advocate if exceptional urgency is being claimed and the application needs to be determined within a certain time scale.

The claimant, or the claimant's solicitors must serve this form on the defendant(s) and any interested parties with the N461 Judicial review claim form.

To the Defendant(s) and Interested party(ies)
Representations as to the urgency of the claim may be made by defendants or interested parties to the Administrative Court Office by fax - 020 7947 6802

In the High Court of Justice Administrative Court	
Claim No.	
Claimant(s) *(including ref.)*	M (by his litigation friend and father N)
Defendant(s)	1. Independent Appeal Panel of X 2. X County Council
Interested Parties	

SECTION 1 Reasons for urgency

The Claimant is a 15 year old boy who has been permanently excluded from school. He is due to go into Year 11 in September 2004. He is halfway through his GCSE courses. He was permanently excluded from school on 15th January 2004. From this date until 22nd June 2004, he was being educated at N Unit. The Independent Appeal Panel met on 21st June 2004 and upheld his exclusion. On 22nd June 2004, he tried to attend the Unit and was told that it could no longer educate him. Since that date, the Claimant has not received any education whatsoever, and has not been offered any alternative. The authority wrote at the beginning of July 2004 indicating that they wanted to abide by their commitment to provide alternative education, but have offered nothing for September 2004 and have done no more than provide the Claimant with a list of schools out of the area to which he can apply.

It is essential that the Claimant receives full time education from September 2004, in order to ensure that he can continue with his GCSE courses and make the most of them. The authority have had over 5 months to plan his integration into an alternative educational environment, but have done nothing. They are in flagrant breach of statutory duty and the relevant guidance.

Interim provision should be put in place for his return to school in September 2004. This matter must be dealt with, at least on an interim basis, by the beginning of September 2004 so that the Claimant can have some education.

SECTION 2 Proposed timetable *(tick the boxes and complete the following statements that apply)*

[✓] a) The N461 application for permission should be considered within _____5_____ hours/(days)

[✓] b) Abridgement of time is sought for the lodging of acknowledgements of service

[✓] c) If permission for judicial review is granted, a substantive hearing is sought by 15th September 2004 _____ (date)

APPENDIX F

SECTION 3 Interim relief *(state what interim relief is sought and why in the box below)*

A draft order must be attached.

The Claimant seeks the following interim relief:
1. A mandatory order compelling the Defendant to provide the Claimant with full-time educational provison in Key Stage 4 from the start of the schol term in September 2004 and to provide him with an appropriate school placement and/or other alternative provision on a full-time basis which meets his educational needs (including his special educational needs).
The Claimant is currently receiving and is being offered no education at all. He has a very strong prima facie case that the authority are in breach of duty.

SECTION 4 Service

A copy of this form of application was served on the defendant(s) and interested parties as follows:

Defendant

☑ by fax machine to
Fax no. 020 8212 3454
time sent 13.10

☐ by handing it to or leaving it with
name

☐ by e-mail to
e-mail address

Date served
Date 29.7.04

Interested party

☐ by fax machine to
Fax no.
time sent

☐ by handing it to or leaving it with
name

☐ by e-mail to
e-mail address

Date served
Date

Name of claimant's advocate
name
Sarah Hughes

Claimant (claimant's advocate)
Signed
S. Hughes

APPENDIX G

Exclusion: judicial review – counsel's grounds

IN THE HIGH COURT OF JUSTICE
QUEEN'S BENCH DIVISION
ADMINISTRATIVE COURT

BETWEEN:

M

(A minor, suing by his father and litigation friend, N)

Claimant

and

(1) INDEPENDENT APPEAL PANEL OF X
(2) X County Council

Defendants

GROUNDS OF REVIEW

SUMMARY

1. This is an application for review of the decision made on 21 June 2004 by the First Defendant to uphold the permanent exclusion of M from S School made on 6 February 2004. This decision is disproportionate and unlawful.
2. Given the age of the Claimant and the nature of the case, the Claimant asks that reporting restrictions apply pursuant to Children and Young Persons Act 1933, s.39.

INTRODUCTION/FACTUAL BACKGROUND

3. The full factual background to this matter is set out in the witness statement of N and the attached exhibits (pp. 23–262). The Claimant is a 15-year-old boy who was in Year 10 at S School, maintained by the Second Defendant. He has one

APPENDIX G

year left of his compulsory schooling. He had just finished his first term of GCSE tuition when he was permanently excluded from school.

4. M was permanently excluded from school on 6 February 2004 (pp. 31–2). This was following an incident which took place on 12 January 2004, in which M had assaulted a fellow student, C. This was captured on CCTV. The assault on this student took place after C had attacked M's younger brother during the lunchtime of 12 January 2004.

5. The witness evidence gathered during the course of the investigation demonstrated that M had returned after school to assault C after having been told to go home twice by members of staff (pp. 64–6) (both of whom noticed how upset M was and what a state he was in) as C attacked his younger brother during the lunchtime of 12 January 2004.

6. The deputy head teacher, in a memorandum about the incident (pp. 49–50), specifically states that M had taken revenge because the victim had assaulted his brother earlier in the day. He mentions that the matter was recorded by CCTV.

7. The behaviour policy of the school (pp. 178–85) sets out that punishments should be fair, just and proportionate.

8. After investigation, the head teacher decided to impose a fixed-term penalty, and so excluded M for 35 days (pp. 28–9) on 15 January 2004. The head teacher does not state anywhere within that letter that this is pending further investigation or that any other penalty may emanate from this incident.

9. It was therefore a surprise to M and his father when the head teacher wrote the letter on 6 February 2004 converting this fixed-term exclusion into a permanent exclusion (pp. 31–2).

10. M's father appealed against the decision to permanently exclude his son to the governing body. Its decision was made on 5 March 2004 (p. 263). It upheld the permanent exclusion.

11. An independent appeal panel hearing was held on 21 June 2004. A witness statement from M (pp. 49–50) and submissions made by solicitors (pp. 46–8) were provided to the panel, along with extensive information from his school. It is clear from this information that M had not been the subject of previous exclusions, and that whilst his attendance was variable, his behaviour had previously been good.

12. The panel decided to uphold the permanent exclusion (pp. 332–7). In its conclusion it states:

   1. The panel considered how well the punishment fitted the crime. They acknowledged that 35 days was particularly harsh and queried whether the head teacher should have informed the parents that the exclusion period could be extended after further investigation of the incident . . . The panel agreed that, while M had no previous history of negative behaviour, the attack was premeditated and the CCTV provided very clear evidence. This was compounded by the fact that a number of teachers had advised M to let the school deal with disciplining C . . .
   2. The panel found as follows:
      (a) that, beyond a reasonable doubt, the panel was firmly satisfied that M had aggressively attacked C in a premeditated and calculated manner;
      (b) that the evidence submitted provided clear evidence of an aggressive premeditated attack. The panel noted the government guidance, which states that a school can permanently exclude a child for a one-off incident of severe violence. The panel agreed that this constituted such an incident;
      (c) that the support and strategies put in place could not reasonably have done any more to prevent this incident;
      (d) that M had not been discriminated against under the Race Relations Act 1976 or the Disability Discrimination Act 1995.

3. The panel decided that the head teacher and the Discipline Committee had reached the correct decision in deciding to permanently exclude M, and had had the appropriate regard to the Secretary of State's guidance on exclusion, and that, in these circumstances, permanent exclusion was a reasonable response.

13. The panel's notes of the hearing have been disclosed (pp. 239–44).
14. Solicitors also wrote to the authority to challenge the decision of the IAP on 1 July 2004, setting out the grounds of review (pp. 246–50). To date, no substantive response has been received at all to this letter.

THE DECISION OF THE INDEPENDENT APPEAL PANEL

15. The decision of the IAP is legally flawed as:
    (a) the panel misdirected itself on the law when dealing with whether or not the head teacher could or could not turn a temporary exclusion into a permanent exclusion in the circumstances of this case, and permitted the head teacher to act in a way which was unfair and/or a breach of substantive legitimate expectation;
    (b) the panel's action in continuing to uphold the permanent exclusion was a disproportionate punishment, in the circumstances of the case.

TEMPORARY/PERMANENT EXCLUSION

16. The head teacher behaved in an unfair manner, and exceeded her powers in turning a temporary fixed-term exclusion into a permanent exclusion, on the basis that no indication was given by the school at the time of the fixed-term exclusion that another punishment would follow. M is being punished twice for the same offence. An individual is entitled to know whether or not a temporary exclusion is or is not going to be made permanent. No such indication was given in these circumstances.
17. By virtue of Education Act 2002, s.52 and the Regulations made thereunder (the Education (Pupil Exclusion and Appeals) (Maintained Schools) (England) Regulations 2002, SI 2002/3178), the panel must have regard to the guidance issued by the Secretary of State. The relevant guidance (which has been altered for exclusions after 22 March 2004, but which remains substantively the same) is 'Improving Behaviour and Attendance: Guidance on Exclusions from Schools and Pupil Referral Units (LAC 87/03).
Part 2, para 1.9 of the guidance says as follows:

> 1.9 In exceptional cases – usually where further evidence has come to light – a fixed period exclusion may be extended or converted to a permanent exclusion. In such cases the head teacher must write again to the parents explaining the reasons for the change. The head teacher may choose to withdraw an exclusion that has not yet been reviewed by the Discipline Committee.

18. The decision of the head teacher in this case does not or cannot fall into this exception. The head teacher's decision was made after 'extensive investigation of events'. The minutes of the IAP hearing indicate the following:

> At this point, Ms M invited Ms T to address the panel and explain why she had deemed it appropriate to increase the severity of the exclusion from fixed term to permanent. Ms T addressed the panel and [refers to relevant paragraph of the Guidance] . . .

APPENDIX G

> Ms T explained that she had initially decided to exclude M for a fixed-term period of 35 days. Subsequent investigation of the incident by the school revealed evidence that suggested the attack had been premeditated and involved other children. Based on this further evidence, and after discussion with the school management team, it was decided that the exclusion should be increased from fixed term to permanent.

19. It is submitted that the circumstances described by the head teacher do not fall within the guidance set out above and/or that the guidance is incorrect in stating that such a punishment can be altered.
20. The head teacher had every opportunity to view the CCTV evidence prior to making her decision on 15 January 2004. The major facts relied upon by the head teacher were all available to her within that timescale. The recommendation of the deputy head teacher (p. 136) set out the salient facts, and she was well aware that other boys were involved. She was aware that the attack had been premeditated at the time of the original investigation. The deputy head teacher informed the head teacher that CCTV was available at the time. Furthermore, as the CCTV footage was available, the head teacher should and/or could have looked at that before making the original decision. The head teacher is under a duty to carry out an adequate investigation before making her decision: she cannot decide, after having not made such an investigation when given an opportunity to do so, to reopen matters and change her mind.
21. What fairness demands depends upon the context in which it is being exercised. In this case, the head teacher has not exercised her powers in a fair manner. In *R.* v *Secretary of State for the Home Department ex p. Pierson* [1998] AC 539 at 591F, a case involving substitutions and changes to a prisoner's sentence, the court found that:

> ... the minimum standard of fairness does not permit a person to be punished twice for the same offence. Nor does it permit a person, once he has been told what the punishment is to be, to be given in substitution for it a more severe punishment

22. Whilst this statement relates, of course, to the circumstances before the court in that case, it is submitted that it is of general application to any case involving punishment in an administrative context.
23. Given this, it is submitted that either the guidance is incorrect, or it should be applied in a strict way to those cases where further evidence has come to light which could not have reasonably been found before the making of the original decision. Given the length of the fixed-term exclusion, it is clear that the head teacher intended this decision to be final.
24. The panel discussed this issue. The minutes of the hearing state that:

> The panel considered how well the punishment fitted the crime. It was suggested that, although the initial punishment of a 35-day fixed-term exclusion was, in itself, harsh, the school acted in accordance with the guidelines of the published behaviour policy and the guidance.
>
> A query was raised as to whether the head teacher should have informed the parents that the exclusion period could be increased after further investigation of the incident. Advice was sought from the legal advisor who stated that although there was no legal stipulation to relay this information, in the circumstances, it would have been beneficial and may be something that the panel takes into consideration.

25. The panel has clearly misdirected itself on this issue. It is manifestly unfair to substitute one punishment for another and to consider that something was 'harsh' but then provide no remedy for what it considers to be unnecessary. Had

the panel directed itself correctly, it should have overturned the exclusion in these circumstances.
26. Furthermore, the head teacher's change of mind emanated from sight of the CCTV evidence. The CCTV footage does not demonstrate an aggressive premeditated attack, rather a blur, as the actual assault is significantly obstructed by a door frame.
27. In the alternative, the Claimant has a substantive legitimate expectation that the punishment will not be altered, and that by doing so the head teacher abused her powers. Given the gravity of the offence, and the consequences of it to M, it was an abuse for her to resile from her original decision.
28. The court (see *R.* v *Dunraven ex p. B* [2000] ELR 156 at 190–4) clearly believes that exclusion proceedings should be subject to fair procedure.

PROPORTIONALITY/FAILURE TO FOLLOW GUIDANCE

29. The DfES guidance at Part 1, para. 4.1 sets out alternative strategies to be used instead of exclusion.
30. The guidance (at Part 1, para. 3.1) also finds that any investigation should look at whether the incident may have been provoked. It is clear that M's attack was provoked by the attack on C, and that, in the witness statements of the teachers who saw M immediately before the assault (pp. 61–7), he was visibly upset. M's witness statement (pp. 49–59) and evidence at the hearing (pp. 33–231) was that he had acted without thinking as a result of the attack on his little brother and he was full of remorse. The IAP decision failed to have regard to this guidance.
31. It is submitted that given M's age, previous good behavioural record, the fact that he was in the middle of his GCSE courses, the 35-day exclusion already imposed upon him, the provocation associated with this incident, and his full and frank admission of the assault and remorse for it, the panel acted in a disproportionate manner. M is also a child with special educational needs. Part 1, para. 3.2 of the DfES guidance states that a school should make every effort to avoid excluding pupils who are being supported at School Action or School Action Plus under the SEN Code of Practice. Whilst the Panel is entitled to exclude for a one-off offence (see Part 1, para. 1.4 of the guidance), this must be looked at in the light of all the other circumstances. There was no evidence presented that M's behaviour would reoccur, or that he would cause a problem if returned to the rest of the school community. The guidance must be followed, but not slavishly (see *S, T and P* v. *Brent London Borough Council* [2002] EWCA Civ 691, CA, at para. 15).
32. The incident log set out in the bundle does not disclose any previous exclusions. The report of M's head of house [*name*], states:

> Since I have been M's head of house, he has not presented any behavioural problems until he was involved in an incident that took place on 12 January 2004.

33. The guidance sets out that restorative justice or mediation can be used as an alternative to exclusion (see guidance, para. 4.1(a)). M was willing to be part of any such process. It is clear from his record that M acted totally out of character, and no evidence was placed before the panel to contradict it.
34. M is in Year 10. It is proving impossible for him to finish his education at a mainstream school. He had the advantage of a specially supported curriculum at S School. He will be significantly and severely disadvantaged and socially excluded if the permanent exclusion is not overturned. The penalty was disproportionate.

APPENDIX G

35. In *R.* v. *Newham ex p. X* [1995] ELR 105, the court indicated that exclusion decisions had to be proportionate to the offence. In *R.* v. *Governor of Bacon's City Technology College ex p. W* [1998] ELR 488 at 500B–D, the court again use the term proportionality, when deciding if the punishment given to one child was reasonable in the context of the other involved. In *R.* v. *Muntham House ex p. H* [2000] ELR 287 at 297H, the court invoked the concept of proportionality when looking at whether or not a permanent exclusion was justified.

36. The concept of proportionality has gained acceptance in the Administrative Court when looking at the imposition and use of administrative penalties (exclusion clearly falling within that ambit): see *R.* v. *Barnsley Metropolitan Borough Council ex p. Hook* [1976] 1 WLR 1052 at 1057. The court has always invoked the use of proportionality in circumstances which involve excessively onerous penalties or infringements of rights and interests and manifest imbalance of relevant considerations.

37. English law will incorporate and deal with the concept of proportionality as: (a) an appropriate balance between means and ends; or (b) something which is either necessary or the least restrictive alternative; or (c) something which is suitable.

38. Further, the ECHR provides that 'no person shall be denied the right to education' (First Protocol, Art 2). This right is in issue in exclusion cases:

    (a) the Court of Appeal regarded the assumption that permanent exclusion without good reason engaged Art 6 as 'perfectly tenable' (*S, T and P* v. *Brent London Borough Council* [2002] ELR 691, at [30]); and
    (b) unlawful exclusion can lead to damages being awarded under the Human Rights Act 1998 (*Ali* v. *The Head Teacher and Governors of Lord Grey School* [2004] EWCA Civ 382).

39. If exclusion can have these consequences under the ECHR it is appropriate to assess its lawfulness under principles deriving from the Convention (proportionality). In the alternative, the proper test under domestic law is either proportionality or a level of anxious scrutiny as to amount to a proportionality test for practical purposes (see *Ghosh* v. *General Medical Council* [2001] 1 WLR 1915, para. 34, which assessed penalty via concepts of proportionality).

40. A proportionality assessment requires the court to assess whether a decision was appropriate and necessary to a legitimate aim (*B* v. *Secretary of State for the Home Department* [2000] UKHRR 498 at 502C).

41. Proportionality may also require a court to assess the balance which the decision maker has struck, to consider the relative weight to be attached to different considerations and to subject the decision to scrutiny beyond the 'heightened scrutiny' adopted in domestic rights cases (*R.* (*on the application of Daly*) v. *Home Secretary* [2001] 2 AC 532, at 547). In the same case, Lord Cooke noted (at 549) that absence of unreasonableness in the *Wednesbury* sense should not be seen as sufficient in any field of administrative law.

42. Given the factual circumstances of this case, it was disproportionate and wrong for the IAP to uphold the permanent exclusion.

PRE-ACTION PROTOCOL LETTERS

43. The Claimant's solicitors wrote pre-action protocol letters on 1 July 2004 setting out the challenge to the IAP decision and on 6 July 2004 setting out the the EA 1996, s.19 challenge. No response at all has been received from the Defendants on the IAP issue. Holding letters were received on 7 and 9 July 2004 indicating

that a response would come in the immediate future. To date (29 July 2004) no such letter has arrived.

DELAY AND RELIEF

44. It is submitted that this claim is brought within the three-month time limit set out under CPR, r.54.5, and that it has been brought promptly. If the Honourable Court thinks otherwise, the Claimant seeks permission for this claim to be extended under CPR, r.3.1. The breach of EA 1996, s.19 is continuing in nature.

APPENDIX H

Special educational needs: appeals checklist

1. Lodge appeal within two months of receipt of decision.
2. Respond to pre-registration directions within time.
3. Arrange for assessments by experts.
4. Arrange and instruct representation.
5. Ascertain which witnesses are to attend the hearing.
6. Consider witness summons applications.
7. Obtain dates to avoid for parents/witnesses/representatives and provide these to the tribunal within time.
8. Investigate schools (Part 4 appeals), obtain placement assessments and the completed provision of place form.
9. Apply to DfES for enabling consent if applicable.
10. Draft case statement within time and attach all documents available at date of case statement expiry.
11. Consider mediation with the LEA once the LEA's case statement has been received and considered.
12. Consider drafting proposed amended statement of SEN for negotiation purposes.
13. Consider late evidence and serve late written evidence on the opponent and tribunal five working days before the hearing at least.

APPENDIX I

Draft Claim under the Disability Discrimination Act 1995 to SENDIST

IN THE SPECIAL EDUCATIONAL NEEDS AND
DISABILITY TRIBUNAL
BETWEEN:

Claim No.

MR A and MRS B	Claimants
and	
(1) C SCHOOL	
(2) A COUNTY COUNCIL	Defendants

DISABILITY DISCRIMINATION ACT 1995 CLAIM

BACKGROUND

1. Mr A and Mrs B are the parents of a pupil K who is now aged 11 years. K is a pupil with Down's syndrome. She has a statement of SEN which has been maintained by A Council since [*date*]. The statement has been amended three times.
2. K had attended at a mainstream junior school, and her parents were anxious for her to transfer to a mainstream secondary school on secondary school transfer. Having done research on appropriate schools, the Claimants were impressed by the Ofsted report on C School and the school's own publicity. They liked the opportunities for small group teaching and access to a broad curriculum which these materials indicated.
3. In May 2004, K's parents contacted C School and A Council and had a number of conversations with people including the head teacher of C School. It appeared from the conversations that initially the school was willing to take K. However, towards the end of the May prior to secondary transfer in September 2004, the school changed its mind. It told K's parents that the school was unsuitable because it had a traditional curriculum with pupils taught in large groups, very few children were withdrawn from class for specialist teaching and it had no arrangements with the local colleges for vocational courses which could be rel-

APPENDIX I

evant to K as she progressed through the school. C School was supported by A Council, which did not agree that mainstream schooling would be suitable for K.

4. The Claimants considered that the information that they had been told by C School and A Council was wrong and/or misleading, not being consistent either with published information in the Ofsted report or the school's own literature, nor with what the parents had been led to believe in conversations with the school. They entered into correspondence with A Council which eventually agreed to name the school in K's statement of SEN as her placement. An amended statement of SEN naming C School in Part 4 was issued in August prior to the September 2004 transfer.

5. The school governors were reluctant to admit K. The head teacher refused to admit K until an LSA was in place, and the governors had approved the recruitment of the LSA. Although the funding for the LSA required by K's statement of SEN had been put in place by the council in effect from September 2004, it took more than a month to place an advert for an LSA for K.

6. The school continued to refuse to admit K until an LSA who could be allocated totally to her had been recruited and was in place. Eventually a suitable LSA was recruited and the school agreed to admit K with effect from the week after half-term. As a result of C School's conduct and A Council's conduct and the failures in the previous three months, K had missed half a term of her secondary school placement. She had missed joining with other pupils who started in September 2004. As K had learning difficulties, it would be more difficult for her than other pupils to make up the lost half a term's work.

DDA 1995 CLAIM

7. The three main elements of the claim are that C School and A Council unlawfully discriminated against K in the following:

    (a) in the admission arrangements which the school operated and/or in the curriculum that 'potentially' could be offered to her;
    (b) by failing to make reasonable adjustments with a view to admitting her sooner than after half-term;
    (c) as against A Council, in failing to discharge its residual obligations as an LEA to ensure K's admission or earlier admission to the school.

8. Section 28A of DDA 1995 provides (in relevant part) as follows:

    (1) It is unlawful for the body responsible for a school to discriminate against the disabled person –

        (a) in the arrangements it makes for determining admission to the school as a pupil;
        (b) in the terms on which it offers to admit into the school as a pupil . . ..

    (2) It is unlawful for the body responsible for a school to discriminate against a disabled pupil in the education or associated services provided for, or offered to, pupils at the school by that body.

    (3) . . .

    (4) It is unlawful for the body responsible for a school to discriminate against a disabled pupil by excluding him/her from the school, either permanently or temporarily.

9. Section 28B of DDA 1995 provides (in relevant part) as follows:

    (1) For the purposes of section 28A, a responsible body discriminates against a disabled person if –

DRAFT CLAIM UNDER THE DISABILITY DISCRIMINATION ACT 1995 TO THE TRIBUNAL

(a) for a reason which related to his disability, it treats him less favourably than it treats or would treat others to whom that reason does not or would not apply; and

(b) it cannot show that the treatment in question is justified.

(2) For the purposes of section 28A, a responsible body also discriminates against a disabled person if –

(a) it fails to his detriment to comply with section 28C; and

(b) it cannot show that its failure to comply is justified.

(7) ... less favourable treatment, or a failure to comply with section 28C is justified only if the reason for it is both material to the circumstances of the particular case and substantial.

(8) If, in the case falling within subsection (1) –

(a) the responsible body is under a duty imposed by section 28C in relation to the disabled person, but

(b) it fails without justification to comply with that duty

its treatment of that person cannot be justified under subsection (7) unless that treatment would have been justified even if it had complied with that duty.

10. Section 28C of the 1995 Act provides (in relevant part) as follows:

(1) the responsible body for a school must take such steps as it is reasonable for it to take to ensure that

(a) in relation to the arrangements it makes for determining the admission of pupils to the school, disabled persons are not placed at any substantial disadvantage in comparison with persons who are not disabled; and

(b) ...

11. Sections 28F and 28G of DDA 1995 impose residual duties on LEAs not to discriminate against disabled persons in respect of the authority's functions under the Education Acts. (See ss.28F(1)(a) and 28G(2).)

12. The DDA 1995 outlaws two types of discrimination:

less favourable treatment (s.28B(1)); and (b) unjustifiable (by reference to s.28B(7) and (8)) failure to make reasonable adjustments to cater for the special needs of disabled people (s.28B(2)). In both cases, discrimination contrary to DDA 1995, s.28B can be justified only if the reason for it is both material to the circumstances of the particular case and substantial (s.28B(7)).

13. For the purposes of DDA 1995, s.28B, before the Defendant's delays in admitting K to the school can be justified, it must first be determined whether the school or the council owed her a duty to make reasonable adjustments with a view to her admission; what those adjustments were; and what the position would have been if they had made the required adjustments.

14. The Claimants submit that the school's delay in admitting K between issue of the statement naming C School and after half-term when it was finally prepared to admit K amounts to both less favourable treatment on grounds of her disability contrary to DDA 1995, s.28B(1) and also a failure to take reasonable steps contrary to s.28B(2), both of which cannot be justified under s.28B.

15. Further, the council's failure to ensure that K was admitted to school pursuant to it having been named in her statement of SEN or, alternatively, the council's failure to take reasonable steps to require the school to admit her, constitutes unjustifiable discrimination against K contrary to both DDA 1995, s.28B and the council's own residual duty provided for in DDA 1995, s.28F.

APPENDIX I

16. In support of these submissions it is put forward as follows:
    (a) The school governors did not convene with any sufficient urgency in order to be able to make arrangements for K to be admitted to the school at the beginning of the term on 2 September 2004 or as soon as possible thereafter.
    (b) The school made no, or no adequate, effort to admit K at the beginning of term or as soon as possible thereafter.
    (c) The school made no, or no adequate, attempts to provide and/or advertise for an LSA for K to enable her to start in September.
    (d) The school took no steps at all to admit K to the school on any basis such as attending part-time or subject to sharing an LSA.
    (e) The school did not even put in place a planning scheme for K until the week after half-term.
    (f) Between August 2004 and the week after half-term, the LEA knew that K had not been admitted to school but failed to act in any way to require or ensure her admission; and further failed to provide her with any alternative suitable educational provision.

EDUCATION ACT 1996 ISSUE

17. By virtue of EA 1996, s.316, children with SEN, including those such as K, who have a statement of SEN, are usually to be educated in mainstream school and the LEA must educate a child in such school where the parents so wish: see EA 1996, Sched. 27 and the SEN Code of Practice, para. 8.60.
18. By long resisting the Claimants' request for K to be educated in mainstream school and only in August 2004 naming such a school, the council has breached its statutory duty under EA 1996. The Claimants submit that in doing so the council has also breached its duties under DDA 1995, subjecting K to less favourable treatment on the grounds of her disability.
19. Further, having named a school in Part 4 of K's statement of SEN, EA 1996, s.324(5)(b) requires the school to admit K immediately or as soon as practicable thereafter. The school failed to do so, and the failure constitutes a breach of DDA 1995 as above.
20. In *R.* v *Chair of the Governors and Head Teacher of A and S School ex p. T* [2000] ELR 274, Jackson J held that it was unacceptable for a 12-year-old boy to be deprived of education for half a term because two public bodies could not agree about the interpretation of a statute. Similarly, here, at a crucial stage of her education, K was denied admission to the school for half a term. It is submitted that this constitutes a breach of EA 1996, s.324(5)(b) and DDA 1995 as set out above.

REMEDIES

21. The Claimants seek a declaration that both the school and the council subjected K to less favourable treatment and/or unjustifiably failed to take reasonable steps to accommodate her on grounds of her disability contrary to DDA 1995, ss.28A–28C and/or ss.28F and 28G.
22. Further, the Claimants request the tribunal to require the school and/or the council to make some extra provision for K, whether out of the resources made available to the school during the period she did not attend or out of extra resources, to make up for her lost education between August 2004 and the week after half-term.

APPENDIX J

Pre-action protocol letter

By post and fax

Dear Sirs

Re: [*name*] (DOB [*date*])

Proposed Claim for Judicial Review – Pre-action Protocol Letter

This letter is sent to you in accordance with the pre-action protocol for judicial review in the Administrative Court.

As we explained in our previous letter, [*name*] is the subject of a statement of SEN, maintained by [*name*] Council. His current statement is dated 12 December 2003 and was issued following a decision of SENDIST. In our earlier correspondence we expressed the view that the authority had failed properly to implement the decision of SENDIST, issued on 7 August 2003, and that the authority was failing to arrange the special education provision specified in [*name*]'s statement of SEN.

[*name*] has recently been assessed by an independent educational psychologist, speech and language therapist and consultant of assistive technology for people with disabilities. Following these assessments it is clear that he is not currently receiving the special educational provision specified in his statement of SEN.

The authority's breaches of statutory duty

- Section 324(5)(a)(i) of EA 1996 imposes a statutory duty upon a local authority to deliver the special educational provision specified in a child's statement of SEN. The authority is presently failing to deliver the special educational provision specified in Part 3 of [*name*]'s statement.
- [*Name*]'s statement specifies that he should receive:
    1. High levels of specialist teaching in literacy using structured, multi-sensory methods, delivered by experienced, trained and qualified teachers of dyslexic children (e.g. holding an RSA, specialist diploma or equivalent).

    No specialist teaching is delivered to [*name*] by an experienced, trained or qualified teacher of dyslexic children.

APPENDIX J

2. The teaching of alternative and written means of recording, including daily access to a computer/word processor and touch-typing tuition sessions on a weekly basis. A laptop computer with voice-recognition is preferential.

[Name] does not have any touch-typing tuition sessions on a weekly basis. His laptop computer has been broken for several months and it has not been mended satisfactorily. [Name]'s computer does not have a voice-recognition facility on it.

3. A carefully structured, multi-sensory approach in mathematics.

[Name] does not receive any multi-sensory teaching to address his difficulties in this area.

4. Additional support with homework. Time and support for completing homework in school will be required.

No after-school homework support is available at [name] School.

5. When planning his learning programme, the advice of an optometrist should be taken into consideration.

This has not happened.

6. Daily access to a learning skills development programme delivered by appropriately qualified or trained staff, in order to develop his visual and auditory short-term and working memory and phonological processing skills.

The school does not practise any 'learning skills development' programme.

7. Adult support to help him develop warm, trusting and secure relationships with other children, both in and outside school. This may be achieved by having access to some form of individual counselling and by participating in small group Circle Time type activities.

There are no Circle Time activities for [name]'s age-group at [name] School.

8. It is important to ensure close liaison between the occupational therapist and [name]'s school to allow for the essential carry-over of therapeutic aims and management strategies in the classroom. The LSA must implement the programme on a daily basis throughout the school year. Compensatory strategies and management of problems must be outlined.

An occupational therapy programme was written in March 2004, but this appears to be more appropriate for home use rather than school use. [Name] School has not apparently received an occupational therapy programme.

9. A programme to reduce tactile sensitivity to develop his ability to respond to the environment is to be delivered across the curriculum by his LSA.

No such programme exists at [name] School.

10. A handwriting programme is required to improve his handwriting. The advice of an occupational therapist should be sought in the planning of such a programme.

The school does not use a handwriting programme and has not sought advice from an occupational therapist concerning this provision.

11. Not less than one session of one-to-one swimming or hydrotherapy each week.

There have been difficulties in arranging regular hydrotherapy for [*name*] and this provision has not been regularly provided.

12. Occupational therapy input using a combined sensory integrative and neuro-developmental approach to address his underlining sensory integrative and neuro-muscular difficulties. A school and home profile must be devised by the occupational therapist to address the difficulties. [*Name*] will require occupational therapy delivered by a qualified, state-registered occupational therapist. He needs one weekly, 45-minute session. It is important to ensure close liaison between the occupational therapist and [*name*]'s school to allow for the essential carry-over of therapeutic aims and management strategies into a classroom situation.

[*Name*] has been receiving weekly occupational therapy sessions of 45 minutes. However, he does not have a school and home programme. Since September 2004 [*name*] has had a new occupational therapist and there has been no liaison between her and the SENCO at [*name*] School.

13. Physiotherapy treatment with a trained therapist each week for 40 weeks of the educational year, plus not less than 35 (30-minute) sessions of physical leisure activity. [*Name*] will require support to participate in a planned programme of physical activity to support his physiotherapy programme. Such a programme should be planned by a physiotherapist in cooperation with his teachers, supporters and family.

Whilst [*name*] receives weekly physiotherapy treatment, no programme is in place and there is no liaison between the physiotherapist and other professionals involved in [*name*]'s schooling.

Remedies sought

The authority should immediately arrange for all of the special educational provisions specified in [*name*]'s statement of SEN to be put in place.

Judicial review proceedings against the LEA will be initiated without any further warning unless we have received adequate and substantive reply to this letter within seven days.

Any correspondence regarding this matter can be sent to us at this office.

Yours faithfully

Solicitors

APPENDIX K

Case digest: exclusions

SCHOOL EXCLUSION APPEAL PANELS

R. (on the application of B) v. *Head Teacher of Alperton Community School and Others* [2001] EWHC 229 (Admin), [2001] ELR 359. Although members were appointed, paid and trained by the LEA, the LEA had the opportunity to make representations to the appeal panel, and the members had no security of tenure, the composition of the appeal panel did not infringe the right of a person under ECHR, Art 6 to the determination of his/her civil rights and obligations by an independent tribunal.

S, T and P v. *Brent London Borough Council* [2002] EWCA Civ 693, [2002] ELR 556. LEA representations should be objective and not urge any particular outcome in the instant case.

Procedures for appeal panels

S, T and P v. *London Borough of Brent* [2002] EWCA Civ 693, [2002] ELR 556. An appeal panel had to be careful when hearing submissions by the LEA not to acquiesce in an endeavour by the LEA or anyone else to determine or influence its final decision.

Consideration should be given to the layout and seating arrangements at panel hearings so as to avoid any impression that the LEA and the school were ranged against the pupil.

Evidence

R. v. *Cardinal Newman's School ex p. S* [1998] ELR 304. Where an issue arises as to the identification of a pupil, the panel must be alive to the possibility of identification evidence being tainted and the interests of fairness require careful consideration of the circumstances of the identification. The appeal panel must inquire how the identification came to be made. A failure to make sufficient inquiry into these matters led to the quashing of an appeal decision.

Content of duty to reinstate

R. (on the application of L) (A Minor) v. *Governors of J School* [2003] UKHL 9, [2003] 1 All ER 1012. The House of Lords held by a bare majority that reinstatement means simply that a pupil is no longer excluded. It does not mean that the status quo is restored.

(A controversial decision which McManus believes was wrongly decided, preferring the minority decision, as otherwise the decision of the appeal panel is deprived of much of its force.)

The House of Lords recognised that the head teacher had acted under threat of industrial action from the staff and accepted that this was a relevant consideration.

THE DECISION TO EXCLUDE – RELEVANT CONSIDERATIONS

Guidance

S, T and P v. Brent London Borough Council [2002] EWCA Civ 693, [2002] ELR 556. The Court of Appeal held that guidance issued by the Secretary of State should not seek to influence individual decisions, but could list factors which the panels should seek to have regard to without indicating any preferred outcome.

If the panel treated the guidance as something to be strictly adhered to it would be failing to exercise its own independent judgement, it would be treating the guidance as rules, and it would be fettering its discretion.

R. v. Northamptonshire County Council ex p. Weighill [1998] ELR 291. Laws J held that the previous guidance (DfE Circular 10/94) was a relevant consideration.

R. (on the application of P) (A Child) v. Oxfordshire County Council Exclusion Appeals Panel [2002] EWCA Civ 693, [2002] ELR 556. Although the guidance on exclusion provides in mandatory terms when exclusion should not be used, it cannot take effect as anything other than guidance, and the decision maker is not bound to follow it.

Proportionality and conduct off school premises

R. v. Newham London Borough Council ex p. X [1995] ELR 303. Brooke J held it was arguable that the behaviour of pupils towards each other off school premises was a relevant consideration and that the penalty had to be proportionate to the offence.

Conduct of parents

Secretary of State for Education and Science v. Tameside Metropolitan Borough Council [1977] AC 1014. Lord Diplock referred to parents as partners with the LEA and the Secretary of State in the education of their children.

R. v. Neale and Another ex p. S [1995] ELR 198. Turner J held that, where the parent's attitude to the head teacher and the governors was defiant, it was not necessarily an irrelevant consideration in deciding whether to make an exclusion permanent.

(McManus believes this is still good law notwithstanding section 5.1(f) of the DfES Guidance on Exclusions, because such guidance is not absolute.)

R. v. Bryn Elian High School Board of Governors ex p. W [1999] ELR 380. Kay J held that it was proper in the circumstances for the head teacher to look at the way the father had behaved and the way in which that would have an effect on the children's behaviour, if they were not excluded; but he also held that the children had been excluded for their own conduct and not that of their father, the latter's conduct only being relevant to the question whether there was a reasonable prospect that the children's behaviour would improve.

APPENDIX K

Effect of not excluding on the victim

R. v. Camden London Borough Council and the Governors of the Hampstead School ex p. H [1996] ELR 360. The Court of Appeal held that the effect on the victim of an assault should be taken into account when considering setting aside a head teacher's decision to exclude. If it was a choice between the victim or the offenders remaining at school then the justice of the case might be to let the victim remain.

Previous conduct

R. v. Camden London Borough Council and the Governors of the Hampstead School ex p. H [1996] ELR 360. Previous conduct is plainly a relevant consideration.

A v. Staffordshire County Council (1996) *The Times*, 18 October. The court held that, having regard to the pupil's poor disciplinary record and the fact that his continued presence at the school would make it more difficult to deliver satisfactory education to the rest of the children, the exclusion was not unlawful.

Degree of injury

R. v. London Borough of Camden and the Governors of the Hampstead School ex p. H [1996] ELR 360. Where the exclusion is based on an assault, it is appropriate to examine the injury actually sustained rather than punish someone for the hurt that may have been caused to a typical victim.

R. (on the application of C) v. Sefton Metropolitan Borough Council Independent Appeals Panel and the Governors of Hillside High School [2001] ELR 393. Medical reports do not need to be obtained as to the precise extent of the victim's injuries.

Educational factors

R. v. Board of Governors of Stoke Newington School [1994] ELR 131. The court held that a decision as to whether the child should be reinstated was essentially one for those concerned with the administration of the school and the education of the child. Those persons should take account of educational factors which the court declared to be outside its province.

R. v. Governors of St Gregory's RC Aided High School and Appeals Committee ex p. M [1995] ELR 290. The court held to be a relevant consideration that the particular school had strict disciplinary standards.

Exclusion for breaches of rules related to dress or appearance

R. (on the application of Roberts) v. Chair and Governing Body of Cwmfelinfach Primary School [2001] EWHC 242 (Admin). Complicated come back (page 330 McManus).

R. (on the application of B) v. The Head Teacher and Governors of Denbigh High School [2004] EWHC Admin 1389, [2004] ELR 374. The defendant school had not excluded a pupil by requiring her to attend school in the requisite school uniform for Muslim female pupils, even though the style of the uniform contradicted her religious beliefs.

WEDNESBURY CHALLENGES

R. v. Governors of St Gregory's RC Aided High School and Appeals Committee ex p. M [1995] ELR 290. The extent to which the court will entertain a challenge to the merits of a decision to exclude was explored. If it cannot be shown that the authority failed to take into or left out of account some material factor, the question becomes one for the court to assess whether or not a reasonable head teacher could have arrived at the decision reached in the present case.

R. (on the application of DR) v. Head Teacher of S School [2002] EWCA Civ 1822, [2003] ELR 104. The Court of Appeal applied the test in employment law of whether the decision under challenge was 'certainly wrong' or 'perverse' rather than being a 'permissible opinion'.

A v. The Head Teacher and Governors of the Lord Grey School [2003] EWHC 1533, [2003] ELR 517. The court reviewed authorities on whether proportionality was necessarily engaged in any decision to exclude because of Art 2 of the First Protocol to the ECHR:
   (a) the right to education in Art 2 does not exclude all disciplinary penalties;
   (b) it would not be contrary to Art 2 of the First Protocol to exclude, provided the national regulations did not prevent the child from enrolling in another establishment;
   (c) the duty in Art 2 was imposed on the State and not on any particular domestic institution;
   (d) Article 2 of the First Protocol did not create any right to an education in any particular institution;
   (e) if the child had no access to any particular alternative educational institution, there might be a breach of Art 2 of the First Protocol, and the school authority might be liable in damages unless the cause of the unavailability was that of the LEA (in which case it would be liable) or the parent's decision (in which case the LEA would not be liable for the breach of Art 2);
   (f) just as compliance with domestic law would not justify a breach of Art 2 of the First Protocol, nor would a failure to comply with domestic law necessarily lead to an infringement of that right.

In the particular case, one exclusion was held to be unlawful because, *inter alia*, it was neither for a fixed term nor permanent, but it was held that this did not render the school liable for breach of Art 2 of the First Protocol to the ECHR.

PROCEDURAL CHALLENGES

R. v. Governors of the London Oratory School ex p. Regis [1989] Fam Law 67. It was held that the rules of natural justice apply to the decision to exclude a pupil.

R. (on the application of AM) v. Governing Body of K School and Independent Appeal Panel of London Borough of E [2002] EWCA Civ 1822, (2002) *The Times*, 19 December. Where there had been an unfairness in the original hearing, it could be cured by the hearing before the appeal panel.

R. v. Board of Governors of Stoke Newington School [1994] ELR 131. The court held rules of natural justice had been infringed when a teacher governor was present at the governors' meeting and was a relevant witness.

APPENDIX K

R. (on application of T) v. *Head Teacher of Elliott School* [2002] EWCA Civ 1349, [2003] ELR 160. Teacher governors who know the pupil should err on the side of caution and not sit on the panel even when a parent fails to object, if there is a reasonable doubt as to their ability to act impartially as a result of their knowledge of the pupil.

R. (on the application of S) v. *Head Teacher of C High School* [2001] EWHC Admin 513. The court held that it was not an infringement of the rule against bias for an appeal panel to be advised by a clerk employed by a local authority when the clerk simply advised on points of law and took no part in the decision-making process.

R. v. *Newham London Borough Council ex p. X* [1995] ELR 303. In the exceptional circumstances of the case it was appropriate to grant leave to move for judicial review against an initial decision of the head teacher despite the rights of appeal available.

In this case the head teacher took the decision to exclude the pupil without giving the parents any opportunity to make representations, the child was in his GCSE year, and every day was critical. Interim relief was granted to ensure that the child was accepted back at school pending further order.

R. (on the application of DR) v. *Head Teacher of S School* [2002] EWCA Civ 1822, [2003] ELR 104. The Court of Appeal accepted the correctness of the decision in *Ex p. X* (above), but observed that it would expect judicial review of decisions below those of the appeal panel to be very few and far between.

R. v. *Governors of St Gregory's RC Aided High School and Appeals Committee ex p. M* [1995] ELR 290. The court considered how an appeal panel should examine evidence. It was held that hearsay evidence could be heard and that the child could give evidence without the parent being present.

R. v. *Staffordshire County Council ex p. Ashworth* (1997) 9 Admin LR 373. Hearsay evidence could be received by the appeal panel.

(Now SS Guidance on Exclusions provides expressly for the receipt of hearsay evidence.)

R. v. *Head Teacher and Independent Appeal Committee of Dunraven School ex p. B* [2000] ELR 156. Where a child had been excluded on the basis of a witness statement he had not seen and oral testimony he had not heard, the Court of Appeal held that this was a breach of the requirements of natural justice because the appellant had not had a fair opportunity of answering the case against him.

However, the court was sensitive about the need to protect confidentiality where there was a fear of reprisals against the informer. It applied the guidance of the Employment Appeal Tribunal in *Linford Cash and Carry Ltd* v. *Thompson* [1989] IRLR 235.

The court held that if the informant's identity cannot be concealed, and that is necessary for his protection, then the appeal panel cannot act on the basis of his evidence and keep it from the appellant.

S, T and P v. *Brent London Borough Council* [2002] EWCA Civ 693, [2002] ELR 556. There might be very good reasons for anonymising witness statements if they were to be disclosed, but the injustice of not using them might be even greater than the injustice of using them. Appeal panels and governing bodies should be prepared to disregard such statements if they were damaging to the pupil in ways with which the pupil could not be expected to deal without knowing who had made the statement.

CASE DIGEST: EXCLUSIONS

R. (on the application of T) v. *Head Teacher of Elliott School* [2002] EWCA Civ 1349, [2003] ELR 160. The panel had to look at unsigned statements and decide whether to give them weight, bearing in mind that it might be unfair to do so in the absence of identification, but decisions in this area were fact-sensitive. The court referred back to the decision in *S, T and P* v. *Brent LBC* (above).

R. (on the application of A) v. *Head Teacher of North Westminster Community School* [2002] EWHC Admin 2351, [2003] ELR 378. The court reviewed the case law and held that it was not unfair to rely on an anonymous statement that identified the appellant as the culprit when there was no reason to doubt its accuracy and that line had not been explored by the appellant before the appeal panel.

R. (on the application of J) v. *A School* [2003] All ER (D) 158. It is fair for an appeal panel not to hear evidence from witnesses who had no first-hand knowledge of the incident which led to the exclusion when the claimant wished them to be called simply for the purposes of cross-examination.

R. v. *Camden London Borough Council and the Governors of Hampstead School ex p. H* [1996] ELR 360. While the governors and the LEA were not obliged on every occasion to carry out searching inquiries involving the calling of bodies of oral evidence, if there were factual issues to be resolved, reasonable inquiries had to be made and these inquiries had to be balanced.

If it was contemplated not to exclude, it was important to obtain information on the effect that this would have on the victim.

EXCLUSION FOR CRIMINAL OFFENCES

Two issues arise from the SS Guidance on Exclusions in regard to criminal offences.

Standard of proof if exclusion for a criminal offence

R. v. *Head Teacher and Independent Appeals Committee of Dunraven School ex p. B* [2000] ELR 156. Brooke LJ stated that if a person was charged with an offence of dishonesty, the law required not that the proof should be on the ordinary balance of probabilities, but that it should be distinctly more probable than not that the excluded pupil had been dishonestly involved. The more serious the allegation the stronger the evidence that is required in order for it to be made good on the balance of probabilities.

R. (on the application of K) v. *Governors of W School and West Sussex County Council* [2001] ELR 311. Hidden J held that *Dunraven* had determined that the standard of proof was not a simple balance of probabilities test where a serious offence was alleged.

R. (on the application of S) v. *Governing Body of YP School* [2003] All ER (D) 202. The Court of Appeal decided, on a concession, that where a criminal offence is alleged, the standard of proof before a pupil can be excluded is not the civil standard, taking into account the inherent improbability of a serious offence having been committed, but the criminal standard, so that the head teacher has to be sure that the pupil has committed the criminal offence that he is accused of before he can exclude.

(This contradicts the Guidance on Exclusions Part 5, para. 1.1, and may also render para 3.4 of doubtful legality. If the criminal standard does apply it would be difficult to see how it would be appropriate for an appeal panel to uphold an exclusion predicated upon an allegation that the pupil had committed a criminal offence when the pupil had been acquitted.)

Appropriateness of excluding a pupil suspected of committing a serious offence

R. v. *Independent Appeal Panel of Sheffield County Council ex p. N* [2000] ELR 700. Moses J held that the panel should accept that it cannot investigate the truth or otherwise of the charge and instead should consider a freestanding separate issue, namely whether it was in the best interests of the school for the pupil to be excluded, bearing in mind that the truth or otherwise could not be determined until the criminal proceedings.

A v. *The Head Teacher and Governors of the Lord Grey School* [2003] EWHC 1533, [2003] ELR 517. Burnton J endorsed remarks of Moses J *ex p. N* (above).

R. v. *Head Teacher and Independent Appeal Committee of Dunraven School ex p. B* [2000] ELR 156. This was a Court of Appeal case in which central issue to be decided from head teacher upwards was whether the pupil had been involved with theft.

(It was difficult to see how the appeal panel could not make a decision on whether the pupil had committed the offence.)

DUTY OF APPEAL PANEL TO STATE THE GROUNDS OF ITS DECISION

R. v. *Hackney London Borough Council ex p. T* [1991] COD 454. Hutchinson J held that it was sufficient if the appeal committee explained its conclusions in broad and simple terms.

R. v. *Lancashire County Council ex p. M* [1995] ELR 136. Macpherson J held:

> There is absolutely nothing wrong with a local authority having a standard form letter which can be modified if required ... the statute requires that grounds shall be given for the decision which is made and it does not, for example, anywhere state that detailed reasons must be given. There is a distinction between grounds and detailed reasons.

R. v. *Northamptonshire County Council ex p. Weighill* [1998] ELR 291. Laws J considered the case law and refused to draw a distinction between 'reason' and 'ground', and held that while it was not the committee's duty to recite all the arguments for and against, or to explain why upon each point it had preferred one view rather than the other, there was a basic requirement to explain, with whatever brevity, the reason for the decision in question.

R. v. *Education Committee of Blackpool Borough Council ex p. Taylor* [1999] ELR 237. There was no obligation upon the appeal panel to state more than reasons why it had reached its decision: 'The need to give reasons is a requirement to give reasons which enable the parents to understand the basis upon which the decision had been made.'

STANDING AND TIMING

R. v. *Camden London Borough Council and Governors of the Hampstead School ex p. H* [1996] ELR 360. The victim has standing to challenge a decision not to exclude.

R. (on the application of A) v. *Head Teacher of North Westminster Community School* [2002] EWHC 2351 (Admin), [2003] ELR 378. In expulsion cases it was appropriate to move at the beginning of the three-month period rather than the end.

R. v. *Neale and Another ex p. S* [1995] ELR 198. Where the child had already gone to another school, the court held that there was no useful purpose to be served by intervening or making an order. The court accepted this passage as accurate:

> The court does not beat the air in vain. It may have become otiose or pointless to grant a remedy because the relevant detriment to the applicant has been removed or because nothing in practice will change if the remedy is granted.
> (Supperstone and Goudie, *Judicial Review* (1991), p. 349)

R. v. *Independent Appeal Panel of Sheffield County Council ex p. N* [2000] ELR 700. An application to clear a pupil's name might be regarded as serving a useful purpose. In this case, it was to clear the name of a child who had made an allegation.

R. (on the application of A) v. *Head Teacher of North Westminster Community School* [2002] EWHC Admin 2351, [2003] ELR 378. A pupil accused of a serious breach of discipline could make an application to clear his name even though he had obtained a place in another school.

APPEAL OR REVIEW

R. (on the application of DR) v. *Head Teacher of S School* [2002] EWCA Civ 1822, [2003] ELR 104. Courts will require statutory rights to be exhausted before any application is made for judicial review, as they are an adequate alternative remedy, except in exceptional circumstances, for example, where there is a need to move quickly by way of interim relief or where serious improper conduct of governors is alleged.

INTERIM RELIEF

R. v. *Newham London Borough Council ex p. X* [1995] ELR 303. The child was expelled in the GCSE year and the parent given no opportunity to make representation before the child was excluded.

INDEPENDENT SCHOOLS

R. v. *Fernhill Manor School ex p. A* [1994] ELR 67. The decision of an independent school could not be challenged by way of judicial review.

R. v. *Muntham House School ex p. R* [2000] ELR 287. The decision in *Fernhill* (above) applied to non-maintained residential schools.

R. v. *Incorporated Froebel Educational Institute ex p. L* [1999] ELR 488. There was also no means of challenging by way of judicial review the decision of an independent co-educational day school.

In these cases, parties can seek a declaration of their contractual rights only.

APPENDIX L

Case digest: special educational needs

STATEMENTS OF SPECIAL EDUCATIONAL NEEDS

Parts 2, 3 and 4

R. v. *Secretary of State for Education ex p. E* [1992] 1 FLR 377, CA. Each need in Part 2 should be met by provisions specified in Part 3.

R. v. *Kingston upon Thames London Borough Council* v. *Hunter* [1997] ELR 223. Part 4 cannot influence Part 3. It is not a matter of fitting Part 3 to Part 4, but of considering the fitness of Part 4 to meet the provision in Part 3.

A v. *Special Educational Needs and Disability Tribunal and Barnet London Borough Council* [2003] EWHC Admin 3368. The decision maker (i.e. the LEA or tribunal) must thus develop Part 2, then Part 3 and then Part 4.

R. v. *Harrow LBC ex p. M* [1997] FCR 761 and *R. (on the application of V)* v. *Cumbria County Council* [2003] EWHC Admin 232. The duty in relation to Part 3 can be enforced through judicial review proceedings.

E v. *Flintshire County Council and the Special Educational Needs Tribunal* [2002] EWHC Admin 388. Where the statement was the subject of an appeal to the tribunal, the court can and will look at both the statement and the tribunal's decision to ascertain the detail of the provision which must be made.

What is educational and what is non-educational?

Special educational needs include:

(a) speech therapy: *R.* v. *Lancashire County Council ex p. M* [1989] 2 FLR 279, CA
(b) occupational therapy and physiotherapy: *B* v. *Isle of Wight Council* [1997] ELR 279
(c) residential provision: *G* v. *Wakefield Metropolitan District Council and Another* (1998) 96 LGR 69, per Laws J.

G v. *Barnet London Borough Council and Special Educational Needs Tribunal* [1998] ELR 480. Being Jewish is not a special educational need for which special educational provision must be made.

A v. *Special Educational Needs and Disability Tribunal and Barnet LBC* [2003] EWHC Admin 3368 and *R.* v. *Secretary of State for Education ex p. E* [1996] ELR 279. Where there were emotional needs which were educational which required the pupil to be with Jewish peers, they were special educational needs requiring special educational provision in the form of appropriate peer group and school environment.

Bromley LBC v. *Special Educational Needs Tribunal* [1999] ELR 260, CA. Whether any particular provision is educational or non-educational is not a question of law. It is a matter for the LEA and, on appeal, the Special Educational Needs Tribunal (now SENDIST).

Part 3 must specify the special education provision

Part 3 should describe all aspects of the provision which differs from the provision normally made in mainstream schools:

(a) class sizes: *H.* v. *Leicestershire County Council* [2000] ELR 471
(b) staff qualifications/experience: *R.* v. *Wandsworth London Borough Council ex p. M* [1998] ELR 424
(c) small group sizes, length and frequency of sessions; also need for one-to-one work: *L* v. *Clarke and Somerset County Council* [1998] ELR 129
(d) input by other professionals such as speech therapists must specify frequency and length of sessions: *R.* v. *Harrow London Borough Council ex p. M* [1997] FCR 761.

L v. *Clarke and Somerset County Council* [1998] ELR 129. 'The real question . . . is whether [the statement] is so specific and so clear as to leave no room for doubt as to what has been decided and what is needed in the individual case.'

M v. *Brighton and Hove City Council* [2003] EWHC Admin 1722, QBD. Part 3 was condemned as impermissibly ambiguous.

E v. *Flintshire County Council and the Special Educational Needs Tribunal* [2002] EWHC Admin 388. The requirement to specify is to ensure that specific needs are not ignored or inadequately focused on, and to allow provisions to be made and enforced.

R(on the application of IPSEA Ltd) v. *Secretary of State for Education* [2002] EWHC Admin 504. The legislative purpose is: 'to require focused and express consideration to be given to the specific needs of a child and then to provide for them in terms which will further and effect its enforceability as a provision'.

C v. *Lambeth London Borough Council* [2003] EWHC 1195. Part 3 can also specify that a child be placed in a different year group to that indicated by his/her age.

Cannot leave specification in Part 3 to a future assessment

(a) *C* v. *Special Educational Needs Tribunal and London Borough of Greenwich* [1999] ELR 5 – extent of disapplication from the National Curriculum
(b) *Re A (A Child)* [2000] ELR 639 – the nature of other provision (speech therapy) which is to be provided
(c) *E* v. *Rotherham Metropolitan Borough Council* [2001] EWHC Admin 432, [2002] ELR 266 – condemned provision for SALT.

APPENDIX L

E v. *Newham London Borough Council* [2003] EWCA Civ 9. It was held that in exceptional circumstances the amount of therapy the child should receive could be left to a future assessment by therapists.

Parents not to be required to make educational provision by statement

R. (on the application of A) v. *Cambridgeshire County Council and Lorn* [2002] EWHC Admin 2391, [2003] ELR 464. A statement cannot lawfully specify (in Part 3 or 4) provision which is to be made by parents.

R. (on the application of KW) v. *Special Educational Needs Tribunal and Rochdale Metropolitan Borough Council* [2003] EWHC Admin 1770. The tribunal should look at what a statement requires of the parents and ask whether it is 'educational' or 'special educational provision'.

DR v. *Sheffield City Council* [2002] EWHC Admin 528. A statement which specified a '24-hour curriculum' (or equivalent) could not lawfully specify only a day placement.

Funding of provisions

R. v. *Cumbria County Council ex p. P* [1995] ELR 337. Part 3 can make reference to the arrangements for funding the provision which is set out (ie how the balance is to be apportioned between the school, the LEA, and the health authority).

R. v. *Oxfordshire County Council ex p. C* [1996] ELR 153; *R.* v. *Hillingdon LBC ex p. Queensmead School* [1997] ELR 331. The LEA remains ultimately responsible for making the provision if the other parties fail to do so.

Part 4 – Placement

Richardson v. *Solihull Metropolitan Borough Council* [1998] ELR 319. There is no need to name a particular school.

The tribunal should consider adjourning before naming an unnecessary expensive provision where other, less costly, provision may be suitable.

T v. *Islington* [2001] EWHC Admin 1029, [2002] ELR 1029. The choice of placement must be informed by appropriate evidence and with due notice to all concerned.

Rhondda Cynon Taff County Borough Council v. *Special Educational Needs Tribunal and V* [2001] EWHC Admin 823, [2002] ELR 290. The LEA should have drawn the tribunal's attention to the possibility of alternatives.

C v. *Lancashire County Council* [1997] ELR 377. If the parental preference is a bit more expensive, the LEA and the tribunal must balance the 'parental factors' against any extra cost.

B v. *Harrow (No 1)* [2000] ELR 109, HL. The efficient resources are those of the LEA responsible it can take into accont:

    (a)   the cost of an out-of-area placement if that is requested; and
    (b)   in a special school funded on a place-led basis, the 'wasted' cost of not placing the child at the school.

Parental preference

C v. *Buckinghamshire County Council* [1999] ELR 179, CA. There was no obligation to give effect to parental preference under EA 1996, s.9.

Oxfordshire Council Council v. *GB* [2001] EWCA 1358; [2002] ELR 8, CA. Under s.9 it is only the additional cost of the placements under consideration which is relevant.

Southampton City Council v. *G* [2002] EWHC Admin 1516. When considering the cost balance, the LEA or tribunal should look at the effect over time of the choice of placement (in this case an extra year needed to complete GCSEs).

S v. *Hackney London Borough Council* [2002] ELR 45. By virtue of ECHR, First Protocol, Art. 2 (via HRA 1998, s.6) parental religious or philosophical convictions in the choice of school must be 'respected', implying a positive obligation going beyond treating them as being merely material.

T v. *Special Educational Needs Tribunal and Wiltshire County Council* [2002] EWHC Admin 1474, [2002] ELR 704. Philosophical conviction in favour of 'inclusive education' seems not to be a 'philosophical conviction'.

CB v. *London Borough of Merton and Special Educational Needs Tribunal* [2002] ELR 441. A statement which names a residential school when the parents wanted a day school is not a violation of ECHR, Art. 8(1) – violation would only arise if a school attendance order was made – such interference can be justified under Art. 8(2).

S v. *Bracknell Forest Borough Council and the Special Educational Needs Tribunal* [1999] ELR 51. When considering if the LEA needs to make out-of-school provision, the first question to be asked is what does the child need (Part 3) and then it should be decided if that can be provided in school.

C (Shirley) v. *Brent LBC* [2003] EWHC Admin 1590, [2003] EWCA Civ 1773. If the provision can be made in a school then there is no power to provide it 'otherwise'.

T v. *Special Educational Needs Tribunal and Wiltshire County Council* [2002] EWHC 1474, [2002] ELR 704. The parental view is not relevant in deciding whether the school can indeed make appropriate provision (although this decision is arguably wrong).

Wandsworth London Borough Council v. *K* [2003] EWHC 1424, [2003] ELR 554. Where a 'home programme' is identified, that should be described in Part 3 and can also be described in Part 4.

R. v. *Chair of Governors and Head Teacher of A and S School ex p. T* [2000] ELR 274. Where a maintained school is named in Part 4 then the school must admit the pupil.

E v. *Hampshire County Council* [2000] ELR 652, CA. In law, the question of whether a child has SLD or MLD is not to be determined by reference to IQ.

Part 6: Transport

R. v. *Hereford and Worcester County Council ex p. P* [1992] 2 FCR 732. Transport must be 'non-stressful'.

APPENDIX L

General

W v. *Gloucestershire County Council* [2001] EWHC Admin 481. When considering what is appropriate (for Parts 3 or 4), the LEA or tribunal must have regard to the curriculum presently being followed by the child and the impact of disrupting that curriculum.

Wilkin and Goldthorpe v. *Coventry City Council* [1998] ELR 345. The LEA or tribunal should not simply look at the short-term needs of a child in drawing up a statement (in this case, they only looked at the one term left in primary school and not at what would happen at secondary school).

Southampton City Council v. *G* [2002] EWHC Admin 1516. There had been an error in not looking at the cost of the whole GCSE course.

SPECIAL EDUCATIONAL NEEDS AND DISABILITY TRIBUNAL CASES

Parents have right to appeal to the tribunal under SENDA 2001, ss.325, 326, 328, or 329.

Procedural matters in the tribunal

O v. *Harrow London Borough Council* [2001] EWCA Civ 2046; [2002] 1 WLR 928, CA. One prior assessment under s.323 was sufficient to ground more than one appeal. Multiple appeals could be controlled by SENDIST exercising its powers to strike out appeals that are scandalous or vexatious.

R. v. *Special Educational Needs Tribunal ex p. J* [1997] ELR 237. The decision of the President on whether or not to extend the time within which an appeal can be brought is only reviewable if the exercise of his discretion was perverse or revealed an error of law.

S and C v. *Special Educational Needs Tribunal* [1997] ELR 242. It is not an error of law to refuse to extend time because of a mistake by advisers who held themselves out as competent so to act, whether or not they were legally qualified.

S v. *SENT* [1995] 1 WLR 1627; (*on appeal*) [1996] 1 WLR 382. It is only the parent who has a right of appeal to the tribunal and thereafter the High Court.

R. v. *SENT ex p. South Cambridgeshire County Council and Chapman* [1996] CLY 2493. It is a clear abuse of process for the child to launch an application for judicial review rather than appeal to the tribunal through his parents, if this was done in order to obtain public funding.

R. v. *Barnet ex p. Barnett* (unreported) 27 November 1995. An application for leave to move for judicial review of a decision of an LEA was refused where there was a dispute about whether the tribunal had jurisdiction to hear any appeal.

Interim relief

R. v. *Oxfordshire County Council ex p. Roast* [1996] ELR 381. Recognised the construction that once an amendment had been made it took effect and subsisted to and beyond the appeal unless the tribunal decided otherwise at appeal, could produce unfortunate results involving the disruption to a child's education.

(Under EA 1996, Sched. 27, para. 11(5), a decision to cease to maintain a statement cannot now take effect if the parent has appealed to the tribunal and the appeal has not been determined or withdrawn.)

Re M (A Minor) [1996] ELR 135, CA. The statutory right of appeal to the tribunal was an adequate alternative remedy.

R. (on the application of MH) v. *Hackney London Borough Council* [2001] EWHC Admin 314. Section 19 of EA 1996, which obliges the LEA to make arrangements for the provision of suitable education at school or otherwise for children who, by reason of illness, exclusion or otherwise, may not receive suitable education unless such arrangements are made for them, does not apply when the parents choose to keep their child at home pending the determination of an appeal to the tribunal.

Challenging decisions of the tribunal in the court

S v. *SENT* [1995] 1 WLR 1627. Where a final, as distinct from interlocutory, decision of the tribunal was challenged, RSC Ord 55 was the appropriate route.

R. v. *Special Educational Needs Tribunal ex p. Brophy* [1997] ELR 291. (*Obiter*) the court lacked the jurisdiction to hear an appeal by way of case stated from a final decision of the tribunal.

Alton-Evans v. *Leicester Local Education Authority* [1998] ELR 237. It was held that the court lacked the jurisdiction to hear an appeal by way of case stated from a final decision of the tribunal.

R. v. *Head Teacher and Governing Body of Crug Glas School and Others ex p. W* [1999] ELR 484. The court refused to intervene in a dispute about a case management decision of the tribunal, holding that it should be very slow to interfere with the working through of a hearing before the tribunal.

Judicial review

R. v. *Special Educational Needs and Disability Tribunal ex p. South Glamorgan County Council* [1996] ELR 326, CA. The Court of Appeal made clear that it would not allow a judicial review to be brought in order to obtain legal aid. The local authority had brought judicial review proceedings rather than an appeal under RSC Ord 55 (now CPR Part 52).

R. v. *Special Educational Needs and Disability Tribunal ex p. F* [1996] ELR 213. The courts will not allow an application to be brought for judicial review in order to evade the 28-day time limit for an appeal (CPR Part 52 Practice Direction, para 17.3)

R. v. *SENT ex p. South Cambridgeshire County Council and Chapman* [1996] CLY 2493. The allegations of unfairness as a result of a third party's inadvertent misleading of the tribunal could, and should, be ventilated by an appeal under what

APPENDIX L

was then RSC Ord 55. It was also held that the fact that legal aid was available for a child for judicial review, but that the appeal under Ord 55 had to be by the parent was a potential source of mischief which should be avoided by requiring an appeal, rather than permitting judicial review.

Scope of CPR Part 52 appeals

South Glamorgan County Council v. *L and M* [1996] ELR 400. The appeal is only on a point of law. It was held that a point of law includes the case where there is no evidence to support a primary finding of fact and where the conclusion of the tribunal is inconsistent with the primary facts it has found so that it can be said the decision is perverse.

(This decision was reaffirmed in *R.* v. *Kingston upon Thames London Borough Council ex p. Hunter* [1997] ELR 223.)

T v. *London Borough of Islington* [2001] EWHC Admin 1029. The tribunal had insufficient evidence to justify its conclusion and therefore an appeal should be allowed on this basis. (But 'insufficiency of evidence' as a point of law within the meaning of s.11 is questioned.)

S v. *Swansea City Council and Confrey* [2000] ELR 315. The dictum in *T.* v. *Islington* (above) was followed:

> ... if a particular school is to be relied upon to meet a particular need, the tribunal must have accurately defined the need ... and must have been able to satisfy itself that the school will be able to provide the special educational provision specified in the statement.

R. (on the application of W) v. *Bedfordshire County Council* [2001] ELR 645. The tribunal had not satisfied itself that the school could meet the needs of the child. The decision was plainly perverse and not just based on insufficient evidence.

A v. *Kirklees Metropolitan Borough Council* [2001] ELR 657, CA. Where information had not been given to the parents by the LEA which was material to their appeal to the tribunal, the Court of Appeal held that the parents' case could be put on the basis either that a material factor had not been taken into account or that the family was denied a fair hearing.

R. v. *Special Educational Needs Tribunal ex p. F* [1999] ELR 417. The tribunal is not entitled to all background information. Ognall J quashed a decision by the chairman of the tribunal that the papers to be placed before it should include those of the current appeal and a previous appeal brought by the appellant a year earlier. (However, there is no general rule that papers relating to earlier appeals should not be considered by a tribunal when hearing a fresh appeal.)

R. (on the application of A) v. *Lambeth London Borough Council* [2001] EWHC Admin 379. The tribunal did have information relating to the earlier appeal.

L v. *Clarke and Somerset County Council* [1998] ELR 129; *H* v. *Kent County Council* [2000] ELR 660; *JD* v. *Devon County Council* [2001] EWHC Admin 958, QBD; *R. (on the application of B)* v. *Vale of Glamorgan County Borough Council* [2001] ELR 529; *Crean* v. *Somerset County Council* [2002] ELR 152. It was now an established practice of the courts to allow appeals where the reasoning of the tribunal is thought to be inadequate.

Parties to CPR Part 52 appeals

Conflicting rulings on whether child a proper party

South Glamorgan County Council v. *Long* [1996] ELR 400. It was stated that a child could be joined as a proper and necessary party under the then existing rules of the court (RSC Ord. 15, r.6).

Sunderland City Council v. *Plumpton* [1996] ELR 283. It was held (*obiter*) that the child was not a proper respondent.

Who is the parent?

F v. *Humberside County Council* [1997] ELR 12. It was held that foster parents did have the right of appeal.

Whether the tribunal a proper party

S and C v. *Special Educational Needs Tribunal* [1997] ELR 242. The tribunal, through the chairman of the relevant panel, was held to be a proper respondent to any appeal.

S v. *SENT* [1995] 1 WLR 1627. The tribunal cannot be forced to give evidence nor does it have any right to appear and be heard.
    In practice, the tribunal only appears where there are issues of general principle as to jurisdiction and procedure raised or allegations of bias against the tribunal.

CPR Part 52 time limits

S v. *SENT* [2002] EWHC 1047, [2003] ELR 85. Time should be taken as running from the date of decision and not the date of receipt of notice of the decision.

Sayers v. *Clarke Walker (Practice Note)* [2002] EWCA Civ 645, [2002] 1 WLR 3095. This practice note concerns the approach to extension of time limits under CPR.

S and C v. *SENT* [1997] ELR 242. An extension was granted where delay was caused by legal advisers being mistaken as to who should bring the appeal prior to the point being settled by *S* v. *Special Educational Needs Tribunal* [1995] 1 WLR 1627, and the wide reporting of that decision. It was made clear that this dispensation was not a precedent for the future.

S v. *SENT* [2002] EWCA 1047, [2003] ELR 85. A similar error to the above led to an appeal being out of time but this was not regarded by Goldring J as an acceptable basis for extending time.

R. v. *Special Educational Appeals Tribunal ex p. J* [1997] ELR 237. The court refused to intervene when the tribunal had refused to extend time for an appeal to it for a short period where the delay had been caused by the ineptitude of the parent's advisers.

Sage v. *South Glamorgan County Council and Confrey* [1998] ELR 525; *Sayers* v. *Clarke Walker (Practice Note)* [2002] 1 WLR 3095. Where the delay was arguably caused by advice from the courts or the tribunal, extensions have been granted, although lawyers were warned not to rely on advice from court staff and to make their own judgement about when to appeal.

Skilbeck v. *Williamson and Oxfordshire County Council* [1999] EWHC Admin 815. Courts have to take account of the substantive merits of the case when deciding whether to extend time.

Sayers v. *Clarke Walker (Practice Note)* [2002] 1 WLR 3095. When arguments for and against extending time are evenly balanced, the prospects of success have to be evaluated in order to see the effect on the parties of granting an extension.

Skilbeck v. *Williamson and Oxfordshire County Council* [1999] EWHC 815 (Admin). The court extended time where the Legal Aid Board had mislaid an application for funding in circumstances where the court accepted that the solicitors had not chased for the decision as early as they should.

S v. *SENT* [2002] EWCA 1047, [2003] ELR 85. The court did not regard as acceptable the delay caused by seeking funding in the name of the wrong person.

London Borough of Bromley v. *SENT* [1999] ELR 260. On the question of whether it was relevant that the respondent to the appeal had suffered no prejudice as a result of the delay, it was held:

(1) The courts are and should be reluctant to extend time in public law cases, where the interests of good administration require challenges to tribunal decisions to be brought within limited timescales.
(2) The court will only extend time where it is satisfied that there is an acceptable reason for the delay; and, if so, the delay is not substantial and has not caused significant prejudice to the respondent. It is argued from this statement of principle that in the absence of an acceptable reason the question of prejudice does not arise.

In this case the extension was allowed because there had been no prejudice to the respondent, and the reason for the need of an extension was ignorance. Only after an acceptable explanation had been established was prejudice relevant.

S v. *SENT* [2002] EWCA 1047, [2003] ELR 85. In the absence of an acceptable explanation for the delay it was not appropriate to extend time even if there was no prejudice to the respondent.

Sayers v. *Clarke Walker (Practice Note)* [2002] EWCA Civ 645, [2002] 1 WLR 3095. The question of prejudice is one of the factors to be considered by the court when deciding whether to extend time under CPR r.3.1(2)(a) and r.3.9(1)(h) and (i), where it falls to be considered whether or not there is an acceptable explanation for the delay.

Interim relief

The Mayor and Burgesses of Camden London Borough Council v. *Hodin and White* [1996] ELR 430. It was held that a stay was not automatic and should not generally be granted unless there was good reason to do so.

CASE DIGEST: SPECIAL EDUCATIONAL NEEDS

PROCEDURAL POINTS ON ALL APPEALS

Taking points on appeal not run below

B v. Harrow London Borough Council and the Special Educational Needs Tribunal [1998] ELR 351, CA. The Court of Appeal allowed a point to be taken on appeal because the interests of justice required it. The court found the case to be one of general importance which might set a precedent.

L v. Hereford and Worcester County Council and Hughes [2000] ELR 375; *S v. Hackney London Borough Council* [2001] EWHC 572 (Admin), [2002] ELR 45; *T v. SENT and Wiltshire County Council* [2002] EWHC Admin 1474, [2002] ELR 704. All appellants wanted to raise on appeal points on the ECHR which had not been ventilated before the tribunal. It was held that in circumstances where the appellant was represented before the tribunal by a highly competent solicitor, and the point sought to be raised was not one of pure statutory construction, nor one of general importance, it was appropriate to distinguish *B v. Harrow* (above).

Evidence

South Glamorgan County Council v. L and M [1996] ELR 400. It was held that it was only in exceptional circumstances that it would be necessary to seek a note of the evidence from the chairman because the point of law should be apparent from the statement of reasons or the general documents in the case.

Joyce v. Dorset County Council [1997] ELR 26. The transcript was voluntarily produced by SENT to counter an allegation of bias. The allegation made on the affidavit was abandoned when the transcript showed it to be groundless.

Sythes v. Camden London Borough Council and Special Educational Needs Tribunal (unreported) CO/3991/95 (Transcript, 21 June 1996). It was held that in order for the chairman's notes to be ordered:

1. the notice of appeal had to raise a permissible ground of attack. Permissible grounds were that:
   (a) there was no evidence to support a particular finding of fact;
   (b) SENT had misunderstood the evidence; and
   (c) the finding of fact was perverse;
2. the party seeking the notes had to specify the exact finding which was attacked or the finding which he/she contended should have been made.

Fisher v. Hughes [1998] ELR 475. On the test to be applied:

(a) it was common ground that the question to be asked was whether it was necessary for the notes and/or transcript to be produced in order to dispose properly of an issue raised in the appeal;
(b) earlier decisions suggesting that an order for the production of notes would only be made in exceptional circumstances were not laying down a rule of law to that effect but merely stating that as a matter of expectation occasions of necessity would rarely arise.

Witness statements

Oxfordshire County Council v. *GB and Others* [2001] EWCA Civ 1358. The court commented on the practice of parties filing witness statements (and reviewed recent case law). It signalled a reluctance to accept further evidence other than that which is relevant to relief.

S v. *SENT* [1995] 1 WLR 1627. It was held that it was proper to receive evidence to provide the court with the full picture when there was an assertion that there was no relevant evidence upon which the tribunal could base its decision.

It was also held that evidence was admissible to expose the true nature of the decision-making process, but not to enable *ex post facto* rationalisation.

Oxfordshire County Council v. *GB and Others* [2001] EWCA 1358, [2002] ELR 8 reiterated the same point.

R. v. *Brent London Borough Council ex p. Baruwa* (1997) 29 HLR 915. Where the decision maker had amplified his reasons in written evidence before the court, it might be appropriate to refuse relief in the exercise of the court's discretion on that basis.

Costs

S and C v. *Special Educational Needs Tribunal* [1997] ELR 242. If the appeal succeeds the view was expressed that the tribunal should be liable for costs only in 'extreme' circumstances.

C v. *London Borough of Lambeth and the Special Educational Needs Tribunal* [1999] ELR 350. The tribunal refused to award costs against the LEA unless it could be shown that its decision was 'unjustifiable and unsustainable upon any view of the facts'. On appeal the court held that the tribunal was entitled to conclude that the LEA decision was not 'wholly unreasonable' and its decision was not perverse or wrong in law.

SUBSTANTIVE POINTS OF LAW ON APPEAL

Wednesbury unreasonableness

South Glamorgan County Council v. *L and M* [1996] ELR 400. The court dismissed an attempt to widen the scope of error of law to include error of fact other than when the error was one of precedent fact.

E v. *Oxfordshire County Council* [2001] EWHC Admin 816, [2001] ELR 256. In principle, a review should be heard by the same tribunal that heard the original appeal where this is possible.

Challenge to the form of the statement

R. v. *Secretary of State for Education and Science ex p. E* [1992] 1 FLR 377. A statement has to identify each and every special education need and the provision for meeting those needs.

Joyce v. *Dorset County Council* [1997] ELR 26. Where the applicant argued that although numeracy had been mentioned in the statement as a particular area of

SEN, it was not specifically addressed when dealing with the child's needs, the court refused to intervene holding that the tribunal must have concluded that the provision met the child's needs as a whole and that the statement, though apparently deficient, was not in truth so.

There was no error of law when a tribunal which could have ordered the amendment of an unclear statement chose not to do so.

Knight v. *Dorset County Council* [1997] COD 256. Even though the tribunal had misdirected itself, the appeal was dismissed on the basis that it was likely that the tribunal would have reached the same conclusion had it adopted the correct approach and thus there was no miscarriage of justice.

E v. *Newham London Borough Council* [2003] EWCA Civ 09, [2003] ELR 286; *R. (IPSEA Ltd)* v. *Secretary of State for Education and Skills* [2003] EWCA Civ 7, [2003] ELR 393. It was held, dismissing both appeals, that although the statement should not be too vague the need for flexibility was a matter of judgment for the tribunal.

Relevance of resources

R. v. *Oxfordshire County Council ex p. P* [1996] ELR 153. It was held that there was no delegation by the LEA of its duties under the EA 1981 so long as the school agreed to meet the costs out of its delegated budget.

R. v. *London Borough of Hillingdon ex p. Governing Body of Queensmead School* [1997] ELR 331. The court held that the needs of the child always had to be met, and that where the LEA proposed a reduction in funding it was obliged to notify the school first so that they could make appropriate representations.

Budgetary considerations had no part to play in the assessment of SEN, although they could be relevant in deciding how those needs could be met.

R. v. *Surrey County Council Education Committee ex p. H* (1984) 83 LGR 219, CA. The Court of Appeal emphasised that LEAs were not obliged to provide the best possible education for the child but merely to meet the needs of the child.

R. v. *East Sussex County Council ex p. Tandy* [1998] AC 714. Suitability had to be determined without reference to LEA means.

Resources were only relevant if there was more than one way of providing an objectively suitable education, not having regard to the means of the provider (this case concerned EA 1996, s.19 and not the SEN context).

London Borough of Havering v. *SENT* [1996] EWHC 73. The court followed *Tandy*, in holding that where a child's SEN can only be met by one form of provision, an LEA is not entitled to refuse to provide it on the grounds that it is too expensive.

B v. *Harrow LBC (No. 1)* [2000] 1 WLR 223. The House of Lords held that reference to resources in EA 1996, Sched. 27, para 3(3) meant the resources of the LEA making the statement of SEN and not those of some other authority which did not have to pay for the provision.

Wakefield Metropolitan District Council v. *Dorsey* [1998] EWHC Admin 96. Social services resources were not to be taken into account by the LEA.

B v. *London Borough of Harrow (No.2)* [2000] ELR 1. The cost of transporting a child to and from school, as well as the costs of occupational therapy, had to be taken into account by the LEA as costs it would bear and not something that parents should fund.

Hereford and Worcester County Council v. *Lane* [1998] ELR 319. The Court of Appeal held that the tribunal erred in law in ordering the LEA to name a school which provided more than the child needed by way of special educational provision.

Therapy

London Borough of Bromley v. *SENT* [1999] ELR 260. The Court of Appeal held that no hard and fast line should be drawn between educational and non-educational provision. It was to be decided on a case-by-case basis by the LEA and the tribunal. In this case, physiotherapy, occupational therapy and speech therapy were all held to be educational.

R. v. *Lancashire County Council ex p. M* [1989] 2 FLR 279; *R* v. *Oxfordshire County Council ex p. Wallace* [1987] 2 FLR 193. Speech therapy is educational.

R. v. *Brent and Harrow Area Health Authority ex p. Harrow London Borough Council* [1997] ELR 187. It was difficult to review the decision of the health authority not to assist in relation to the provision of speech therapists.

Duration of the LEA's responsibility

R. v. *Dorset County Council and Further Education Funding Council ex p. Goddard* [1995] ELR 109. Once the child had been the subject of a statement, the LEA had to continue to maintain the statement after the child had reached the age of 16 and could not rely on it automatically lapsing when the child left school.

Wakefield Metropolitan District Council v. *E* [2001] EWHC Admin 508, [2002] ELR 203. This case illustrated the need for a child over the age of 16 to be registered at a school rather than a college of further education in order to enjoy the protection of a statement of SEN. It was held that a tribunal that refused to name a college of further education for a child because had it done so, the child would not have remained the responsibility of the LEA, was correct to do so.

Parental preference

Catchpole v. *Buckinghamshire County Council* [1999] BLGR 321. Where there are two adequate schools, but one is markedly more suitable than the other for the child's needs, the tribunal is not obliged by s.9 to give effect to the parent's choice for the least suitable of the two schools.

W-R v. *Solihull Metropolitan Borough Council and Wall* [1999] ELR 528. Once a tribunal has compared the two schools contended for and concluded that the material before it showed one was preferable for meeting the child's needs, s.9 could, thereafter, have little significance.

T v. *Special Educational Needs Tribunal and Wiltshire County Council* [2002] EWHC Admin 1474, [2002] ELR 704. Section 9 was merely a general principle to be taken into account and, where the dispute was between school and non-school provision, it could not override EA 1996, s.319 which empowered the LEA to make non-school provision only if a school was not appropriate.

S v. *SENT* [1995] 1 WLR 1627. Where the parents want their child to go to an independent school they have to persuade the LEA or the tribunal that the child's needs cannot be met in a maintained school.

Sunderland City Council v. *P and C* [1996] ELR 283. Where a child was over the approved age range for a maintained school, it was held that the tribunal could not lawfully make an order which had the effect that the conditions for approval at the school were not complied with.

Ellison v. *Hampshire County Council* (unreported) 24 February 2000. Where the decision was whether a child with average intelligence should go to a school for children with moderate learning difficulties, the Court of Appeal held that it was open for the tribunal in the exercise of its judgment to conclude that a child with average intelligence nevertheless had moderate learning difficulties, and that therefore there was no breach of regulations in the child going to that school.

Fairness

Porter v. *Magill* [2001] UKHL 67, [2002] 2 AC 357. The test for bias in this House of Lords decision was:

> The question is whether the fair-minded and informed observer, having considered the facts, would conclude that there was a real possibility that tribunal was biased.

R. (on the application of Opoku) v. *Principal of Southwark College* [2002] EWHC Admin 2092. *Magill* (above) was applied.

Locabail (UK) Ltd v. *Bayfield Properties* [2000] QB 451, CA. This case gives authority for the principle that bias can arise from the tribunal members having published, in an academic capacity, views on the law which indicate to a fair-minded observer that they are not impartial.

E v. *Oxfordshire County Council* [2001] EWHC Admin 816, [2002] ELR 256. It was not inherently unfair for the same tribunal to hear the review as made the original error and that the regulations contemplated this course.

White v. *Ealing London Borough Council* [1998] ELR 319. The Court of Appeal held that the members of the tribunal could act on the basis of their own experience, and it was preferable, if that led them consider that a particular course of action was appropriate, to canvas that with the parties, but failure to do so did not render the decision procedurally unfair.

Religion

R. v. *Secretary of State for Education ex p. E* [1996] ELR 312. Whilst culture and religion are not SEN in themselves, if a child has other needs which are SEN and they

APPENDIX L

cannot be met in a non-denominational school, there is a duty to educate the child at a denominational school.

Duty to name a school

White v. *Ealing London Borough Council* [1998] ELR 319 CA. The Court of Appeal held that there was no absolute duty on the LEA or the tribunal to name a school as part of the special educational provision where it was of the view that such provision should be made in a special school.

R. v. *Hackney London Borough Council ex p. GC* [1995] ELR 144, [1996] ELR 142. If the SEN of the child were so unusual that they could only be met by specifying a particular school, the LEA might have to name the school.

R. v. *Barnet London Borough Council ex p. B* [1998] ELR 281, CA; *R.* v. *Secretary of State for Education and Science ex p. Davis* [1989] 2 FLR 190. Where there is a duty to name a school, the tribunal is concerned with the present and future needs of the child, and an order by it that a particular school should be named does not have retrospective effect, with the consequence, in relation to a fee-paying school, that the LEA is liable for fees incurred by the parents since the child was placed in the school, but before the order of the tribunal that that school should be named in Part IV of the statement.

REASONS

Summary duty

S v. *SENT* [1995] 1 WLR 1627. Reasons for the decision should be in writing, deal with substantial issues raised, and state what evidence was preferred. It was not necessary to deal with every argument but the conclusion on the issue had to be intelligible.

South Glamorgan County Council v. *L and M* [1996] ELR 400. *S* v. *SENT* was approved.

Staffordshire County Council v. *J and J* [1996] ELR 418. There was a duty to give reasons in summary form, but it was essential that parties knew why they had won or lost and what the tribunal's conclusions had been in relation to the major issues.

Defect not error in law

S v. *SENT* [1995] 1 WLR 1627. A failure to give reasons was not an error in law, but if the reasoning was inadequate the court might conclude that the tribunal had misdirected itself and remit the matter.

South Glamorgan County Council v. *L and M* [1996] ELR 400. There was no jurisdiction to intervene on the basis of a mere defect of reason and it would be only in a rare case that the court would seek additional reasons in order to dispose of the case. It was better to ask the tribunal to review its own decision in the interests of justice under what is now reg.39 of the Special Educational Needs Tribunal Regulations 2001, SI 2001/600.

L v. *Clarke and Somerset County Council* [1998] ELR 129. The judge allowed an appeal and remitted for a fresh tribunal a case where he held the reasoning was inadequate.

H v. *Kent County Council* [2000] ELR 660. The court set aside a decision of the tribunal because it did not sufficiently identify the basis of the decision. (See also *R. (on application of B)* v. *Vale of Glamorgan County Borough Council and Confrey* [2001] ELR 529.)

Re A (A Child) [2000] ELR 639. The court quashed the decision of the tribunal on the basis of inadequate reasoning. The tribunal had failed to reach a conclusion on a significant issue.

Evidence

S v. *SENT* [1995] 1 WLR 1627. The court will admit evidence to explain the reasons already given for the decision; however, the court will not admit evidence which is an ex post facto rationalisation of the decision.

Oxfordshire County Council v. *GB and Others* [2001] EWCA Civ 1358. The Court of Appeal cautioned against the general admission of evidence in tribunal appeals.

S v. *SENT* [1995] 1 WLR 1627. Evidence will be admitted to add to the reasons given, providing these were the true reasons at the time.

R. v. *Northamptonshire County Council ex p. Weighill* [1998] ELR 291. Evidence was admitted where the court was confident that there was no shift of ground between the reasons in the decision letter and the subsequent affidavit.

R. (on the application of Nash) v. *Chelsea College of Art* [2001] EWHC Admin 538, (2001) *The Times*, 25 July. Circumstances in which late reasons for earlier decisions could be accepted by the court were set out.

ABUSE OF PROCESS

G v. *South Gloucestershire Council and the Special Educational Needs Tribunal* [2000] ELR 136. The tribunal should not exercise the power to strike out if that involved the determination of factual issues because evidence was not to be considered under these rules.

R. (on the application of A) v. *London Borough of Lambeth* [2001] EWHC Admin 379, [2002] ELR 231. The court upheld a decision of the tribunal to strike out an appeal which was an attempt to relitigate an issue determined in a previous appeal where the evidence relied upon could have been obtained for the earlier appeal.

APPEALS BY CONSENT AND ALTERNATIVE DISPUTE RESOLUTION

R. (on the application of Cowl) v. *Plymouth City Council* [2001] EWCA Civ 1935, [2002] 1 WLR 803. A failure by the parties to seek to settle their disputes by alternative dispute resolution procedures even after an appeal has been launched may lead to a denial of relief or, at the very least, adverse cost consequences.

PRIVATE LAW ACTION IN DAMAGES (SPECIAL EDUCATIONAL NEEDS CASES)

X v. *Bedfordshire County Council* [1995] 2 AC 633, HL. The LEA did not owe a direct duty of care to carrying out its statutory duties as this would replicate remedies already available under the statute.

The LEA did owe a direct duty of care once the decision was taken to provide a service as long as it was not merely part and parcel of its statutory duty. However, this may be limited or excluded so as not to impede the due performance by the authority of its statutory duties.

Educational psychologists, and other members of staff of the LEA, owed a duty of care to use reasonable professional skill and care in the assessment and determination of the pupil's SEN, and the LEA was vicariously liable for breach of such duties.

In each case, the test to be applied is not that of the reasonable parent but that applied to professional persons, the *Bolam* test; those persons were bound to exercise the ordinary skill and care of a competent professional working in their profession.

Phelps and Others v. *London Borough of Hillingdon and Others* [2001] 2 AC 619, HL. The LEA was vicariously liable for negligence of employees in connection with its duties in relation to children with SEN. If the LEA is to contend that such vicarious liability would interfere with the performance of its duties it was for the LEA to establish that; it could not be presumed, and the circumstances in which it was anticipated that it would be established would be exceptional.

Professionals concerned with children who had SEN might owe a duty of care to people whom it could be foreseen might suffer damage if injury or damage was caused by their failure to exercise reasonable skill and care.

Psychological damage caused by the failure of the educational psychologist to take reasonable care was damage for the purpose of the common law. Where there was a failure to diagnose a congenital condition and take proper action, as a result of which a child's level of achievement was reduced, loss of employment and wages was recoverable damage.

The standard of care for the relevant professional was the ordinary skill and care of an ordinary competent man exercising that art (*Bolam* v. *Friern Hospital Management Committee* [1957] 1 WLR 582 approved).

RECENT CASES

Oxfordshire County Council v. *M and Special Educational Needs Tribunal* [2002] EWHC Admin 2908; [2003] ELR 718, QBD. The tribunal named the independent school requested by the parents in the child's statement, following an adjournment to see how best the child's needs could be met outside school, given the Part 2 identification of a 24-hour management programme that was 'systematic and explicit and applied rigorously by all care givers'. The LEA had the opportunity to show how its preferred placement could meet the child's identified needs. It was held that there was no error in law to consider behaviour of child at home, nor any error in considering funding from the social services department, as it was not a relevant consideration in the decision itself. The tribunal's reasons supported the approach it took.

DM and KC v. *Essex County Council and the Special Educational Needs Tribunal* [2003] EWHC Admin 135, [2003] ELR 419. The statement provided for an educational programme to be used which required the parents not only to participate but to formulate and deliver the programme. It was held that responsibility for provision had in part been placed on the parents without their permission. The LEA had failed to fulfil its statutory duty to arrange appropriate provision and thus the tribunal erred in law.

R. (on the application of M) v. *Brighton and Hove City Council and Special Educational Needs and Disability Tribunal* [2003] EWHC Admin 1722, [2003] ELR 752. Inadequate reasons were given for the tribunal's decision. It was essential that the tribunal resolved precisely what teaching need the child required and the extent to which it must be specialist. It was not enough to say 'J needs to be taught by specialist teachers trained in teaching pupils with severe specific learning difficulties', as this was too ambiguous. The sentence needed to be addressed in order that the tribunal could go on to decide the appropriate placement.

Regardless of the cost of the school, which all agreed was very expensive, the only question was whether that school could meet the child's needs. If it did not the cost became irrelevant.

Wardle-Heron v. *Newham London Borough Council and Special Educational Needs Tribunal* [2002] EWHC Admin 2806. Where a significantly erroneous cost comparison was used between two placements by the tribunal, a substantial wrong or miscarriage had been occasioned and the appeal would be allowed.

R. (on the application of W (Jane)) v. *Blaenau Gwent Borough Council and Another* [2003] EWHC Admin 2880, [2004] ELR 152. The LEA proposed to cease to maintain a statement preferring to put the child on School Action Plus. Consideration was to be given to whether the objectives of the statement had been met, and whether the child's needs could in future be maintained under the resources of the school she was attending. The tribunal answered both these questions in the affirmative. However, the evidence suggested that the child's needs plainly could not be met within the school's resources. The tribunal's decision was flawed and had to be set aside.

R. (on the application of L) v. *Waltham Forest LBC* [2003] EWHC Admin 2907, [2004] ELR 161. There was a burgeoning line of cases on the duty of SENDIST to give reasons.

The reasons given had to deal with the substantial points raised so that parties could understand why the decision had been reached.

SENDIST could use its expertise in deciding the issues but where it rejected expert evidence before it, it should state so specifically; it also might be required to say why it rejected the evidence.

Mere recitation of the evidence was no substitute for giving reasons.

Where the specialist tribunal used its expertise to decide an issue, it should give the parties an opportunity to comment on its thinking and to challenge it.

It was held that what was stated in the tribunal's reasons was not sufficient, there had been an error of law in not stating briefly why expert evidence was not accepted, and the appeal was allowed.

R. (on the application of S) v. *Norfolk County Council* [2004] EWHC Admin 404, [2004] ELR 259. An interim injunction was granted continuing the funding of a placement at the residential school (where concerns about child abuse had been reported), until the outcome of an appeal against a decision to cease funding the placement. The child was doing well there, another child was still allowed to stay there, and no proper alternative has been offered in the interim.

A v. *SENDIST and Barnet London Borough Council* [2003] EWHC Admin 3368. The parents wanted the placement in Part 4 of the statement to be an Orthodox Jewish school. The court held that, although it was not persuaded that the tribunal had decided the placement first and then allowed that to influence its decision on needs and provision, it was essential that the tribunal's decision was intelligible to all and not merely to experts in the field. The failure to provide a summary of reasons for reaching its conclusions on the child's SEN was a fundamental defect of the decision. If the tribunal rejected the view of an expert, it was required to say so specifically and to give brief reasons why it had done so, especially where the expert evidence was directly related to the crucial issues and there was no expert evidence produced on behalf of the other party. These omissions lead to the conclusion that the impact of the child's Jewishness on her SEN and the provisions to be made for them was not fully considered by the tribunal. The decision of the tribunal was quashed.

Index

Ability
   admission criteria and 46, 48–9
Academic failure 107
Academies 3
   educational negligence 107
   establishment of 18–9
Accessibility strategies 161–2
Additional schools 17
Adjudicator 9–10
   admission to school disputes and 50–1
Administration and decision-making 3–12
   adjudicator 9–10
   governing bodies 10–2
   Learning and Skills Council 7 8
   local education authorities 5–7
   school organisation committee 8–9
   Secretary of State 4–5
Admission to school 41–59
   adjudicator 50–1
   admission arrangements 44–50
      additional powers 49–50
      admission criteria 45–7
      admission numbers 44
   appeal panel 169
   disability discrimination and 155
   judicial review remedy 56–9
      examples 57–9
      preliminary considerations 56–7
   parental preference 42
      exceptions to obligations to comply with parental preference 42–3, 47–9
   statutory appeals 51–6
      arrangements for appeal 52
      composition of panel 52
      decision-making 54–5
      hearing procedure 53–4
      infant class size appeals 55–6, 59
      preparation for hearing 53
      preparatory procedural issues 52
   statutory framework 41–4
      admission forums 44
      Codes of Practice 43
      parental preference 42–3
   who is the client 41
Alternative dispute resolution
   educational negligence cases 106–7
Appeals
   admission to school 51–6, 169
      arrangements for appeal 52
      composition of panel 52
      decision-making 54–5
      hearing procedure 53
      infant class size appeals 55–6, 59
      preparation for hearing 53
      preparatory procedural issues 52
   disability discrimination
      admission appeal panel 169
      case law 164–5
      exclusion appeal panel 169
      factors to be considered 165
      orders that can be made 167–8
      preparing case 164
      Secretary of State direction 168
      SENDIST 163–8, 185–6, 205–8
      strike out 165–7
      time limits 163–4
   exclusion from school 79–85, 169
      decision 83–4
      grounds 187–8
      hearing 82–5
      preliminary procedural issues 80–1
      preparation for hearing 81–2
      role of independent appeal panel 79–80
   special educational needs 133–47
      adjournments 144–5
      after case statement period 140

INDEX

Appeals—*cont.*
case statement 139
checklist 204
concessions by LEA 147
costs 145
date of hearing 138
determination 145
directions 142
draft claim 205–8
enforcement of tribunal
    determinations 146
hearing 143–4
late evidence 140–1
parental statement to tribunal
    185–6
post-registration requirements 138
public funding 147
reasons for appeal 182–4
registration of appeal 137
representations 142–3
review of determination 146
statutory appeal 147
statutory framework 133
timescale and procedure 134–7
transfer of LEA 135–6
views of child 143
which decision can be appealed 134
whose right of appeal 134
witnesses 141–2
Aptitude
admission criteria and 46, 48–9

Behaviour
admission criteria and 47
Bullying 108

Catchment areas 46, 58
Categorisation of schools 1–3
City technology colleges 2–3
educational negligence 107
Class sizes
admissions appeals and 55–6, 59
Closure of schools 20
Codes of Practice
admission to school 43
disability discrimination 149–50
special educational needs
    identification and assessment 114–5
Commissioner for Local Administration (Ombudsman)
challenges to planning and policy
    decisions 22–4

exclusion from school and 86
Community schools 1
Complaints procedure 85–6, 168
Confidentiality
disability discrimination and 161
Conscience
freedom of 40
Contributory negligence 105
Costs
judicial review 36
special educational needs appeals 145
Criminal offences
exclusion from school and 65, 70

Damages
for educational negligence 102–5
    quantum 104–5
human rights issues and 31
judicial review 31
pupils out of school 96
Decision-making *see* Administration
    and decision-making
Declaration 30
Disability discrimination 148–70
accessibility strategies 161–2
appeals
    admission appeal panel 169
    case law 164–5
    exclusion appeal panel 169
    factors to be considered 165
    orders that can be made 167–8
    preparing case 164
    Secretary of State direction 168
    strike out 165–7
    time limits 163–4
Codes of Practice 149–50
coverage of provisions 155–6
definition of disability 150–3, 164
    long-term effect 151–2
    normal day-to-day activities 152–3
    physical/mental impairment 150
    substantial adverse effect 151
Disability Rights Commission (DRC)
    169–70
educational settings 153–5
    responsible body 154
exclusion appeal panel 169
less favourable treatment 156–7
    defences 160–1
    justification 157
local authority's residual duties
    162–3

240

pre-school provision 161
public funding for claims 170
reasonable adjustment duty 157–61
  alternation removal of physical features 160
  case example 158–9
  defences 160–1
  exceptions 159–60
  nature of duty 157–8
  reasonableness 158
special educational needs and 149
statutory framework 149–50
test 156–61
who is the client 148
Disability Rights Commission (DRC) 169–70
Disabled pupils
accessibility strategies 161–2
exclusion from school and 68–9
see also Disability discrimination; Special educational needs
Discrimination 39
disability *see* Disability discrimination
exclusion from school and 85
Distance
admission criteria and 46
Duty of care 101–2

Early years providers
identification and assessment of special educational needs 111–2
Education
duty to educate 88
right to 38–9
Educational negligence 97–108
contributory negligence 105
damages for 102–5
  quantum 104–5
duty of care 101–2
independent schools 107
information needed from client 100
limitation 101
mediation/alternative dispute resolution 106–7
other causes of action 107–8
procedural issues 105–6
public funding for claims 108
statutory framework 99
what client needs to know 100–1
who is the client 99
Enlargement of schools 21

Establishment of schools 17–20
Ethnic minorities
exclusion from school and 68
Evidence
disability discrimination appeals 164
exclusion from school and 74–5
expert *see* Expert evidence
special educational needs appeals 140–1
Examinations
disability discrimination and 154–5
exclusion from school and 64–5
Exclusion from school 60–87
appeals 169
  decision 83–4
  grounds 187–8
  hearing 82–5
  preliminary procedural issues 80–1
  preparation for hearing 81–2
  role of independent appeal panel 79–80
case digest 212–9
decision to exclude 65–72, 78–9
  burden of proof 69–70
  challenging 75–6
  early intervention and alternatives to exclusion 66–7
  parallel criminal proceedings 70
  responsibilities flowing from decision to exclude 71–2
  steps before taking decision 69
  steps preceding exclusion 67
  vulnerable pupils 68–9
  when to exclude 65–6
  who can exclude 66
disability discrimination and 156
during public examinations 64–5
evidence and 74–5
fixed-term exclusions 63
further remedies 85–6
governing body and 71–9
  meeting 76–9
  preparing for meeting 73–6
independent schools 62–3
judicial review 86
  application for urgent consideration 195–6
  claim form 189–94
  counsel's grounds 197–203
lunchtime exclusions 64
managed moves 67
permanent exclusions 49–50, 64, 66

INDEX

Exclusion from school—*cont.*
reinstatement on appeal 83, 84–5
pupils out of school 88–96
damages 96
finding another school place 94–5
guidance on 90–2
individual tuition 92
pupil referral units 93
pupils with statement of SENs 95–6
reintegration 93–5
school's duty to excluded pupils 92
statutory framework 88–9
removals 65
school's duty to excluded pupils 92
statutory framework 61–3
who is the client 60–1
see also Pupils out of school
Expert evidence
disability discrimination appeals 164
educational negligence 106
exclusion from school and 75
Expression
freedom of 40

Fair trial right 39
Family life
right to 39–40
Foundation schools 1–2

Gifted pupils 111
Governing bodies 10–2, 72–3
complaints to 85–6, 168
constitution 72
disability discrimination and 154
exclusion from school and 71–9
meeting 76–9
preparing for meeting 73–6
special educational needs and identification and assessment 111–2
when it meets 73
Grant-maintained schools 2

Health and safety issues
exclusion from school and 65
Hearings
admissions appeals 53–4
exclusion from school
governing body meeting 76–9
independent appeal panel 82–5
judicial review 36

special educational needs appeals 143–4
Human rights issues 38–40
damages and 31

Inclusive schooling 127–8
Independent schools 3
disability discrimination and 154, 160
educational negligence 107
exclusion from school 62–3
inspection and regulation 14–5
Individual education plan 115–6
Injunctions 31
Inspection and regulation 13–5
independent schools 14–5
maintained schools 13–4
Interviews
admission criteria and 46–7

Judicial review 24, 26–38
admission to school claims 56–9
examples 57–9
preliminary considerations 56–7
alternative remedies 27
basic requirements 27–30
exclusion from school 86
application for urgent consideration 195–6
claim form 189–94
counsel's grounds 197–203
forms of relief 30–1
planning and policy field 37–8
pre-action protocol 32
letter 208–11
procedure 32–7
acknowledgement of service 34
commencement of proceedings 33–4
costs 36
letter before claim 32–3
permission stage 34
post-permission procedure 35–6
pre-action protocol 32
refusal of permission 35
renewal of applications 35
settlement and consent orders 36
substantive hearing 36
public funding 29–30, 36–7
time limits 27–8
timing of bringing challenge 28–9
who can bring claim 27

242

INDEX

Learning and Skills Council 7–8
  establishment of sixth forms and 19–20
Learning difficulties *see* Special educational needs
Legal Help Scheme *see* Public funding
Letter before claim
  judicial review 32–3
Limitation *see* Time limits
Local authorities
  admission forums 44
  alterations to school provision 20–1
  challenges to planning and policy decisions 21–6
    judicial review 24, 26–38
    Ombudsman (Commissioner for Local Administration) 22–4
    Secretary of State 24–6
  children in care 69
  decision to cease to maintain schools 20
  disability discrimination and 154
    residual duties 162–3
  duties and powers 5–7
  duty of care 101–2
  establishment of schools by 17–20
  exclusion from school and
    advice to governing body meeting 76
    informing of exclusion decision 71–2
    inspection and regulation by 13
  maintained schools 1
    inspection and regulation 13–4
  Ombudsman (Commissioner for Local Administration)
    challenges to planning and policy decisions 22–4
    exclusion from school and 86
  school organisation committee 8–9
  school organisation plan 16–7
  school transport and *see* Transport
  special educational needs and
    concessions of appeal 147
    identification and assessment 111, 113, 118–9
    SEN officers 113
Lunchtime exclusions 64

Maintained schools 1
  inspection and regulation 13–4
Maladministration 22

Managed moves 67
Mandatory orders 30–1
Mediation
  educational negligence cases 106–7

Negligence
  educational *see* Educational negligence
  negligent teaching 107
Non-additional schools 17–8
Nurseries
  disability discrimination and 153

Office for Standards in Schools (Ofsted) 13
  inspection by 13–4
Ombudsman (Commissioner for Local Administration)
  challenges to planning and policy decisions 22–4
  exclusion from school and 86

Parent partnership officers 113
Parents
  admission to school and parental preference 42
    exceptions to obligations 42–3, 47–9
  exclusion from school and 71
    governing body meeting 73–9
    prosecution under EA 1996 s.444 173
  special educational needs and
    parental preferences 125–7
    request for assessment 118–9
    statement to SENDIST 185–6
  transport and parental preference 174–5
Particulars of claim 177–81
Planning and policy decisions 16–40
  challenges 21–6
    Commissioner for Local Administration 22–4
    funding 24
    human rights breaches 38–40
    judicial review 24, 26–38
    Secretary of State 24–6
  human rights breaches 38–40
  judicial review 24, 26–38
  school provision 16–21
    decision to cease to maintain schools 20

243

Planning and policy decisions (*cont*).
  establishment of schools by LEA 17–20
  prescribed alterations 20–1
  school organisation plan 16–7
Playgroups
  disability discrimination and 161
Pre-action protocols 32
  letter 208–11
Pre-school provision
  disability discrimination 161
Private life
  right to 39–40
Private schools *see* Independent schools
Prohibiting orders 31
Provision of schools 16–21
  decision to cease to maintain schools 20
  establishment of schools by LEA 17–20
  prescribed alterations 20–1
  school organisation plan 16–7
Public funding 24, 26
  disability discrimination claims 170
  educational negligence claims 108
  exclusion from school claims 87
  judicial review 29–30, 36–7
  special educational needs appeals 147
  transport claims 176
Public schools *see* Independent schools
Pupil referral units 93
Pupils out of school 88–96
  damages 96
  finding another school place 94–5
  guidance on 90–2
  individual tuition 92
  pupil referral units 93
  pupils with statement of SENs 95–6
  reintegration 93–5
  school's duty to excluded pupils 92
  statutory framework 88–9

Quashing orders 30

Religion
  admission criteria and 58
  freedom of 40

School Action Plus support 117
School Action support 116–7
School organisation committee 8–9
School organisation plan 16–7

School records
  exclusion from school and 75
School transport *see* Transport
Secretary of State for Education 4–5
  challenges to planning and policy decisions 24–6
  decision to cease to maintain schools 20
  establishment of academies and 18–9
  establishment of schools by direction of 19
  guidance on exclusion from school 61–2
  guidance on pupils out of school 90–2
Selection process 48–9
Siblings
  admission criteria and 45–6, 58
Sixth forms
  disability discrimination and 154
  establishment of 19–20
Special educational needs
  admission criteria and 47
  appeals 133–47
    adjournments 144–5
    after case statement period 140
    case statement 139
    checklist 204
    concessions by LEA 147
    costs 145
    date of hearing 138
    determination 145
    directions 142
    draft claim 205–8
    enforcement of tribunal determinations 146
    hearing 143–4
    late evidence 140–1
    parental statement to tribunal 185–6
    post-registration requirements 138
    public funding 147
    reasons for appeal 182–4
    registration of appeal 137
    representations 142–3
    review of determination 146
    statutory appeal 147
    statutory framework 133
    timescale and procedure 134–7
    transfer of LEA 135–6
    views of child 143
    which decision can be appealed 134

whose right of appeal 134
witnesses 141–2
case digest 220–38
disability discrimination and 149
educational negligence 97–9
exclusion from school and 68
pupils out of school 95–6
identification and assessment 109–32
   annual reviews 131–2
   Code of Practice 114–5
   decision to assess 121–2
   definitions 110–1
   local authorities and 111, 113, 118–9
   personnel 112–3
   responsible bodies 111–2
   school-based support 115–7
   statement of needs 122–7, 128, 129–31, 132
   statutory assessment 118, 119–22
   statutory framework 109–10
   transfer between phases 131
inclusive schooling 127–8
special schools 2, 126–7
statement of needs
   ceasing to maintain 132
   draft 122–7
   final 128
   maintenance 129–31
   transfer 132
transport and 129, 175

Special Educational Needs and Disability Tribunal (SENDIST) 112, 163–8
draft claim 205–8
factors to be considered 165
orders that can be made 167–8
parental statement 185–6
preparing case 164

Secretary of State direction 168
strike out 165–7
time limits 163–4

Special educational needs co-ordinator 112–3

Special schools 2, 126–7

Teaching
negligent 107

Thought
freedom of 40

Time limits
disability discrimination appeals 163–4
educational negligence 101
judicial review 27–8

Transport 171–6
nearest available route 174
parental preference 174–5
policy changes 175
prosecution of parents under EA 1996 s444 and 173
public funding for claim 176
remedies 176
special educational needs and 129, 175
statutory framework 171–2
types of assistance/arrangements 172
who is the client 173

Tuition
pupils out of school and 92

Voluntary schools 2

Witnesses
exclusion from school and 75
expert *see* Expert evidence
special educational needs appeals 141–2

Domestic Violence, Crime and Victims Act 2004

A Guide to the New Law

Claire Bessant

The Domestic Violence, Crime and Victims Act 2004 makes substantial amendments to civil and criminal law: it increases support for victims of crime and bolsters the framework for bringing offenders to justice.

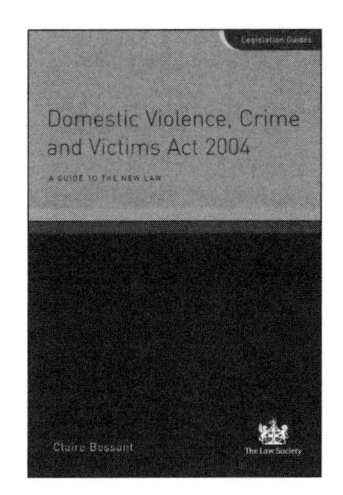

Written by a solicitor for busy practitioners, this book provides practical guidance on the impact of these changes, clearly outlining how the new rules interact with the existing provisions.

Key features include:

- relevant sections and schedules of the Act reproduced in full
- detailed guidance on the practical impact of the changes to criminal and civil law
- explanation of how the new rules interact with the existing provisions relating to domestic violence
- a concise summary at the beginning of each chapter highlighting the main points covered.

Available from Marston Book Services:
Tel. 01235 465 656.

1 85328 902 7
208 pages
£29.95
Mar 2005

The Law Society

Child Law Handbook

Guide to Good Practice

Liz Goldthorpe with Pat Monro

Published with the Association of Lawyers for Children

The interdisciplinary approach to child law is the cornerstone of good practice and decision-making. It is also increasingly important in the wake of the Children Act 2004, which emphasises comprehensive safeguarding and integrated services.

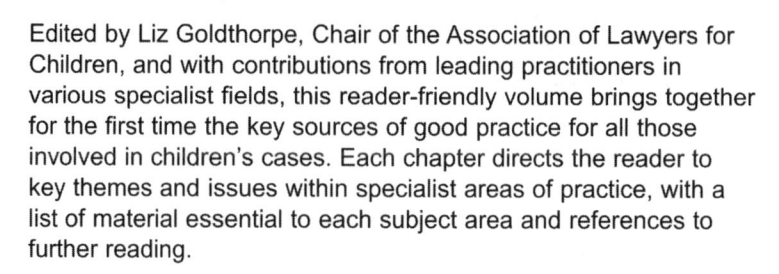

Edited by Liz Goldthorpe, Chair of the Association of Lawyers for Children, and with contributions from leading practitioners in various specialist fields, this reader-friendly volume brings together for the first time the key sources of good practice for all those involved in children's cases. Each chapter directs the reader to key themes and issues within specialist areas of practice, with a list of material essential to each subject area and references to further reading.

Available from Marston Book Services:
Tel. 01235 465 656.

1 85328 712 1
508 pages
£49.95
November 2005

The Law Society